SMART KIDS, BAD SCHOOLS

ALSO BY BRIAN CROSBY
The $100,000 Teacher

SMART KIDS, BAD SCHOOLS

38 Ways to Save America's Future

Brian Crosby

THOMAS DUNNE BOOKS
St. Martin's Press   New York

THOMAS DUNNE BOOKS.
An imprint of St. Martin's Press.

Excerpt on page 217 is from an editorial piece by Sheryl Boris-Schacter in *Education Week,* © 2006.

www.thomasdunnebooks.com
www.stmartins.com

Book design by Ruth Lee-Mui

Library of Congress Cataloging-in-Publication Data

Crosby, Brian (Brian Franklyn)
    Smart kids, bad schools : 38 ways to save America's future / Brian Crosby.—1st ed.
      p. cm.
    ISBN-13: 978-0-312-37258-3
    ISBN-10: 0-312-37258-2
    1. Public schools—United States.   2. Educational change—United States.
    I. Title.

LA217.2.C755   2008
370.973—dc22

                      2008017615

First Edition: August 2008

10 9 8 7 6 5 4 3 2 1

*Dedicated to my mom, Ruth Crosby, God bless her soul,
who always introduced me to complete strangers in this way:*

"This is my son Brian. He is an English teacher."

She said it as if I were president of the United States.

Contents

viii   Contents

Do you care about this country's future?
If not, put this book back on the shelf.

You may not have any school-age children. In fact, you might not have given a second thought about this country's public education system since you graduated so many years ago. Here's an amazing realization: Nearly one out of every five Americans attends or works in a public or private kindergarten-through-grade-twelve (K–12) school. So, what happens in this country's schoolhouses affects millions of people.

The people who we interact with daily are products (if I may use such a cold term) of America's public schools. Think of the last time you were in a retail store, a market, a bank, a gas station. Were the employees at these establishments helpful and able to answer your questions? Or did you think to yourself, "Did they even graduate from high school?"

You're in your car at a drive-through fast-food restaurant, placing an order via the speaker box: "I'd like two cheeseburgers." And the person on the other end reads back, "You'd like a taco and a shake?" in broken English.

Have you ever wished the person you were speaking to over the phone regarding your credit card bill was a tad smarter? Or at least located in the United States instead of India?

Once, in a Barnes & Noble bookstore, I asked an employee where I could find a copy of *Macbeth*. "Who wrote that?" she asked me.

Every citizen is impacted by public education. Before you put this book down, I need you to ask yourself some basic questions:

Do you wish for America to remain strong economically?

Do you wish for America to stay on the cutting edge of technology?

Do you wish people were better informed and that more participated in the voting process?

Do you wish for a prosperous future?

Are children the future of our country?

If you answered "yes" to any of these questions, then you obviously do care about how we educate our young people.

This book presents a plan of action, thirty-eight steps toward a better way of educating kids and, in turn, securing America's prominence in the world.

Young people entering the job market today will have to ensure a place in it for themselves by either strengthening their education or filling a niche in America's economy. And how well are schools preparing the youth for this kind of future? Let's take a look at some statistics from recently conducted surveys:

- The United States ranks ninth out of twelve industrialized nations in math skills, tied with Latvia (wherever that is*).
- One out of every four American children reads below grade level.
- Two-thirds of eighteen- to twenty-four-year-olds cannot find Iraq on a map; one-third can't find Louisiana.
- American businesses spend an estimated $50 billion on training their employees in basic skills that should have been taught in school.
- One-third of all high school students, and one-half of African-American and Latino students, do not graduate—and this hasn't changed for thirty years, despite reforms.
- Half of all high school dropouts are unemployed.
- Two-thirds of imprisoned Americans are high school dropouts.
- In the future as many as one-third of the country's total available jobs may be outsourced. That's forty-two million jobs.

*Give up? It's located in Europe, north of Poland and south of Finland.

- Almost half a trillion dollars is spent on K–12 education each year. That's not a misprint—$500,000,000,000 is spent on education every year. For many, that's not enough.

According to a *Time/The Oprah Winfrey Show* poll in March 2006, 64 percent of people believe we are spending too little on education. Au contraire. In the past thirty years, the amount of per-pupil spending has doubled. *Doubled.* And look at the results! What company would continue spending more and more money on a product if sales remained stagnant over a quarter of a century? Putting more coal in the firebox is not going to make the education engine go further.

Headline after headline about how bad America's schools are fill the media daily. An outsider would think, "Wow, with all that money, how come that country can't educate their children right?"

Here's a multiple-choice question for you. (Remember, choose the *best* answer.)

What do the horrific statistics about America's schools prove?
a. There are many dumb students.
b. There are many dumb teachers.
c. There is a disconnect between what schools give and what students need.
d. All of the above.

Why A *is incorrect.* While some students do struggle in school, the reality is that children do the best they can in the system that exists. Kids tend to be a lot smarter than grown-ups realize.

Why B *is incorrect.* Any time you're looking for a juicy conversation at a party, bring up the topic of teachers, especially bad ones. They are an easy target. After all, they get paid whether they do a good job or not, can leave work early in the day, and have all those days off. Are there dumb teachers? Absolutely. But not as many as one would think.

Why C *is correct.* Okay, so if America's teetering-on-collapse school system is not the fault of student or teacher incompetence, just what or who is to blame? *The System.*

Kids could thrive if given a different system. Teachers could thrive if given a different system. If the numbers were reversed, and suddenly 68 percent of twelfth graders were reading at an advanced level instead of below proficiency, imagine the positive reverberations in America's economy.

You see, improving schools is everyone's business, not just the business of teachers, parents, and politicians. America is not that far away from slipping off the cutting-edge radar. Don't forget that your taxes, whether you like it or not, whether your children attend public or private schools, go toward paying for public schools. It's an investment we all make, and so it's an investment we should all care about.

What's holding students back from fulfilling their potential is an outdated, musty, politicized organizational behemoth that continues to keep going and sputtering and gasping, teaching kids in the same virtually unchanged way from the little red schoolhouse of 150 years ago.

Today's educational system is yesterday's educational system. Imagine if medical care today employed remedies of a century ago. "Oh, that finger hurts? Let's cut it open and let it bleed." We treat people differently today, thank goodness, so why shouldn't we educate them differently as well?

Yet no one seems to have the foresight or fortitude to create a new vision for public schools, from the buildings that house students to the subjects taught and the food served to them.

After twenty years of teaching high school English and journalism to over three thousand students, mentoring dozens of new teachers, teaching university credential courses, and becoming a National Board Certified Teacher, I see what works and what's wrong, and so I have a plan.

Public school is dysfunctional. It needs to go through more than a simple makeover. It needs to be torn down, with a new foundation put in its place.

Like a dilapidated ramshackle fixer-upper that is more cost-effective to scrap than to renovate, now is the time to bulldoze America's public school system. The expiration date has passed. Forget CPR. It smells, it stinks. Discard the carcass. Start fresh.

In education, change moves at a snail's pace. Walk into any school, and you're bound to discover the books you used as a child still on the shelves; the chalkboards may have not yet been replaced with whiteboards; you may even discover the same desk or chair you sat in. When journalist Joel Stein came to visit my journalism classes, he was quite surprised to discover teens using the same literature anthology he had nearly twenty years ago.

Public school lags behind the times. For example, as long ago as the 1930s researchers discovered that when students had access to typewriters, they learned faster and better than those without. Did schools then provide all students with typewriters? No. And in today's times, do schools provide all students with computers? No.

One of the great ironies about America is how such a rich country could house such a poor public education system, especially when compared to its enviable university system, which attracts students from around the world.

As J. Martin Rochester said about America's education systems, in college, the classroom is the castle; in K–12, the classroom is the dungeon.

It's no longer a question of if America's schools will continue to fail students, but of how far the schools will fall. The 2005 National Academia report "Rising Above the Gathering Storm: Energizing and Employing America for a Brighter Economic Future" warns that the United States is on the verge of losing its economic, technological, and scientific advantage over other countries.

How many more companies must seek out better workers overseas to fill positions?

Must Wal-Mart take over every city in America to ensure that a bounty of jobs remain here (albeit low-paying ones)?

What's going to happen to one-third of the kids, who don't graduate?

What's going to happen to half of the kids, who don't finish college?

What's going to happen to the college graduates who can't get a job?

What's going to happen to America then?

Americans need to look deep down and figure out where they want the United States to stand in the world in ten, twenty, thirty years from now. The only position that counts—number one—is not a sure thing. Something has to change in our schools to prevent further decline; otherwise, this country will be going from a "nation at risk" to a "save America now" telethon. According to Wyoming senator Michael B. Enzi, ranking member of the Senate Health, Education, Labor, and Pensions Committee, "Without an educated workforce, we are certain to lose our pre-eminence in the world."

The change that is needed in public education must be huge, along the lines of the civil rights movement. The same fervor people exert in antismoking and antiabortion campaigns needs to be replicated in efforts to transform public schools.

Yes, *transform,* not *reform.* "Reform" means to change to a better state while "transform" means to metamorphose, to completely alter an existing condition into a different form altogether.

But no one does anything to alter the system. And when I say "no one," I'm directly referring to the governors and president, the most powerful politicians in the country who really are the CEOs and CFOs of the nation's school system. We, the stockholders, should fire them for "reforming" public education. None of the recent reforms including the highly touted No Child Left Behind (NCLB) Act of 2002 have made public schools any different from what they were decades ago. You still have kids responding to bells like Pavlov's dogs, schlepping books from room to room. You still have teachers teaching the way they were taught. The framework of public education has not altered. NCLB and all the programs that came before it have acted as Band-Aids, not cures.

Let's face it. Wealthy people don't send their own children to public schools unless they live in a district with heavily financed donations.

And look what goes on right underneath the noses of the U.S. Congress: More than half of fourth and eighth graders do not read or do math at basic levels, and four in five schools are not meeting NCLB achievement goals.

How ironic that the area in which politicians live and work, Washington, D.C., has always had one of the worst-performing districts in the nation. Perhaps one of the prerequisites for election of any U.S. representative, senator, or president—or, at the very least, any politician who serves on education committees—should be that all their children must attend public schools.

It may take a group not privy to the power to truly think outside the classroom box.

Since politicians control the way schools operate, it will take an honest-to-goodness political leader willing to give up power and transfer it to those who do the teaching: the three million public school teachers. That is one source of imagination and genius that largely goes untapped for its input. Even when eliminating the bad ones, the mediocre ones, the average ones, you are still left with a hefty number of gifted people who, because they actually go through the system day in and day out, have the best vantage point to drive the transformation. "Educrats," bureaucrats whose specialty is education, i.e., those who wield power in education and wish to maintain the status quo and thereby are out of touch with the reality of the classroom, enjoy freely referring to teachers as stakeholders or shareholders, but it's just a bunch of malarkey to make teachers feel good. Teachers have no real power. Educrats know it and they like it that way; otherwise, they would have no jobs.

Dear Mr. President. Call to you the best teachers in America. Put the smartest minds in the country in a room and have them map out a long-term strategy. Then be willing to give them control over it. Don't forget—those teachers are with our children for the bulk of their waking youth. If parents entrust their own children to teachers, then so should the government entrust teachers with knowing what's best in education. Because what's good for students will lead to what's good for America. The future depends on it.

Do we want high schools to continue graduating young people who are capable of doing less and less? This means that they will do less and less for this country.

Throw away the kitchen sink and reinvent the wheel. Start with a blank slate and come up with a visionary blueprint. Nothing should be sacred.

- How should the buildings appear?
- Is it okay for students to fail a grade and be promoted on to the next one?
- Should parents pay for public schools?
- Should good teachers be paid more than bad ones?
- Is there any point to homework?
- Should teachers work four days a week?
- Should holidays be eliminated from the school year?
- Is special education sucking away money from the rest of the students?
- Should teachers unions be banned?

By the title of this work I am not implying that all children are A+ students and that schoolchildren own zero accountability in the matter of their education. I'm saying that the system does not work and that young people could and should be achieving much more after thirteen years of education than they do now. They should be better prepared to enter society as contributing, responsible citizens who have future paths clearly "Mapquested." Yes, there are students who misbehave, who don't do their work, who are apathetic and don't want to be there any longer, as one-third vanish before the marathon race is over with. But it's the system that doesn't want to rethink itself. It's incapable of reflection, of looking inward.

So, as highfalutin as it may be, as pie in the sky as it may come across, as Pollyanna as some will dismiss it, here is one teacher's vision for America's schools.

This book serves as a blueprint of what public education in America could look like. It's not meant to be a technical manual. It is not meant to answer all the questions; it is not meant to give all the details and provide all the solutions. It is a complete vision, however, doing something that all other proposals and reforms have neglected to do: look at the whole picture, not just one piece. It's time to think *big*.

These thirty-eight ways to overhaul our public schools would make America's K–12 system the envy of the world and would make it equal the excellence of our country's universities.

It would be very easy to look at these ideas and quickly point out why they can't be implemented. Broken up, sliced and diced, each idea on its own is insufficient to transform the way students are schooled. All the actions in this book are interconnected. For example, merely starting school at a later time in and of itself will not do that much in the grand scheme of things.

To put any vision into action will take a long-term commitment. To enact certain changes and expect results after just a couple of years is foolhardy. Change isn't easy. But then educating people isn't, either.

Despite billions upon billions of dollars, years of reform proposals, intense testing of students, countless hours of training, nothing has changed.

The situation is desperate but not hopeless. View this book as an insurance policy against the current free fall of America's economic future. The teaching of America's youth should be viewed as a bulwark against democracy's demise. It's no good to just let students "get by." We must demand excellence. Our country's economic future rests on it.

Yes, national security is a top priority (though many don't know where Iraq is), but the best form of homeland security is education security. Without a sound education system in place for the twenty-first century, the other issues are secondary. Do we want our military to have poorly educated people in its ranks? You can't outsource an army.

Therefore, sit back, read the following with an open mind, and don't be too quick to cut down the ideas. Even if you think it can't be done, ask yourself, "Shouldn't it be done?"

PART ONE

The Way Schools Need to Be Restructured

1

What Building Is Drab-Looking, Has Gates All Around It, with Bells Ringing All the Time? (Hint: It's Not a Prison)

When you enter a hotel lobby or the reception area of a restaurant, the first impression is extremely important. What is your first impression upon entering a public school? Is it inviting, does it put a smile on your face, make you comfortable, stir your imagination? Actually, quite the opposite. And people wonder why kids hate school.

What a shame that each school morning forty-seven million children are dropped off at a place where they spend most of their waking youth in buildings that are often bleak, fostering the attitude that school is a prison.

Why can't America's schools be designed with architectural flair? Wouldn't children want to be at a place that is pleasing to the eye rather than institutional beige–painted warehouses?

We can't just warehouse kids, but need to truly *house* them. Children deserve imaginative environments that allow their minds to contemplate, places where their spirits can soar. Why is it okay for children to go to schools where toilets and water fountains are not working properly? Why is it okay for students to be corralled into overcrowded classrooms? Why is it okay for students to spend up to ten hours a day on campuses that resemble fortresses? Just what kind of community does America want for its children?

In California, because of one parent's complaints that led to a landmark legal decision against the state in 2004, commonly referred to as the Williams case, every school must provide sufficient textbooks for its students and a clean and safe facility. Imagine that.

It took a lawsuit to guarantee that each student had a book and that each school had a properly running toilet. Wow!

And even when there is a new building, problems arise. Since districts typically go with the lowest bidder, shoddy construction ensues. At the school where I teach, all the air-conditioning units had to be replaced, and all the carpeting pulled out, within the first three years after construction.

Let's compare how closely schools resemble prisons—and at a lot less cost, too:

Prisons	Schools
bells	bells
wardens	administrators
gates and walls	gates and walls
one unlocked door for access	one unlocked door for access
timed schedule of activities	timed schedule of activities
high inmate-to-guard ratio	high student-to-teacher ratio
lots of inmates	lots of students
a cafeteria	a cafeteria
drab-looking facades	drab-looking facades
lockdowns	lockdown drills
cramped quarters	cramped quarters
socialization mentality	socialization mentality
mass showers	mass showers (at secondary level)
cell mates	classmates
cost per prisoner = $24,000	**cost per student = $9,000**

Who holds the keys in a prison? Guards. Who holds the keys in a school? Teachers. And just as guards turn their keys in before the end of the day, teachers likewise have to do the same at the end of the school year.

And think about the kids living in urban centers. They attend institutions that resemble the places where some of their friends or family members reside. Even the word "institution" can be used interchangeably with a prison as well as a school.

Another example of how schools resemble prisons is the tardy sweeps many secondary schools employ. A tardy sweep is when administrators and security personnel branch out (like throwing out a net) around the campus to catch wandering students who are out and about after the tardy bell rings. Teachers are to lock their doors when the bell rings to prevent students from gaining entrance to classrooms. Hmm, similar to a prison lockdown, right?

Struggling students need an aesthetic boost to their sensibilities more than the self-motivated ones do. Inner-city schools tend to be larger, staffed with less-experienced teachers, are maintained less, have less parent involvement, and—bingo!—have higher dropout rates. Minority students have more negative feelings about school than white children. No kidding.

When they go from poor living conditions to a ramshackle school, how can their spirits be lifted? Why should they go to school and work hard if they are ensconced in depressing surroundings? No wonder these kids don't achieve at a higher level.

Children living in poverty should be attending Taj Mahal–like education settings. We should be inspiring these children, not depressing them.

Recently, some schools have attempted to be innovative and imaginative.

When architect Daniel Cecil designed the Kennebunk Elementary School in Kennebunk, Maine, winning the 2005 DesignShare Recognized Value Award, he purposely imagined the school with a child-size perspective. Everything from windows to doorknobs is at a child's height level. Images of children at play are placed throughout.

North-Grand High School in northwest Chicago, where 90 percent of students are Latino and 90 percent of students graduate, features a two-story atrium, a culinary program, engineering and medical classes, and an indoor swimming pool. An *Edutopia* article on the facility comments that "so much natural light pours into North-Grand that energy costs are significantly reduced, but the oversize windows are designed to prevent glare, which cuts down on air-conditioning costs." Design director Trung Le said that "from a psychological standpoint, a transparent school filled with natural daylight will improve security." So often schools go unused after 3:00 P.M. However, North-Grand High serves the community in the evenings and on weekends.

Many new schools consider environmental issues in their design. The nonprofit U.S. Green Building Council (USGBC) issues LEED (Leadership in Energy and Environmental Design) certification, a seal of approval for a green school. Since 2002, over thirty K–12 schools located from Massachusetts to Oregon have such recognition; close to three hundred have applied for it.

Common components of a green school include a system for collecting rainwater for reuse in toilets and landscaping, a roof where plants are grown that serve as not only insulation but as botany lessons, and windows that are glare-proof to cut down on electricity use.

USGBC's vice president Peter Templeton told *Edutopia* that "we want to create the optimum environment for learning, one that ensures students can concentrate and be free from distractions." And what are the distractions? "Mold, bad air quality and circulation, which often cause drowsiness, and inadequate lighting, known to hamper learning by diminishing a child's ability to concentrate."

One of the schools receiving a LEED certificate is Tarkington Elementary School on Chicago's southwest side with its use of low-toxic paint and caulking. The school's lights have sensors that adjust to the natural light flowing into the building.

Although Tarkington cost 6 percent more to build than a non-green school, its environmentally friendly design paid for itself within a few years, according to a 2003 study conducted for California's Sustainable Building Task Force.

Would brightly colored buildings with more natural light and ventilation boost test scores? The California Board for Energy Efficiency discovered that they do. Test scores rose as much as 26 percent when compared to scores achieved in classrooms with the least amount of natural light. Plus, energy bills decreased.

Clearview Elementary School in Hanover, Pennsylvania, uses 40 percent less energy than a more conventionally built school. So how much more did it cost to build? $150,000 more. However, the school is saving about $18,000 a year in energy costs, so the added initial expense will be paid for within nine years. Therefore, not only does energy get conserved, but the district saves money, and the students do better academically. Would that be called a win-win-win situation?

Here's a helpful hint when building new schools. Whatever the standard may be for the size of classrooms and the width of hallways, *double them*. Yes, space costs money. However, squeezing thirty-five to forty students in rooms equipped for twenty to twenty-five doesn't make any sense. And as kids get older and bigger, they need more space to pass by one another, especially when carrying forty-pound backpacks. Why increase the likelihood of conflict by having students brush up against each other, especially when they are frantically trying to get to their next class in five minutes?

Also, why not provide students with comfortable chairs? In over one hundred years we've progressed from stiff wooden chairs to stiff plastic ones. How many years now has the private sector shopped for ergonomically correct furniture for their offices? It's common sense that if an individual is physically comfortable sitting, the likelihood of that person performing well will increase.

Once a student-friendly building is in place, children should be taught to respect their school and view it as a haven away from the rest of the world. If students believed that school was a fun and safe place to be, they would be less likely to litter or vandalize school property.

And protecting the campus is a major concern these days. Officials in a school district outside Fort Worth, Texas, had their own idea of protecting students when they paid for training that instructed teachers and students to throw any object at a gun-toting attacker. It only took eighteen months for the district to come to their senses and stop the program.

Another brilliant idea of keeping students safe came from Bill

Crozier, a Republican candidate for state superintendent of schools in Oklahoma, who recommended that students use thick textbooks to deflect bullets during school shootings. He lost the election. I wonder why?

Once the physical plant presents a pleasing air, the adults working there need to foster a nurturing environment and not push kids away with their dictatorial, controlling attitude.

Students are bombarded with negatively worded messages from administrators broadcast throughout the entire school over the PA system, poisoning the environment. "Get to class on time!" "Any student found with a cell phone will have it confiscated!" "Students not following directions will face severe consequences!"

While these messages only pertain to a low percentage of students, all students hear the negativity and rarely get recognized for their part in doing what is expected of them. I wouldn't want that happening to my son or daughter.

In an *Education Week* piece, Robert Epstein shared a discovery made while researching his book *The Case Against Adolescence: Rediscovering the Adult in Every Teen* that "teenagers today are subject to ten times as many restrictions as are mainstream adults, to twice as many restrictions as are active-duty U.S. Marines, and even to twice as many restrictions as are incarcerated felons."

The tension and hostility adults have toward young people is frightening. I can't keep track of how many times I have overheard a teacher or an administrator yell at a student, shouting "Shut up!" at the top of his lungs. And with such histrionics we expect these kids to like school and perform well?

One time an assistant principal was chastising a class for not being quiet and noticed one student who was smiling. In front of everyone present the assistant principal screamed, "You think it's funny? I'll teach you the meaning of funny!" That's not a healthy environment for either the kids or the administrator.

I once observed the librarian strongly reprimanding one student for eating food and not bringing something to read during a silent reading period. "There is no eating in the library. Put that food away," she yelled from across the room. "Get out a book or a magazine, if you know how to read." Such a tactic is not going to encourage this student to do as he is told. He will rebel even further.

Teachers play a role in encouraging a positive atmosphere through what they display in their rooms. Which classroom would you rather have your child in, one where the walls are decorated by student work or by school rules? In one environment students express themselves; in the other, students follow behaviors to stay in line. Having lots of signs with long lists of "don'ts" posted leaves no doubt that student misbehavior is expected.

It reminds me of a posted sign in front of a famous amusement park that greets all incoming customers, NO REFUNDS ON PARKING. Such a screaming notice isn't that welcoming. You figure there must have been a whole bunch of folks who demanded their money back in order for such warnings to be made.

The adults working at a school need to be firm but at the same time keep their cool. Students who don't follow rules can be a pain, but there is a reason why adults are in charge and not children—in order to show them how to act, not act like them.

Finally, implementing a mandatory dress code would help make young people understand that school is a place for learning, not for fashion. While I have long opposed the idea of school uniforms in a public school (thousands of kids all dressed alike scares me), having all students follow an outline of proper clothing with a certain color scheme is a nice compromise.

At schools that have such a dress code (not a negatively worded "you will not wear these one hundred items" code but a positively worded one, like "Good grooming contributes to a healthy learning environment"), principals and teachers have found that kids connect better to their schools.

If all kids follow the dress policy Monday through Thursday, then on Friday they can have a casual wear day. However, if even one or two students are found not abiding by the policy, then Casual Dress Friday is canceled. Ahh, the wonders of peer pressure.

Maybe if the students dressed more appropriately, so would the teachers who often come to work as if they are doing a home improvement project. How can an educator look at herself* in the mirror dressed in shorts and flip-flops and conclude, "I'm ready for work"? Would any of us respect our doctor or lawyer dressed that way? Even plumbers have a certain way of dressing for their job.

One first-year teacher I observed was dressed like she was trying to get the part of Sharon Stone's stand-in in *Basic Instinct*. That probably was the only way she was able to keep the young boys in her ninth-grade class awake since it was clear she had no idea of a lesson plan. If all teachers dressed professionally, respect for them would increase.

If a solid foundation for an individual is a good education, then that schooling must be done in conditions conducive to maximizing learning. It's often said that a nation's most precious resource is its children. If so, then let's show kids that adults care about them. Build schools like cultural landmarks.

---

*Because 75 percent of public school teachers are women, I'm using female pronouns when referring to teachers, and since most secondary school principals and superintendents are men, I'm using the male pronouns for them.

2

Size Does Matter: Larger Class Sizes, Fewer Teachers, Smaller Schools

What parent wouldn't want her child in a classroom with only a handful of other students being taught by one teacher? Parents wish to hold on to the belief that if a teacher has fewer students their children will receive more one-on-one attention.

Here's one tiny example that debunks this assumption. My son's first-grade teacher could not remember if his school photos had arrived even though she had a small class. As she told me, "With twenty students it's difficult for me to keep track." Boy, did that response make me nervous. What about the high school teacher with five classes of forty students each? Now for that teacher not to easily remember if photos arrived or not, *that* I could understand.

Research remains inconclusive whether or not small class sizes have a positive effect on student achievement. Japanese students continuously outperform American students despite much larger class sizes. Of course, there are large classes and then there are enormous classes. Physical education classes in the United States tend to run humongous. One PE class in Los Angeles had 123 students. At some point the number should be limited just as there are fire codes regarding the maximum number of occupants in a public space.

Teachers unions back smaller class sizes for one reason: More teachers translate to more union dues. Why not take the money earmarked for additional teachers and apply it toward paying good teachers more?

No one thinks through the reality of smaller class sizes. First, more teachers need to be hired. Class size reduction places an enormous drain on the talent pool. Limiting the student/teacher ratio to twenty-to-one in every grade would produce the following dilemma. Take a 2,600-student grade 9–12 high school with 110 teachers, each of whom already teaches 5 classes of 30 students for a daily total of 150 students. Reducing the student/teacher ratio by one-third would reduce each teacher's client load to 100 students. So for every two teachers with a diminished workload the school would need one additional teacher, thereby increasing staffing needs by 50 percent.

If the remaining grades went in the same direction, you're looking at a 38.5 percent increase in teachers in grades four through twelve, possibly a million more instructors. Where on God's green Earth are these people going to sprout from?

It's not like any licensed teacher has ever been unable to locate employment. In education, there is no waiting list. Quite the opposite. The federal government's No Child Left Behind proclamation of a "highly qualified" instructor in every classroom across America sounds good as a sound bite but in district offices anything goes. Principals need a noncriminal, college-educated adult (preferably with a pulse) in every classroom. Quality has nothing to do with it. Commitment to mediocrity is public education's credo.

There's also the logistical problem: Where is the space to house the additional million teachers? Too many times overcrowded schools have held classes in storage rooms and cafeterias, not the best accommodations. Therefore, more classrooms would need to be built.

Is it possible that a real teacher is advocating larger class sizes? That's like a legislator proposing campaign reform.

I used to be a proponent for class size reduction. As an English teacher, how can you *not* be for it? Think about the difference: forty essays versus thirty versus twenty. If each two- to three-page paper takes ten minutes to grade, one is looking at a difference of two hundred minutes or three and a half hours of extra work for the teacher with forty rather than twenty essays to read through. This is a major reason why teachers don't assign as much writing as they need to—who has the time to evaluate it properly? Over the years journal writing has replaced more formal writing because it gives practice to the student without taxing the teacher.

You see, it really boils down to the key in every classroom—the quality of the teacher. If a teacher has ten or one hundred students, she still has to teach an effective lesson that connects to the class.

The notion that a larger class is harder to control than a smaller class is bogus. I have taught a class of forty-three honors students who have exhibited no behavior problems just as I have taught a summer school class of fifteen kids repeating tenth-grade English that forced me to use my complete arsenal of classroom management tricks.

I actually prefer larger classes because they have more energy than smaller ones where fewer students participate. When a teacher has put much time into planning a lesson and then exerts much energy into delivering it, why not expose as many kids as you can to it?

Which is better: a child in an overcrowded classroom helmed by a masterful instructor, or a child in a smaller classroom taught by an incompetent neophyte?

It is not possible to have three million highly effective teachers. All efforts to transform all teachers into master teachers will fail just as badly as forcing all students into four-year colleges. There are simply too many teachers for all of them to be outstanding.

When districts across the country reduced kindergarten through third-grade classes to a twenty-to-one student to teacher ratio in the 1990s, teacher quality suffered. Novices without teaching credentials got teaching jobs. So what if there were fewer kids? The teacher was of lesser quality.

The answer to the quality issue is simple: Limit the number of teachers. It would go a long way toward professionalizing teaching if fewer people were allowed to do it.

Districts would save money on health insurance and other benefits if they had fewer teachers on the payroll. Some of the money saved could go toward paying excellent teachers more money.

Another advantage of fewer teachers is that the teacher shortage

would be shortened. Districts could have the luxury of being more se-
lective in whom they hired. And teachers would be viewed more
highly since there would be fewer of them.

The main focus needs to be on the size of the campus, not the
size of the class. Why do we have schools in America that house as
many as five thousand students? With so many kids it's no wonder
they quietly drift toward gangs or become misfits or outcasts. The
American Legislative Exchange Council discovered that "small
school size was even more important than small classroom size in
the performance of students."

The idea behind the smaller school movement is to concentrate
on downsizing the big, bad school in order to personalize the learning experience for students.

Ideally children should attend four different campuses: kindergarten through third grade, fourth through sixth, seventh through
ninth, and tenth through twelfth. Dividing students into smaller
groupings would decrease friction and bullying between younger
and older children. Logistically this can be done at existing campuses by having all one grade level in one building. For new construction, smaller campuses should be built to accommodate these
configurations.

Due to space limitations, many high schools are just rearranging the existing campus, labeling each building as a "small school."
Doing this has limited impact on student interaction issues because
at snack or lunch all five thousand students are out there at the
same time, so where's the "small"?

It's not so much the size of a school's population but the number of students within a certain number of acres. Where I work
there are about 2,400 students. Nearby is Occidental College, which
has about 1,800. The difference is that the high school is restricted
to 18 acres while Occidental is spread out over 120. And when the
high school changed configuration from grades ten through twelve
to nine through twelve, suddenly hallways and green space became
congested. Add the raging hormones of male teens and, to no one's
surprise, fights increased.

Allowing adolescents space, both physical as well as emotional, is critical to their well-being. Therefore, schools need to be designed with this in mind.

In studies on people who work in smaller organizations, several positive characteristics emerge: fewer absences, more punctuality, frequent participation, and more leadership behavior demonstrated. Most important, people tend to view their work as more meaningful.

New York and Chicago public schools are pushing toward the smaller school concept. Two hundred small schools have opened recently in New York, and several dozen in Chicago. These schools have been credited with retaining high school students who otherwise would drop out. In 2004 Mayor Richard M. Daley introduced the Renaissance 2010 initiative, which plans on opening one hundred small schools by decade's end. Most of these schools are scheduled to be run independently of the district either as charter schools or by outside companies.

Arne Duncan, the chief executive officer of Chicago Public Schools, told *Education Week* that each of the new smaller schools has a waiting list. "[Families] are desperately looking for better options."

A few studies have looked into whether or not smaller schools make any difference. A study done by the Consortium on Chicago School Research and Mills College on Chicago's small schools revealed increased attendance—students attended school six to nine more days—and a decreased dropout rate—7 percent lower—compared to traditional schools. Teachers at the smaller schools felt they had more of a say in how the school was run. Plus, parents participated more in the PTA at the smaller schools.

New York City's New Century high schools, which deliberately enroll a high percentage of poor and minority students, posted higher graduation rates compared to other high schools, 78 percent versus 58 percent. Policy Studies Associates, Inc., the research group who conducted the 2007 study, also found that the graduate rate at the smaller schools was higher than at larger schools with similar demographics.

Another study conducted by Michigan State University claimed that students attending smaller schools earned no advantages. However, this study and others like it focus on the wrong things, such as higher test scores, to come to such conclusions. Remember, if more students are staying in school, the would-be dropouts who tend to be low performers on tests lower the overall school score by continuing to attend. Did the researchers make observations about student interactions, or conduct interviews with students? Most likely no. The fact that fewer people are moving around in a set space decreases the chances of students bumping into other students, something that often causes friction, especially in the upper grades where teenagers literally brush shoulders with one another as they walk down a hallway. These are things that can't be easily measured.

3

No More Malcolms in the Middle

Could there possibly be a connection between lower student achievement in middle and high schools, and students having up to seven different instructors, unlike the one nurturing elementary school teacher they had the entire day? Imagine having seven different bosses and having to deal with a variety of egos.

Typically troubles brew in middle schools when young people go through the puberty metamorphosis. Adding a new school with a slate of different teachers overwhelms a young teen's absorption factor.

Where did the junior high or middle school concept originate? In the last quarter of a century, junior high schools with grades seven through nine began transforming into middle schools with grades six through eight or just seven and eight, with ninth grade added to senior high schools. The original idea behind this change was an interdisciplinary approach to teaching in a middle school where teachers from different departments such as history and English would intentionally develop lessons incorporating both disciplines. For example, as students read *The Grapes of Wrath* they would also study the dust bowl in America during the Great Depression.

Well, this idea never quite got off the ground. The end result is that instead of having fourteen- and fifteen-year-olds as heads of their domain, they are now the babies in a high school setting. It is now time to admit that the middle school experiment has been a failure and is just another example of how education takes old ideas, repackages them, shines them up, and publicly announces the coming of *the answer* to all that is wrong with public school. This is not the first time there have been middle schools, and just wait for the next new craze that will be tried—junior high schools!

Here's a troubling fact: Only one of four middle school teachers has any kind of special expertise in middle school pedagogy. It seems that no one knows what to do with the Malcolms in the Middle.

A survey by the World Health Organization revealed that out of all grade levels middle schoolers have the most negative views of the climate of their schools and peer culture.

Another survey conducted by the Council of Urban Boards of Education showed that middle schoolers were more likely than students in any other grade level to witness bullying and fighting. Clearly these eleven-, twelve-, and thirteen-year-old tweens do not feel safe in their middle school environment. Actually, few adults have fond memories of these years; people tend to have pleasant remembrances of a grade school or a high school teacher. Most parents would prefer keeping their children in the friendlier confines of elementary schools rather than watching them advance to the scarier, negative influences of middle school.

Kids advancing from elementary to middle school go from one teacher all day long to classes that run less than an hour taught by seven different teachers. Why should anyone be surprised that difficulties arise?

Why have different teachers for different subjects when one teacher does fine with all subjects in elementary school? Supposedly it is because each subject becomes increasingly more challenging, thus requiring an instructor of higher expertise. However, that doesn't seem to have stopped many folks from becoming math or science teachers, since 40 percent of them never majored in the fields they teach. And a study by William H. Schmidt of Michigan State University revealed that American math teachers entering middle schools took half as many math classes as teachers in South Korea and Taiwan. So why bother with subject matter teachers? For decades physical education teachers have taught health classes. Couldn't an English teacher teach history as well? Why not have science instructors do math lessons? When it's time for real high school, students will be mature enough to handle different teachers, and it will be a good transition to college.

Besides having several teachers each day, can you think of anything else that makes middle schools different from elementary schools? The security guards. Rare is it to feel their presence at a grammar school; common to see it in the upper grades. Does that mean more kids misbehave as they get older? The fact that schools even have real police on campus (often referred to as resource officers) gives the impression that there is the expectation that students will get into trouble. And some studies do show a near doubling of reported violent incidents from elementary to secondary school.

The Rand Corporation came out with a report in 2004 called "Focus on the Wonder Years: Challenges Facing the American Middle School" that showed "more than half of eighth graders fail to achieve expected levels of proficiency in reading, math, and science on national tests." And, as is so typical whenever U.S. students are compared with those in other countries, American children do okay in elementary school, start sinking in middle school, then fall off the radar come high school.

Then this sobering conclusion from the Rand report: "Research suggests that the onset of puberty is an especially poor reason for beginning a new phase of schooling." Exactly. Their bodies are changing, their minds are expanding, and instead of providing them a nurturing environment, a sense of sameness as they deal with rapid change, what do schools do? Give them more rapid change. After six years with one teacher, how about forty-five minutes with seven different teachers in seven different rooms, moving around crazily every hour in a tizzy, increasing their heart rate, hearing stern PA warnings to "get to class *on time*." What a place for learning!

Luckily, a trend has begun where districts are creating K–8 schools, eliminating middle schools altogether, along with their problems. According to *Time,* "The change is driven largely by a series of studies that depict U.S. middle schools as the 'Bermuda Triangle of education' . . . the place where kids lose their way academically and socially—in many cases never to resurface."

Milwaukee, Wisconsin, has seen such great success with students performing much better in K–8 settings that the district plans on reducing middle schools "from forty-six in 2003 to eight by 2008, while upping K–8s from 10 to 120." Other cities making the shift include Philadelphia, Baltimore, and San Diego. When asked if they want their children to remain at elementary schools over middle schools, parents overwhelmingly favor the K–8 model.

Many students who seem lost in middle schools become the leaders at K–8 institutions, mentoring the younger children, exhibiting a sense of responsibility not evident in middle school. At one school, third and seventh graders worked together in writing letters to soldiers stationed in Iraq.

The fact that the seventh and eighth graders know that their kindergarten teacher is still on campus might make them behave better as well. The warm and fuzzy that is no longer cool in eighth grade can still continue. Give that thirteen-year-old a hug!

4

The Good News: No More Summer School; the Bad News: No More Summer

Think of all the new information students today must master compared to their counterparts from the nineteenth century. Yet both generations share one thing in common: Both attended school virtually the same number of days.

In olden times when children helped on their family's farm it made sense economically not to have them in school all the time. But things have changed; a long, long time ago, they changed. Yet schools continue much as they have from the past, despite the multiplication of knowledge that has resulted over several decades.

Of the 260 Monday-through-Friday weekdays in a year, 180 of them are school days. This means that kids don't go to school nearly one-third of all weekdays. Put another way, kids attend school 49 percent of the entire year.

Why does America provide a part-time education for its children? Who came up with the six hours a day, nine and a half months a year workload? If education is so vitally important, then more time needs to be spent on it.

If twenty more days were added to the school calendar to make it an even two hundred, as is the case in countries that continuously surpass the United States in basic skills comparisons, the percentage of Monday-through-Friday school days would rise from 69 to 76 percent. Kids would still get eleven weeks off each year. There would be a two-week vacation period after each of the first three quarters, then five weeks off during summer.

Look at the advantage students in other countries have over American schoolchildren. A school year in European countries typically lasts between 200 and 220 days; in Japan 240. Just 20 more days may not seem like much, but when multiplied by the thirteen years of schooling, that equates to 260 extra days, or more than another school year and a half of instruction. Is it any mystery why America's children score lower than their foreign counterparts? U.S. kids are taught subjects at crash-course speed.

With a longer school year, summer school would be eliminated, as would some minor holidays.

As of now, many kids already attend summer school, typically a six-week session (minus one day off for Independence Day), meaning that they are actually enrolled in school for 209 days. A year-round schedule would actually provide those kids with nine more days off than they currently have.

The main complaint parents have against school during the summertime is that it infringes on family vacations. But who actually takes a three-month vacation these days? Plus, traveling during the summer means visiting places when they are the most crowded and during the hottest recorded temperatures. A year-long schedule with more frequent breaks would give families a chance to visit New England Octobers and Gulf Coast Marches.

Having children at school longer is not only beneficial for their education, but beneficial for child care as well considering the number of dual-income households. For many parents the last day of the school year signals a red flag: What do you do with the kids now? Usually what happens is parents start scrambling in the spring to line up summer day camps for their children.

Most workers in the United States get six paid holidays: New Year's, Memorial Day, Independence Day, Labor Day, Thanksgiving, and Christmas.

Look at the holidays schools typically have by the month in a single year:

Months	Holidays	No. of Days Off
September	Labor Day	1
November	Veterans Day, Thanksgiving (2)	3
December	winter break	10
January	Martin Luther King, Jr., Day	1
February	Lincoln and Washington's birthdays	2
April	spring break	5
May	Memorial Day	1
	Total	**23 days off**

Plus, there are anywhere from one to eight pupil-free days when teachers have meetings all day and students remain at home.

October and March are the only holiday-free months, though pupil-free days tend to get scheduled during that time. So, in effect, there is no month when students attend school every Monday through Friday.

Consider as well that time is carved away from the 180-day schedule for school assemblies, minimum days, and testing. These interruptions break up any learning rhythm established.

And with all the increased testing, teachers are covering less material than they used to in order to give practice tests.

Where I work I receive the Orthodox Christmas off on January 6 (referred to as Feast of the Epiphany or Three Kings' Day) because of the large Armenian population. We also have the day before and the day after Thanksgiving, meaning school is open for just two days that week—how productive. In Beverly Hills, where one-fifth of the residents along with its mayor are Persian, the schools close on the Persian New Year.

There is one day I would like to see added to the list of holidays for children. Why not give kids the day off after Halloween, the only day of the year strictly for them? I've never understood how we expect young children to get up early the next day and go to school after being out at night past their bedtime, getting candy or visiting relatives dressed in their costumes, enjoying themselves. Making November 1 a nonschool day (teachers can have meetings) makes sense. Children are very tired on this day and are still in the afterglow of their festive evening.

Summer school is for two types of students: those who failed classes during the regular school year and those who wish to take enrichment courses.

Both types of students would benefit from a longer school year. Absences would not have as much of a negative impact as in a shorter year. A student with fifteen absences in a ninety-day semester versus fifteen absences in a hundred-day semester might still be able to salvage a passing grade in the class, avoiding the need to repeat the class. If a student does need to repeat a class, or would like to take an enrichment class, he can take the course online.

The Washington-based Center for American Progress did a study on high schools that had a longer school day and year and found higher achievement at those institutions.

Here's how the school year calendar would look. Using the 2008–09 year, school begins on Monday, July 21, 2008, and runs for ten weeks (forty-nine school days), completing the first quarter on Friday, September 26. There is only one holiday during this quarter: Labor Day. School is closed for two weeks.

The second quarter begins on Monday, October 13, and ends on Friday, December 19 (forty-eight school days). There are only two holidays: Thanksgiving and the day after. School is closed for two weeks, which would normally be winter break (or Christmas vacation, right, Mr. O'Reilly?).

The second semester or third quarter begins on Monday, January 5, 2009, and finishes up on Friday, March 13 (forty-nine school days). There is one holiday: Presidents' Day. School is closed for two weeks, which would normally be spring break.

The fourth and final quarter starts on Monday, March 30, and the school year ends on Friday, June 12 (fifty-four school days). There is one holiday: Memorial Day. Note that the last quarter is one week longer to accommodate testing.

In all, school covers forty-one of the fifty-two weeks of the year, giving children eleven weeks off of school, five of which are summer vacation.

As a bonus, by not having nearly three months off in the summer, students are less likely to forget everything come the start of school.

Let the Kids Sleep In

6:30 A.M.	Mom:	*Time to get up.*
	Child:	*Five more minutes.*
6:45 A.M.	Mom:	*Time to get up.*
	Child:	*A few more minutes.*
7:00 A.M.	Mom:	*You better get up.*
	Child:	*A couple more minutes.*
7:15 A.M.	Mom:	*Your breakfast is getting cold.*
	Child:	*Coming!*
7:30 A.M.	Mom:	*If you don't get up now, you'll have to walk to school.*
	Child:	*Okay! I'm up!*

Why do we still insist on children getting up early in the morning and going to school when their minds are still asleep? There are no more cows to milk, no more fields to till. The vast majority of children in America arrive at school between 7:30 and 8:00 A.M., often bleary-eyed. In 1850 there was a reason for children to wake up at the crack of dawn. But not in the twenty-first century.

Medical studies show that children, especially adolescents, function better when they wake up later; having them rise early interrupts their normal sleep cycles. Since their bodies are still growing, they require more sleep.

Only one out of every five eleven- to seventeen-year-olds sleeps the recommended nine hours a night. Over a quarter of adolescents admit to falling asleep in class at least once a week.

A later start time makes sense during daylight savings time

months in the fall when the school year commences. Waking children up while it's pitch-black outside isn't easy to do.

For working parents it's better for children to arrive at school later. Because the vast majority of married-couple families have both parents working, having school hours that mirror adult work schedules would aid parents; they could use the extra child care.

Usually parents quickly drop their students off at school, then head back home to finish getting themselves ready for work. Wouldn't it be easier on parents if everyone left the house all at once?

Plus, a later start time would give families time to actually eat a real breakfast instead of swallowing Pop-Tarts. So many kids barely wake up, put clothes on, and fly out the door with empty stomachs that negatively impact their learning capability. It is difficult for families to regularly find a meal of the day when they all can sit together and talk about anything (remember the Ozzie and Harriet days of family suppers?). Allowing families to be together for even a half hour has a positive impact on the children.

Elementary schools would start at 9:00 A.M. and last until 4:00 P.M. for all grades. In Massachusetts, some schools are part of the Expanded Learning Time Initiative, which provides extra money in order to lengthen the school day. Much of what used to be imbedded in elementary school—music and art and even physical education—is making a comeback.

An ideal high school schedule would have longer class periods, seventy minutes long, and a forty-five-minute lunch.

While some advocate block scheduling where students go to three or four classes one day, then other classes the next, with periods lasting 90–120 minutes, it is important that students make a daily connection with all their teachers.

Here's a sample high school schedule:

Period 1	9:00–10:10
Break	10:10–10:15
Period 2	10:15–11:25
Break	11:25–11:30

Period 3	11:30–12:40
Lunch	12:40–1:25
Passing	1:25–1:35
Period 4	1:35–2:45
Break	2:45–2:50
Period 5	2:50–4:00
Break	4:00–4:05
Period 6	4:05–5:15

Yes, a longer and more concentrated day, but then the children are finished. No homework, as discussed later in chapter 13. Each teacher would budget a minimum of twenty minutes per class to help students with their work. Paraeducators (discussed in chapter 28) can help out as well. After 5:15 P.M. children can enjoy their families and their friends until the next day.

Note the ten-minute passing period after lunch to give students enough time to get to class. And the "breaks" are in-class ones, as explained in the next chapter.

Parents who need child care earlier or later than school hours could, for an additional fee, drop off their children at the school's study/tutoring center manned by teachers for one hour before or after school, or in any enrichment program on campus.

What often happens is that parents enroll their children in after-school programs since they can't pick them up until dinnertime. It's been estimated that over six million kids are enrolled in some form of after-school program, but that still leaves fifteen million who are on their own. The longer school day would keep them occupied if a productive program were in place.

At many elementary schools private companies offer chess, music, science, and dance lessons, extending the day for many students. Chicago has the After School Matters program where, as reported in *Edutopia,* "High school students are given paid apprenticeships in fields such as technology, journalism, and sports, in which they design Web sites, work at local newspapers, or at the studios of the city's cable-access network." The Navigators program in Alliance,

Ohio, has classes in robotics, fitness, and cooking for middle school students.

A 2004 Harvard Family Research Project reported that "higher levels of attendance in out-of-school-time programs have been significantly correlated to scholastic achievement, higher school attendance, more time spent on homework and on positive extracurricular activities, enjoyment and effort in school, and better teacher reports of student behavior."

Eliminating nutrition break (what a funny name to give to a time in the day when kids buy junk food) has several benefits. One, it means that students won't scarf down chips and soda, weakening their alertness and concentration for class. It would also remove one of the two major breaks when all students congregate in a small area such as the cafeteria, which would make administrators' jobs less stressful. Plus, no snack break would cut in half the number of times students can litter the campus, meaning less clean-up for the custodial staff (maybe they will finally have the time to deep clean the classrooms more frequently than once a year for Open House).

Lunch, however, would be forty-five minutes long, allowing a decent amount of time for everyone, students and adults alike, to eat a meal. Teachers especially would appreciate a lunch break that allows them to chew food at a rate that permits their digestive tract to work properly.

Schools in Minnesota and Kentucky already start forty-five minutes later and have seen positive results: increased attendance, less tardiness, more alert students.

A longer school day is not so foreign to the higher-achieving students who typically spend after-school time in band practice or science study groups. Even student athletes spend more time on campus practicing their sport. Such extracurricular activities could more easily be part of the regularly scheduled longer school day.

It's no coincidence that half of all juvenile crime happens between 2:00 and 8:00 P.M. when many children are without adult supervision. A later end time for students would help put a dent in this statistic.

By the way, making school an hour longer would translate to an extra 200 hours of schooling, equivalent to adding 25 more days, meaning the current 180-day school year, if increased by 20 days as suggested earlier, would transform into a 225-day school year, but in only 200 days of attendance. Imagine how this extra time could positively impact the learning of young people.

6

For Whom the Bell Tolls

Ring. Students rush to their Period 1 class.

Ring. Tardy bell for Period 1.

Ring. Students rush to their Period 2 class.

Ring. Tardy bell for Period 2.

Ring. Bell that starts snack.

Ring. Snack ends and students rush to their Period 3 class.

Ring. Tardy bell for Period 3.

Ring. Students rush to their Period 4 class.

Ring. Tardy bell for Period 4.

Ring. Students rush to their Period 5 class.

Ring. Tardy bell for Period 5.

Ring. Bell that starts lunch.

Ring. Lunch ends and students rush to their Period 6 class.

Ring. Tardy bell for Period 6.

Ring. Students rush to their Period 7 class.

Ring. Tardy bell for Period 7.

Ring. School's out.

Whew! Exhausting, isn't it? And in this frenetically paced environment we expect great things from our children?

Just how many more years will it take before someone sane realizes the craziness of this human shell game, shuffling kids from room to room as if they are laboratory rats.

Bells ring throughout the day, contributing to the factory feeling of schools. This Pavlovian method may work wonders at an automotive assembly plant, but at a school it creates tension. It is disconcerting to sit in a room and hear loud bells throughout the day, every hour in the upper grades.

Why can't schools just have teachers excuse students without any bells?

Some of my favorite days at work over the past couple of decades have been the times when the bell and PA system weren't working. What a pleasure not to hear noise blaring from the speakers above. How calming it was to just tell the students, "You're excused," as they politely left the room, unlike the scrambling hell that normally breaks loose when their ears hear that buzzer.

Without the constant chiming of bells, everyone will calm down to focus more on classwork.

Besides the annoying noise pollution, another issue is the mass movement of students from classroom to classroom in middle and high schools.

Once students exit the comforts of the single classroom setting in elementary school and enter the funhouse in-one-door-and-out-the-other concept in secondary schools, a whole new level of anxiety prevails. The time between classes, though often only five minutes long, creates undue interruptions in the school day. Having students schlep from one room to the next opens up opportunities for tardies and truancies, not to mention fights. It creates a revved-up environment where students hurriedly rush to their lockers and to their next classes.

As it is, school officials expend excessive energy on trying to get students to class on time. With all the strict tardy policies and unending PA admonitions one would think half the students weren't prompt. However, if anyone did a poll they would discover that over 90 percent of students are on time. That's probably a better on-time performance than adult workers. Yet this one issue is focused on to the point of distortion. Hey, sometimes it isn't easy for kids to go from one end of a large high school to another in a sprint-like five minutes. Even for responsible students, such short time spans to get to the next class present a challenge. So why rush them?

Having students move around less by having them stay in one

classroom all day as they do in elementary school would alleviate this problem immediately.

It's interesting that as children get older and supposedly more mature schools give students more teachers and more interruptions. It should be the other way around. Younger children's attention spans are briefer. It makes more sense for them to move around from classroom to classroom in shorter time increments. Have third graders go to the music room for half an hour, then on to the art room for about an hour; next, move outside for some physical activity. Have the older kids stay in the rooms all day long.

Indiana's Shelbyville High principal Tom Zobel told *Time* magazine that students who dropped out of school said in exit interviews that "I'm just done with this process—fifty minutes, bell, fifty minutes, bell."

By simply moving the teachers around, as they do in Japan, schools could make an amazing assortment of long-time ills in public education vanish. Since teachers represent a much smaller group of travelers than the entire student body, they can watch the clock, stop the lesson, then move on to the next room of students. There would be no need for adrenaline-rushing, heart-stopping bells.

Think about it. No more tardies, no more loitering at lockers. A calming effect would envelop a school with the absence of bells blaring or children scampering from one end of the campus to another.

Students can take a breather instead of becoming breathless during the five-minute break between classes, contemplating what was just learned. As they remain in the room waiting for the next teacher to arrive, students can get up from their seats, walk around, stretch or go to the bathroom, or merely do nothing. Their minds will be fresher to take in more information for the next class without their hearts beating out of their chests from barely making it through the door in time for class.

Oh, and who would supervise the kids while teachers switch rooms? Each classroom would be manned by paraeducators, as described in chapter 28. They will provide supervision during the five-minute breaks until the teachers arrive.

And such a situation allows teachers frequent breaks out of the classroom, allowing them to use the restroom if they need to.

The only complication with this plan of keeping students in one room all day is what to do if they all don't take the same classes. Well, with the push toward more academic rigor, why can't they take the same classes? The students in advanced classes are already tracked together; those who would be in a vocational track (see chapter 11) would likewise be taking the same coursework.

7

Full-day Kindergarten

So much attention is given to preschool programs that some people forget about the most underutilized grade level of all: kindergarten (K).

What used to be a three-hour introduction to the world of schooling for five-year-olds is now becoming an integral building block in the foundation of learning. First-grade content has now transferred down to kindergarten.

Close to two out of every three children in America are enrolled in full-day kindergarten programs, a figure that has doubled during the past twenty years. Hillsborough County, Florida, has had full-day K classes for nearly thirty years.

Full-day kindergarten, typically six hours in length, works for a number of reasons.

Children today are used to staying at school all day because of preschool. Nearly 70 percent of children have gotten accustomed to a full-day school setting by the time they are five years old due to preschool experience. It's a smoother transition for children to go from full-day preschool to full-day kindergarten. Since children already know their ABCs and 123s, they are ready to learn more.

There are fewer transitions in a full-day program than a half-day one. The most common misconception about full-day kindergarten is that it doubles the workload. This is not true. Instead of having children spend a quick hour on reading skills, then switch over to math skills, teachers can work at a more leisurely pace, spending more time on each subject, decreasing the number of changes.

This benefits young learners who have difficulty settling down when transitions occur.

Children have more time to think about what they are learning. You can't rush development. Going through the kindergarten standards in three hours allows little time for children to think or play or have the lessons soak in. Full-day environments relieve the rush-rush-rush of the three-hour setup. Teachers who teach full-day have the luxury of time to play music or read books out loud. Reading a book to a class benefits the children's growth as independent readers.

Schools have already cut back on such nonstructured time as recess. Full-day K allows children more time to play with one another with longer recesses, furthering their social development.

As an unfortunate side note, some schools have banned playground games such as tag supposedly because of accidents as well as the harm to little kids' self-esteem. How crazy is that? Children have excessive energy to burn off. It's wiser to have them play outside exerting themselves than inside a classroom bouncing off the walls.

Full-day K provides more learning opportunities. Children who attend full-day kindergarten demonstrate greater reading knowledge than children in half-day programs, and are likely to reach third and fourth grade without having to repeat a grade.

The National Center for Education Statistics reports that 68 percent of students in full-day programs spent more than an hour per day on reading instruction, compared to 37 percent in half-day programs. They also spent more time on math instruction.

Full-day K benefits children with limited English skills as well as those from lower-economic areas, helping to decrease the achievement gap between white and nonwhite students.

By the way, the phrase "achievement gap" refers to the noticeable difference in the academic performance between white students and nonwhite students, and between higher-economic students and lower-economic students. It is because of these differences that governments categorize students by ethnicity in order to track progress among the struggling subgroups. According to the U.S. Census Bureau, the number of Latino and African-American children living in poverty is more than twice the number of white children, which partly explains those minorities' higher dropout rate.

California's Superintendent of Public Instruction, Jack O'Connell, made headlines in 2007 when he called attention to the higher scores of poor white and Asian students compared to nonpoor Hispanics and blacks. "These are not just economic achievement gaps, they are racial achievement gaps," O'Connell said.

Full-day K provides all-day child care. There is also a practical reason why there should be full-day kindergarten across America: June Cleaver is no longer a typical American mother. The majority of family households have either a single parent or both parents working. These families typically place their children in full-day preschools, sometimes starting as early as a few months old. There is no longer the mystery of that first day of school, the first day of kindergarten, the dramatic first separation of parent and child with many crying hysterically for Mommy. They have already acclimated themselves to being at a school all day, in some cases as long as ten hours a day. For these children to go from a full-day program of preschool to three-hour kindergarten sessions is actually a step backward socially and academically, not to mention the intense stress it places on parents to find after-school care. Is it better for children to go to their main school for three hours, then be transported by bus to a child-care facility for the rest of the day? Why not keep them safely in one place all day long? And if the school doesn't provide a full-day program, then they need to have options in place for those parents who need them.

I'll never forget what one school board member told me at a meeting when I addressed my local district regarding this issue. "We are not in the child-care business," she said with a straight face. Well, someone needed to remind her that the school district that she ran has its own full-day child-care center. So what does she mean the district isn't in the child-care business? What a ludicrous statement for a school board official to make.

Additionally, having children in school longer means less time for students to spend vegetating in front of a television, or with a nanny who chats on her cell phone uninterested in the well-being of the child.

Full-day K keeps children in public instead of private schools. Full-day attracts parents who might otherwise opt out of public schools in favor of private ones that more regularly offer all-day kindergarten. Often parents choose a private school for their child's kindergarten year, then transfer the child to a public school for first grade. And some, after getting a taste of private school, never go public.

Full-day kindergarten should be mandatory in order to maximize the learning potential of all children. While it's comforting to know that the majority of kindergartners attend full-day programs, that still leaves over one-third of children receiving only three to three and a half hours of instruction each day for a whole academic year.

School districts that don't seriously study implementing a full-day kindergarten program are living in the past.

If districts need an additional incentive to offer full-day programs, study after study shows that the majority of parents are in favor.

And while we're at it, how about making kindergarten mandatory? Amazingly, eleven states do not make kindergarten enrollment compulsory.

I know what you're thinking. Full-day K costs more. True, it does cost a little more to implement. In Oregon it costs $5,200 annually to educate a half-day kindergartner and $6,700 for a full-day one, but that's only a 20 percent increase, not a doubling of costs, as some claim. Besides, in some areas full-day K can save a district money by reducing the need for crossing guards in the middle of the day.

Some districts give parents the option of paying for the extended program. In Paradise Valley Unified School District in Phoenix,

Arizona, voters gave themselves a property tax increase to provide their children with full-day K.

Not one study exists showing half-day students achieve at a higher level than full-day students. So what are districts and states waiting for?

8

Healthy and Wise, with No Fries

Children are fatter than ever before. Walk onto a school campus, especially a middle or high school one, and observe the snacking that occurs all day long. I've seen kids with teacher's passes under their arms supposedly going to the restroom but instead making a beeline to the vending machines for chips and soda while listening to their iPods and talking on their cells (teenagers are the all-time multitasking champs).

Unhealthy food is easily accessible at schools and is commonly eaten throughout the day in classrooms, adding to the obesity problems of the youth, an epidemic already in progress.

When I was a child, my mom had to buy my pants in the May Company's "husky" section because I was overweight. Back then I had my own version of NCLB: no chip left behind. Sometimes I was the object of ridicule, being the only heavy kid in class. Boy, would I have company today.

During the past thirty years, the rate of obesity has doubled among preschoolers, tripled among six- to eleven-year-olds, with diabetes and heart disease on the rise. Almost one-third of children ages twelve to nineteen are either overweight or at the risk of being obese.

The medical cost of obesity in the United States is $75 billion. In California, nearly every third child in grades five, seven, and nine is obese despite the Golden State's reputation for health fanaticism.

Obese people live less and cost society more. A UCLA/Rand

study found that being fat ages a person and increases the chances of other chronic medical problems more so than being a slim smoker or drinker.

It is projected that one in every five health dollars spent for people ages fifty to sixty will be for ailments due to obesity. Between 1990 and 2002, deaths related to bad eating and scarce exercise rose 33 percent. According to former Health and Human Services secretary Tommy G. Thompson, "Our poor eating habits and lack of activity are literally killing us."

Here are some recent headlines regarding obesity among young people:

- In 1994, fewer than 5 percent of diabetic children had Type 2 diabetes, the disease in which the body loses its ability to use insulin. Today, that number is above 30 percent.
- Since 1970, fast-food consumption among children has increased fivefold.
- Each day, one out of every three children eats a fast-food meal, adding an extra six pounds of weight per year to their bodies.
- Heavy kids miss more school than thin ones, leading to lower academic performance.
- One-quarter of overweight teens have considered killing themselves due to ridicule about their size.

With childhood obesity and diabetes at all-time-high levels, why do schools still have vending machines spread all over their campus grounds? Although they provide a source of income for clubs and athletics, vending machines should be banned. Why is it necessary for children to be eating and drinking all the time throughout the day? And, by the way, whatever happened to drinking fountains? It seems that some students cannot go more than one hour without putting something into their mouths.

And what about teachers who, as a way to get on their students' good side, allow the twenty-ouncers of Cactus Cooler and grab bags of Nacho Doritos to sit on desks during class? How good is that for an effective learning environment? Boundaries need to be reestablished for when it is okay to eat. Food belongs in the cafeteria, not in the classroom.

As with education, good nutrition begins at home. If breakfast consists of Hostess Donettes and a Mountain Dew, who can blame teens for wanting to be consistent in their eating habits at school? Students need to understand that schools are a special place to learn, not an extension of home where they can open the fridge any time they want.

In my unscientific study of observing teens for nearly twenty years I have definitely noticed more pants cutting into bellies and more "muffin tops"—young ladies whose midriffs have drifted a bit too much, 360 degrees around their middles.

Is there a connection between eating in class and overweight kids? From what I've seen it is usually the heavy kids who are munching.

Beyond the health issues, having students snack continuously hinders their concentration. What they are consuming is full of sugar and sodium, which worsens their focus. Many states, including Connecticut and New Jersey, have enacted legislation banning junk food. Some schools limit the use of vending machines, making them inoperable during classes. Maryland has timing devices on them to restrict access during school hours. Some districts go further by instituting healthier cafeteria offerings.

There is a misconception that preparing healthier food costs more. What's interesting is that the cost for cafeterias to switch over to a healthier menu heavy on fresh vegetables is negligible.

Cafeterias can substitute wheat bread for white, baked for fried. Schools that have made the transition to a healthier menu find that initially students resist buying the more nutritious offerings, but soon they get used to it.

Private business is waking up to the obesity alarm as well. In May of 2006 the Alliance for a Healthier Generation, a joint effort of the William J. Clinton Foundation and the American Heart Association, ironed out an agreement with the three largest beverage companies—Coca-Cola, PepsiCo, and Cadbury Schweppes—to limit portion sizes and reduce the number of calories available to children during the school day, affecting close to thirty-five million students. By school year 2009–10, light juices and sports drinks, replacing soda pop, will be sold in twelve-ounce containers, each with no more than one hundred calories. This is significant since 13 percent of adolescents' calories come from sweetened drinks.

However, economics still plays a part in deciding which foods stay and which ones go. Often, the company or group that has the most convincing lobbyists wins. For example, in 2007, California schools no longer sold chocolate milk even if the milk was of the 2 percent, low-fat variety. However, Pop-Tarts were deemed okay. While low in cholesterol (0 mg), each Pop-Tart contains 16 grams of sugar and 170 milligrams of sodium, with 98.8 percent of its 254 calories derived from fat. Unlike Pop-Tarts, chocolate milk contains vitamins A and C. And one study comparing chocolate milk with Gatorade found that cyclists had much more energy from the milk than the energy drink. Oh well, I guess the Dairy Council of California did not persuade as well as Kellogg's of Battle Creek.

It is somewhat understandable why schools are reluctant to change to healthier selections. For years middle and especially high schools in districts all across America have desperately tried to look for new revenues, as any business would. With districts allocating less general funds to schools and with decreased student participation in purchasing student ID cards, principals have been left to figure out where to hunt for money for student programs, so they tapped into hawking soda pop and junk food, the primary diet of teenagers. What MBA graduate could argue with that business concept of exploiting the market?

With lucrative exclusive contracts offered by the two big bottlers, Coca-Cola and PepsiCo, how could schools turn down such deals, especially when they enable schools to directly impact students in a positive way, from school dances to band uniforms to yearbook budgets?

Many schools raise over $50,000 in vending machine sales per year to help student programs. Jefferson High in Los Angeles made over $88,000 one year. With teens' voluminous appetite for soda, how is selling fruit drinks, sports drinks, and water going to make up for the loss in revenue? Where I work the student store began losing hundreds of dollars a week when they made the transition toward healthier snacks.

The ways in which schools choose to promote healthier lifestyles are inconsistent. It is hypocritical for a school to ban junk foods from being sold in its cafeteria and student stores, yet allow clubs to sell candy bars for fund-raising in every classroom. Is anyone proposing to do away with this practice?

Then there are times when it should be okay for kids to have a treat. Case in point, rest in peace, birthday parties at school. Across the nation it is no longer permissible for the parent to bring in cupcakes or cookies if a child's birthday falls on a school day. Now I'm not saying cupcakes are healthy; we all know they're not. But there is something special about a class celebration for a child. One school district official said that a birthday doesn't have to include cake; substitute carrots instead. Try telling that to Chuck E. Cheese. This is just another example of robbing children of pleasant school memories. I'm sorry, but celery sticks instead of cookies are not fun for kids.

At my son's school a note went home during the first couple of weeks of the school year informing parents that treats would no longer be allowed to celebrate a child's birthday; however, if a child so wished, he could bring in a favorite book and read it to the class. Well, quite frankly, such an activity should be happening anyway regardless of birthday celebrations. I doubt a child will jump out of his socks when he finds out that instead of eating cake he will read about it instead. Come on. What's next on the list? Outlawing Girl Scout cookies? (Heaven forbid; where else could one buy the Samoas?)

Sure enough, groups have surfaced protesting new antisnack policies. The Texas Legislature recently passed the so-called Safe Cupcake Amendment (I kid you not), which guarantees parents' right to deliver unhealthful treats to the classroom, such as Sweetheart candies on Valentine's Day and candy corn on Halloween. Representative Jim Dunnam sponsored the legislation after a school in his district booted out a father bringing birthday pizzas to his child's class.

Even treats given by teachers are being considered verboten. The Santa Clara Unified School District in Northern California has already done that. What's going to happen to the teacher? Will there be a chart with varying punishments? A Snickers mini = a verbal warning; a full-size Snickers = a day without pay. And you know what happens when adults try to keep things away from children, don't you? The kids get them anyway; in fact, it makes them desire the forbidden things even more.

The old adage about everything in moderation is the rule to follow. Banning all sweets will backfire. Why not allow elementary classrooms to hold a single monthly celebration for all children's birthdays during that time period?

Limiting junk food in schools is half the job of improving student health; the other is implementing daily exercise regimens for young people. The number-one way that children spend most of their waking hours is using electronic equipment such as computers, cell phones, and iPods—over five hours each day—none of which requires any physical exertion.

Physical education doesn't always mean running laps or playing football. It could mean an aerobics or isometrics class, yoga, martial arts, or just plain walking. Just as a school's track team runs out in the neighborhood, so too can a group of children take to walking in the streets for an hour daily instead of hiding out in PE class chatting with buddies.

At the high school level only the jocks are receiving the right level of conditioning, mainly due to their participation in an organized sport. The National Federation of State High School Associations discovered that "kids in organized sports are more likely to maintain a healthy body weight, develop strong bones . . . [have] respect for authority and teamwork, . . . tend to stay in school, get better grades and have fewer disciplinary issues."

The rest fall by the wayside. Many PE teachers partially blame

Title 9 (established in 1972, opening full access to girls in school sports) for fostering fatter kids, for in making classes co-ed, coaches have had to lower their physical standards so activities can be performed by both male and female students.

Since physical education is no longer a required class as in the old days, nearly half of all teens do not take it. Think about this: It is very possible for some children never to exercise on a daily basis while they are in the prime of their youth.

The term applied to academically weak students is "at risk." But "at risk" now has a whole new meaning in terms of life and death among obese children. There is a 75 percent likelihood that obese teens will turn into obese adults.

Shockingly, some health experts predict that for the first time ever we may end up seeing younger generations with shorter life-spans.

As a way to counteract inactivity, a few states such as Kentucky (preschool through twelfth grade) and North Carolina (K–8) require each student to perform thirty minutes of physical activity daily. All states should have such a stipulation.

Some schools have a quiet reading period as part of the daily schedule. The idea behind this period, often called SSR (Sustained Silent Reading), is to improve students' reading ability and habits. Perhaps a variation of SSR is in order, something like Sustained Silent Running/Walking. That's what kids need—more opportunities to exercise. If they worked their bodies more, their minds would be clearer for their academic classes.

Some school districts have begun including each student's BMI, or body mass index, on report cards so that parents know the health of their child.

Of all the subjects children should have to take every year in school, one of the most vital is physical education. Their future literally depends upon it.

It's not just the food sold in the cafeteria and vending machines, nor the inactivity among teens. It's a bad-habit lifestyle that many parents model for their children. Pick up fast food for dinner, kids connected to their iPods as they watch TV or IM on their computers, all the while sitting, sitting, sitting.

The supersizing of food has been much discussed lately in both book and film form, yet little has changed Americans and their children from gorging themselves to the hilt at fast-food time. Is there any science to explain this? Yes. Studies have shown that people expect to eat the portions provided them, called "unit bias," so when you have an apple or banana, you end up eating the whole thing because of its size. When you drink from a 20-ounce bottle of soda you tend to drink the whole thing whether you're still thirsty or not. Interesting how Coke's original bottles held 6.5 ounces, then bottle size increased to 8 and again to a whopping 10 ounces in the 1950s. Today, the 20-ounce bottle has become the norm.

Remember a few years back when suddenly six-packs of soda disappeared from supermarket shelves, replaced with twelve-pack cases? Bravo to the soda companies for that ingenious way of making people buy more soda. Now the only two sizes available are two-liter bottles or twelve-packs. What will be the options in the future—gallon size or twenty-four-pack cases?

Containers for foods such as yogurt tend to be smaller in Europe than here, which may partially explain why American kids are in worse shape.

Over half a century ago during the Eisenhower era the President's Council on Youth Fitness was established. (Later its name was changed to the President's Council on Physical Fitness and Sports.) Its purpose is to promote good health habits. How are schools promoting good health habits by serving unhealthy food in cafeterias and vending machines, and on top of that not requiring young people to exercise regularly?

Considering all of the evidence, it is astonishing that more is not being done beyond substituting Gatorade for Sprite.

9

MBA Principals

Poor communication skills, constantly uses intimidation, power hungry, always angry, and enjoys yelling at people. A description of Simon Cowell of *American Idol*? No. If these traits match your personality, congratulations, you, too, can become a school administrator.

Parents are under the assumption that principals are the leaders of a school, responsible for running it and making all decisions. Nothing could be further from reality.

Sad to say, but the folks running America's schools tend not to be the brightest, savviest, most knowledgeable, or most visionary people. With few exceptions, school administrators are not the best of the teaching force who through talent ascended up ambition's ladder. No, many administrators are teacher flunkies (I hope my boss doesn't read this).

There are two different types of principals: control freaks who were average teachers themselves, and teacher-friendly principals who were excellent instructors and don't easily forget what it is like to teach in a classroom. These latter principals really should be at the top rung of teacher positions on a career ladder and not in a separate category of administrators.

The scarcity of outstanding principals is not completely the fault of those in such positions. Logic dictates that principals have authority over their schools and teachers. However, that is not so. One would think an individual school's budget would be controlled by the principal. Wrong! A principal's arms are tied behind his back when it comes to which job applicants apply to his school, how much money may be spent on staffing, and so on. Even problematic teachers cast off by their schools must be found positions elsewhere in a school district. Being an administrator is a position of power without real power. How frustrating must that be? It's been estimated that school administrators control only 25 percent of the decisions made at a school. The school district's central office is just that—centralized power.

Such impotency creates frustrated administrators, and that frustration gets passed on to the teachers.

Now before I get accused of espousing typical teacher gripes about their bosses, let me say that the principal of today has a heavy load to carry. Principals are asked to focus on data, focus on getting the school accredited regularly, focus on meeting NCLB standards, as well as know how to handle the media in case a shooting erupts on campus on their watch. Principals need to foster relationships with parents, teachers, and the surrounding community.

And people scratch their heads wondering why better people don't apply to become principals.

Many teachers have the necessary leadership skills; they just don't want to take on such thankless positions.

There are only two reasons why teachers become administrators: They want to earn more money, or they want to get out of the classroom. Or, looking at it from a different view, the people in charge of America's schools are there in order to make a few extra bucks and/or because they wanted to get the hell out of teaching to kids. How inspirational.

Too often mediocre teachers become administrators. That is why they try to escape from the classroom, a place where many of them lacked greatness. And the greatest teachers have little interest in the job of administrating since it would mean giving up doing something they excel at. This is good because you don't want the best teachers leaving the classroom, no longer reaching young people. On the other hand, you do want to rid the teaching ranks of ineffectual instructors, which is the only good thing about paying administrators more money than teachers—it acts as bait.

Districts desperately try to promote after-school workshops for teachers who wish to join the administrative ranks. Huge teaching shortages are always predicted, but hardly anyone mentions administration shortages—yet half of all school districts report not having enough candidates to fill positions. Let's face it. It's an impossible job, plain and simple. When you are a principal, students don't like you, teachers don't like you, and parents are constantly trying to get something out of you. You are at the beck and call of district brass. All this at a salary not worth it all except that it is more money than the highest-paid teacher receives.

An ad for Edison Schools, a private company that operates schools in partnership with school districts, compares the average annual salary of a principal, $80,000, with the average annual salary of an airline captain, $240,000. Just as with teacher salaries, you get what you pay for. Higher pay for such an important job would go a long way toward attracting a higher caliber of people.

You know the old saying "You can't see the forest for the trees"? Well, public school administrators can't see the future for the students. Their vision of how best to teach children is all blurry, so consumed are they in a fog of policies and paperwork.

School administrators get bogged down in minutiae. More time is spent taking attendance at faculty meetings than making sure real teaching is happening in the classroom.

In education, there are plenty of managers but few leaders.

It's easy to find an administrator "administrating," checking up on teachers—when they leave work, why a form wasn't turned in. None of these things constitutes great teaching or great administrating. Nor does it lift up teachers' spirits to have staff constantly looking over their shoulders.

Instead, too often principals mistrust teachers. Because of the freedom from close supervision that teachers enjoy (how many of you go to work each day and barely come in contact with another fellow worker?), the thinking is that those teachers are up to no good. There is also a layer of jealousy. Administrators typically arrive at work earlier and leave later. They need to open and close the campuses, with many high school administrators working the night shift at dances, games, and meetings.

Don't they wish they could leave as early as 3:00 P.M. to go to the dentist or pick up their children or go to the market? Once their audience has left, teachers don't need to physically be at their work site to grade papers or create lesson plans. They can easily do such tasks at home.

At one meeting of all department heads, an assistant principal wanted to talk about photocopy paper that was missing from a cupboard. She said that it was clear some teachers were taking paper for their own private use. If need be, she was going to go into every single teacher's room and unlock all the cabinets to see if anyone was hoarding paper. Sounds like Captain Queeg's search for the strawberries aboard the USS *Caine*.

I got the following message e-mailed to me from an administrator the day after an after-school faculty meeting took place: "Brian, I noticed that you left seven minutes early."

Yes, I admit it. I have left meetings early in order to, God forgive me, pick up my children from school. The question that begs asking is not why would a teacher leave a meeting early, but why would an administrator take the time to document it? Think of the effort it would take to do this type of surveillance. First, the administrator has to keep an eye out for anyone leaving the room. Next, write down the person's name and time of departure. Then, go to a computer and type an e-mail and send it off. Why is any administrator wasting his time tracking the goings and comings of each teacher? What is the point of it? All it does is breed bad feelings and mistrust. It also shows why the union contract needs to be abolished. If the teachers unions want the exact minutes a teacher is expected to be on the job explicitly written in a contract, then the administrators end up following every dotted *i* and crossed *t*.

Forcing people to attend ineffectual and boring meetings is not going to endear teachers to an administrator. Anyone with an ounce of leadership ability knows that in order to win over employees, first, treat them with respect and, second, realize that employees will gladly put in more time and do more than what is required if they feel good about their bosses and about their role at their workplace. Principals shouldn't lead through fear. It's plainly a control issue, a way of putting a teacher in her inferior, subservient place: "Me, Principal; you, Teacher."

Principals quickly get out of touch with the reality teachers face daily. Typically, administrators haven't been in the classroom for years, having taught for as little as a few years, and it shows in their words and in their actions. Most of their careers are spent outside of the classroom, not teaching kids, yet somehow administrators are seen as the experts on how to teach to them.

One time administrators proposed eliminating the fifteen-minute morning snack due to rowdy student behavior and littering. This would have meant that students and teachers would have gone from 8:00 A.M. to 12:15 P.M. without a break except for five-minute passing periods. At least students could make a quick trip to the bathroom, but what about the teachers who by law must never leave their rooms unattended with students present? The administrators didn't think about this because they can go to the bathroom whenever they need to. Canceling snack would have meant one less time for them to supervise students. This decision would have benefited five people and highly inconvenienced over a hundred others. The administrators forgot what it's like to be trapped in a classroom. Besides, can't the teachers just "hold it" for four and a half hours?

At least children at one Southern California school were able to go to the bathroom despite not being able to leave the classroom. The principal, in trying to prevent students from leaving campus to join immigration rallies in March of 2006, put the school in lockdown mode. This meant no students were allowed to go to the bathroom. Students were forced to use buckets in the classroom instead. You see, she was following the district handbook for a lockdown . . . *in case of nuclear attack!* How did a district administrator respond to all of this? He declared the principal's action an "honest mistake. She just misread [the handbook]." He said that the district would update its policy to give principals more explicit directions. Excuse me, but whatever happened to common sense, especially coming from the leader of the school? Did having kids pee in a bucket in the corner of classrooms really make sense to her? She didn't have second thoughts about this one?

One administrator opposed offering teachers immediate access to photocopying if they were to have a brainstorm at night and desire to come in the next morning and make copies. He claimed that teachers should have everything planned out days ahead of time. The notion that someone could come up with an idea the night before or the morning of a lesson was evidently a foreign concept. The proverbial lightbulb going off above a student's head, an image that puts a smile on a teacher's face, is evidently not allowed to occur to the teacher.

You would think that as head of the English department I would be in the loop regarding decisions made affecting English teachers and English courses. Nope. Administrators consult teachers when it's convenient for them, not out of a sense of viewing a teacher as a school leader. Often I'm asked my opinion on something to give the appearance that I'm collaborating. I'm back to being just a teacher, however, when it comes to my own schedule. More than once I was informed of changes to my slate of classes literally the last day before the school year commenced, something not uncommon with many teachers.

How does anyone expect quality work from a management style of flying by the seat of one's pants?

Principals often overlook the most important role they can fulfill, that of a model teacher. It is the most underutilized aspect of an administrator. Instead of coming across as an opponent, an excellent principal should be a supportive and motivational colleague, someone to look up to.

If all principals still taught part of the time in order to maintain relevancy as a leader and be fully aware of the current classroom environment, then going into school administration would have an appeal for brilliant teachers.

Think of how powerful it would be to have a principal stand in front of his faculty and say, "Everyone try this teaching strategy." Then he actually tries it in the class he teaches, and at the next teacher meeting shares, along with the other teachers, how the lesson went. Talk about practicing what one preaches. For truly, a great principal should be a great teacher, the lead teacher on campus.

What schools need are visionaries who are professionally trained in management skills. School administrative techniques should be modeled on the best MBA programs such as those at Northwestern or Wharton. Then, as their final project, have student principals create a vision of a school.

Put principals through corporate training. That's what Boston did with its top brass, incorporating leadership strategies that Dow Chemical, the area's largest employer, used. The result? Boston has done the best job in the nation in closing the achievement gap.

One of the more promising administrator training programs is the New York City Leadership Academy. Begun in 2003 and modeled after private sector leadership programs such as General Electric's John F. Welch Leadership Center and the Ameritech Institute, the Academy states on its Web site that it desires principals "who are true instructional leaders, who can inspire and lead teachers, students and parents in their school community."

A somewhat famous graduate is Verone Kennedy, principal of Granville T. Woods School for Science and Technology, located in the impoverished area of Crown Heights, Brooklyn. Kennedy told *Time* magazine that his leadership style has two parts: "example and teamwork." He is a believer in liberating students from the confines of schools by taking them to museums and Broadway plays, a philosophy echoed in chapter 20.

What's interesting is that he himself was a struggling student in the public school system until he explored his artistic side. Once he discovered something he was good at, art, he had the self-confidence to do better in his other classes, not a coincidence when viewed in light of studies about the importance of the arts to academic achievement (see chapter 18).

The question each principal needs to ask himself is this: What have you done for your teachers lately? Administrators need to learn bedside manners. If I were principal, I would allow teachers plenty of freedom to do the job they can do. Truly empower them with the most precious tool there is (and it doesn't cost a cent): trust. Trust the teacher. The teacher is a well-educated individual who has a heart. Why not trust these people, their judgments, their decisions, their ideas?

The best principals are maverick types who have a strong sense of themselves and are not intimidated by their superiors. If a new policy will not work at a particular school, these principals sometimes defy what the school board or superintendent desires.

Just as with teaching, make administration attractive through salary, bonuses, and better working conditions. Principals in New York City can earn up to $50,000 extra depending upon where they work and how well the school does.

And districts need to free up power and allow those in charge of a school to make most of the decisions. The principal-as-cop needs to be transformed into the principal-as-teacher.

PART TWO
The Way Children Need to Be Taught

10

What One-third of All Seventeen- and Eighteen-year-olds Are *Not* Doing This Year (and It Has Nothing to Do with Sex or Drugs)

> Three thousand students will drop out of high school today.
>
> —Alliance for Excellent Education, 2003

> The United States ranks eleventh among nations in the share of its population that has finished high school. It used to be first.
>
> —Organization for Economic Cooperation and Development, 2006

One-third of today's high school students *do not* graduate. Half of today's African-American and Latino students *do not* graduate. Inner-city high schools are perceived as dropout factories.

Here's a scarier thought. Those same kids who are not served well by the public schools will, like it or not, serve all of us, with all their inadequacies and deficiencies, repairing our cars, fixing our homes, taking care of our bodies.

What should be done about this? The answer to that question is one of those "is the glass half full or half empty?" situations.

The educrats believe this is an atrocious statistic and that all efforts must be sought in order to ensure every single person graduates with a high school diploma.

Others look at this number that astonishingly has remained unchanged over the past thirty years despite billions of dollars of reforms to observe something that others don't see—school is not for everybody.

It's time to end compulsory education after the ninth grade. After ten years in the system, if school isn't their strength, then students need to do something else.

Most states make school compulsory up to age sixteen, others until seventeen or eighteen. New Mexico is the only state in the union that legally requires high school graduation.

Between ninth and tenth grades is when most students drop out of school, never to be seen again, disappearing into a kind of public school black hole. It's no surprise that students who struggle with class material quickly lose interest in school. Isn't it natural that as subject matter increases in complexity some students will get it and others will not, no matter the programs, teachers, or money you throw at the system?

California has the second-lowest high school graduation rate in the nation right ahead (or behind, depending on how one looks at it) of Mississippi. In California for the 2005–06 school year, 546,911 students were in grade nine. That number dropped to 515,675 in grade ten, 467,239 in grade eleven, and 423,237 in grade twelve. Where did the 123,000 students lost between ninth and twelfth grade end up?

About 60 percent of dropouts do eventually earn a high school diploma or equivalent degree, many by taking the General Educational Development test, or GED. Over four hundred thousand certificates were issued in 2004, making the American Council on Education testing service the largest organization in the country giving out high school diplomas.

Is it just possible that young people who struggle in school may not have entirely given up on their education? Yes, many stop doing work, stop attending classes, and become disruptive. But hasn't the system failed them? If 60 percent of dropouts eventually earn a diploma, doesn't that prove that they are motivated and that they recognize the importance of an education? If most dropouts were good-for-nothings then very few of them would return to the system where they had a complete failure.

No one disagrees that children who drop out of school have

negative impacts on the rest of society. These people tend to commit more crimes, drain more money from welfare and health care. If graduation rates rose 1 percent, UC Berkeley economist Enrico Moretti estimates, 100,000 fewer crimes would be committed, saving about $1.4 billion a year. Dropouts even live shorter lives, on the average of nine less years than high school graduates.

There has always been a pecking order like this in America. In the early part of the twentieth century, a person who finished high school really accomplished something. Such a person could be assured of a good-paying job and decent life. Then, in the middle of the century, earning a bachelor's degree was considered the pinnacle and only those who graduated from college were accorded certain levels of jobs. Nowadays, as college degrees become more plentiful, a master's or Ph.D. is considered necessary in order to remain competitive for the top positions.

If everyone is able to achieve at a certain level, doesn't that mean that there needs to be an even higher level to attain in order for the brighter people to rise to the top?

Teachers, think about a situation where you have a disruptive student in your room, who after repeated reprimands and referrals still doesn't bring a book to class, still doesn't do homework, still thinks he can get away with using profanity and disturbing other students around him. Does it make sense to force him to come back day after day when clearly something isn't working right? Wouldn't it work well for everybody if this unmotivated student was doing something else?

As discussed later in chapter 31, schools are funded based on the number of students in attendance, which frankly is the only reason why problematic kids aren't kicked out. It's not politically correct to say this but schools don't want to teach to troublemakers. If each child didn't have a bounty on his head, these kids would have no school to go to.

Parents, think how nervous you would get if faced with the possibility that your child would no longer be under the free child care of the public school system. What would you do then? Would you take more of an interest in whether your child went to school, brought necessary materials, and completed assignments?

Former high school principal and director of credential programs at UC Irvine Dennis L. Evans said in a recent *Education Week* editorial that "we should tell these students that not only do they no longer have to attend school, but that they can't: they will not be allowed to continue to waste teachers' time and effort and interfere with the right of other students to learn."

Paul D. Houston, executive director of the American Association of School Administrators, views high school as a place "to keep teenagers off the streets and out of adults' hair until they can move on." Houston ponders, "Are schools a farm team for corporate America or should [they] serve a broader goal of molding educated citizens who can pursue their dreams?"

This brings to mind an essential question: What is the goal of public education?

Is it for all kids to get college degrees? Many don't.

Is it for all kids to go to college? Some don't.

Is it for all kids to get A's? Several don't.

Is it for all kids to take AP courses? Most don't.

Is it to socialize kids? Not very well.

Is it to excite kids about the world? Few programs do.

Is it to ignite a desire to learn? Fewer do.

Is it to prepare them for life? Not enough.

Is it to take care of children while their parents work? That's probably the biggest benefit public schools do provide.

So much effort in school is made toward socializing young people; not a bad thing on the whole, but often the rigid rules we expect all students to follow just aren't realistic. The zero-tolerance policies that have sprung up in recent years have proven flawed. You know what I'm talking about: A school that has a zero-tolerance policy toward sexual harassment suspends a first grader for giving another first grader a hug. It is ridiculous.

I'm not suggesting public schools become "free schools," those places that became famous in the 1960s and 1970s where rules were completely thrown out, and children were running the place. However, teachers, especially those in the earliest grades, need to have knowledge about child development, knowledge about the differences between boys' and girls' social growth so that they aren't clamping down on, let's say, a seven-year-old boy who is full of Mexican jumping beans and can't sit still for more than fifteen consecutive minutes. Should that child be punished as an unruly child? Or can an alternative solution be employed such as having him stay in a specific area rather than in an uncomfortable plastic chair? Or is there a way to expend the energy in a positive way like running errands for the teacher?

There is a distinction between "school" and "schooling." For some students, less schooling is preferable.

Schools print up posters that encourage students to be independent thinkers, but look at how the system trains them. A good student is an obedient student who arrives to class on time, turns in work on time, speaks only when called on, works well with others.

There is a misconception that smart kids do well in school. Actually, it is passive, obedient children who succeed at school. Or at least recognize school culture and are willing to play the game, get their good grades, then leave.

However, not all people thrive in a system like this. For some, school is toxic. It just doesn't work. Much of what goes on at schools is behavior modification, not learning about life. This might explain why some kids act out. They are placed in such small vestibules of acceptable behaviors that they just want to break out of the straightjacket.

Students are squeezed through the constricted aperture at the end of the twelfth grade and, in so doing, several figuratively die during the process. Wheaton College education professor Kirsten Olson believes that school leaves "painful psychological and spiritual lacerations that are raw and unhealed."

Joe Teller of the famous magic/comedy team Penn and Teller said in an *Edutopia* magazine interview that school should not be compulsory. "Children are taught from an early age that learning is something they're stuck with. . . . Making something compulsory negates all value and joy."

At the adolescent level I know why some students act out. They're bored. Why? According to many surveys, either because they don't see how what they are learning relates to their lives or because they feel that their teachers don't care about them.

A Gates Foundation study discovered that 88 percent of dropouts actually had passing grades but left school due to boredom. According to a National Governors Association survey, 36 percent left school because they were "not learning anything," and 24 percent claimed, "I hate my school." Almost two-thirds would have worked harder if classes were more interesting.

Do you hear that, public school system bureaucrats? Kids are willing to work hard if they are interested in what is happening in the classroom. What a mind-blowing concept!

At one Los Angeles school made up of nearly three-quarters Latino students, Spanish was the only foreign language offered. Some people might think this is okay, how easy for the students. Not so. The students said that they thought the Spanish language classes weren't challenging enough. Additionally, several colleges do not accept Spanish as a foreign language so these kids were at a disadvantage. So incensed were they with the limited choice of one foreign language that they surveyed their peers as to what languages they would prefer learning (French, German, Italian) and presented their findings to the school administration. Again, this is an example that shows that students *want* to be challenged. They really, really do.

Educators sometimes live in an idealistic world, believing to the bone that all students are teachable and can be successful, that every kid can succeed in an Advanced Placement class (they can't; see chapter 19), that every kid can go to a four-year college. Well, I like listening to the Louis Armstrong song "What a Wonderful World" just like anybody else but that doesn't mean that all the ideals are real. It's one thing to have high expectations but another to have unrealistic goals.

There have always been and will continue to be students who don't finish high school. Some of them become successful without college, others remain unreachable. At some point, as hard as it is to say it, a teacher has to give up on a student. A teacher, no matter how gifted she may be, cannot overcome a student's personal problems, family crises, or, worse, doggedness to not learn in an academic setting.

I had this one student in my advanced English class named Alberto. Each day he arrived with a backpack on and fifty-five minutes later left with it on, never once removing the straps from his shoulders and unzipping the contents. Despite all attempts to talk to him, to tutor him, to speak with his parents, nothing changed. The one thing I could count on with Alberto was that he would show up to class each day and keep to himself. For such apathetic participation he received an F, which meant nothing to him.

There is no real way of finding out how many Albertos there are in classrooms around this country who similarly have tuned school out. It's not a show they're interested in viewing anymore.

The National Education Association proposed in the fall of 2006 for there to be "high school graduation centers" for students aged nineteen to twenty-one, asking the federal government to pay $10 billion over ten years for such institutions.

They just don't get it. For young people who struggle through school, attending more school is not the solution. They don't like the institution called "school." Period. The four walls, the controlling environment, the factory conditions. Thirteen straight years of following the ringing of bells, sitting in uncomfortable seats, sitting in nonstimulating surroundings, hearing a litany of rules, having teachers constantly correct their behavior, having administrators blare over bullhorns and PA systems about how to act. And we wonder what's wrong with these kids who struggle in such a system? New strategies and new slogans do nothing to change the way things are.

A survey done by the Council of Urban Boards of Education in 2006 showed that two-thirds of students enjoy learning at their schools. Well, how about the other one-third who aren't enjoying themselves? It's interesting to note that this number matches the two-thirds graduation rate.

To repeat, one out of every four students who drop out does so because he hates his school. So what's being done about this, to rectify such a shameful statistic? The only plan schools have come up with has to do with ways to keep them in school—a place where they continue to fail—forcing more college prep classes down their throats. If a person fails to make a mortgage payment, does the bank send the homeowner even more bills on the blind faith that soon the bills will be paid?

If America truly wants to demolish the achievement gap and deliver on No Child Left Behind and have all minority and poor children succeed as well as white and middle-class children do, then those disadvantaged kids don't need only nice-looking schools and outstanding teachers, they need another way to succeed besides sitting obediently in a chair all day in a room and listening. It simply doesn't work for everyone.

Young people shouldn't be forced to go to school if they choose not to. Eliminate compulsory high school education and offer alternative pathways in place of three more years of hell. Let young people sit down with their parents or other trusted guardians such as counselors and decide what course of action would best serve their needs. And what else is there besides college? Read on and get reacquainted with vocational education.

11

Vocational Education: Public Schools' Neglected Stepchild

What do Bill Gates, David Geffen, Steve Jobs, and Ted Turner have in common besides a billionaire portfolio? None of them have college degrees. How many celebrities went to college? Then there are all the talented athletes who may have college degrees but are not always the strongest people academically. The lesson here is that college is not necessary to be successful in life.

When students don't feel that school provides them with anything, they act out in antisocial ways, from not doing work to creating a disturbance in class to vandalizing the school. A crucial area of connecting students to their schools is making sure there are enough choices to satisfy most students' interests. Currently in high school this is not the case.

Why are students brought up on the belief that they can accomplish any goal, yet when they get to high school their options are limited to "you will go to college"?

The only diversity that receives attention at schools is ethnic diversity. But diversity in thought or diversity in approach to educating kids is verboten.

Despite everyone's best intentions, not everyone goes to college and earns a degree. Even for those who do, it takes longer than it used to. Over 80 percent of entering college freshmen finish earning their degrees in six, not four, years. Maybe they should be referred to as "stalemen."

The United States ranks fifth among twenty nations in students participating in college, but fifth from the bottom in students completing college. What's the problem? The problem is that many students, once enrolled, realize that college is not the place for them. Perhaps they only enrolled because it was hammered into their heads that the one and only path to their future was college.

Any commuter who drives can tell you alternate routes to get to work in the morning besides taking the freeway or expressway. You know what? It doesn't matter whether you travel surface streets or take subways or trains to get to work, as long as you get there, right? And students need options as well in preparation for life after school, be it a job or college.

Public schools are trying to make all kids college-ready, but the colleges aren't ready for all kids. There is no room at the inn. Even if by some miracle all students graduating from high school could meet the requirements to get into four-year universities, there aren't enough spaces for colleges to accept everyone.

A few years ago the University of California (UC) had to turn away many students because of overcrowding. These students were asked to attend two-year colleges until slots opened up. Typically the UC accepts the top 12.5 percent of high school graduating seniors. Where will all the other students go? In the most recent year available, about 120,000 students enrolled in the University of California and California State University systems. That means 300,000 high school seniors went somewhere else. That's a huge number. In academic year 2005–06, over 76,000 California seniors applied to UC campuses; just over 50,000 were accepted.

How will students deal with the knowledge that all their hard work won't pay off?

All the effort that goes into funding intervention classes in order to get every single child up to a certain level is a complete waste of energy, not to mention money.

The question that needs to be asked of every high school student is "What are you interested in doing?" instead of "Did you know that college graduates make X amount of money?" If a youngster can't stand spinach, the solution isn't to give him a heaping portion of it. You try to find alternative nutritious foods he will eat.

Instead of higher education, why not "hire" education?

The whole system would be better off using that intervention class money for reviving vocational education. Schools need to provide viable alternatives (besides military service) to college.

An Oprah Winfrey poll showed that 88 percent of the public think students should have a vocational ed option instead of a college-only track.

What happened to voc ed classes and programs, which were a major part of public schools for the majority of the twentieth century? Number one, the 1980s Back to Basics movement began, driven primarily by the 1983 report "A Nation at Risk." The three Rs—reading, writing, arithmetic—were back in vogue. Two, critics of voc ed classes thought such tracks of educating young people pegged them for a lower-class lifestyle, preventing them from reaching the white-collar world and its riches. As a result, many former shops where classes such as auto, electronics, printing, and wood were once taught have been redesigned into classrooms and conference rooms.

Over the past half century, changes in the workforce have taken place. In 1956, 60 percent of the jobs were unskilled. In 2000, 15 percent were unskilled. But "unskilled" doesn't mean no college, it means just what it says: no skills. Schools can train students to have the necessary skills for decent-paying jobs.

Voc ed, or industrial arts, is now referred to as career or technical education. What's with the name change? Since when did "vocation" become a dirty word? As so often happens in the education world, the thinking is if you change the name of something it becomes something new. And something with a new name gets more attention. The vocal proponents behind today's minor voc ed comeback want everyone to be assured that the coursework is rigorous and of a certain academic pedigree.

Funded at over $1 billion, the Carl D. Perkins Career and Technical Education and Improvement Act is the main federal resource for vocational education. Since 2000, enrollment in voc ed programs has risen 58 percent. Schools with vocational ed programs have lower dropout rates, and students tend to go on to college at a higher rate.

By the time students are old enough to drive a car, their educators have—through hundreds of graded assignments and dozens of report cards—compiled a thorough track record of performance, enabling them, along with counselors, to make intelligent decisions on the students' futures. "Here are the results of your educational experience. If you continue growing this way, here are a couple of options for you. If you don't improve, here are a couple of other options for you." What is so wrong with that? Isn't that the way public schools should serve their clientele? No one is saying we should label these children: "You, voc ed, stand back there, and you, college prep, stand up here."

Let the child and parents confer with each other and make the final call. If a mother believes her F-student son is best taking AP classes, so be it. He should not be prevented. Nor should an honors student who has a knack for construction be excluded from taking an apprenticeship over college prep classes.

It is time to stop forcing every single student to go to college. Should students be pushed academically? Yes, all the time. But that doesn't mean there is only one door to pass through after high school and that door is more school. Whatever happened to providing young people with choices? They may not make the same choice the educator made for herself, but so what?

As people who thrived in the public school structure, educators are dumbfounded when others don't succeed. There is something within them that craves having others follow in their footsteps. If they did okay with school, shouldn't everybody?

Educators do an awful job of not seeing past their noses. They have gone through the system, graduated from it, now work in it, but never question it.

The usual tactic of motivating high schoolers to go to college is by showing them a salary comparison of what high school graduates earn versus college graduates. No one is denying that on the whole the more education you have the higher your earnings. Those not finishing high school earn two-thirds the salary of those with diplomas, and those with college degrees earn three-fourths more than those with solely diplomas. These are the facts.

However, just how many high-paying white-collar jobs are there in America? And second, how many young people really, really desire to do those jobs, beyond making a lot of money?

It takes the average college student six years to finish a four-year degree these days. You know why? Between one-third and one-half of entering freshmen need to take remedial classes in math and English; many can't read a freshman-level textbook. The cost to re-educate these students is $17 billion, according to the nonprofit organization Achieve.

If so many students are taking remedial classes in undergrad schools, then isn't there a domino effect on those entering grad schools? You don't hear about remedial grad classes, but if high schools are graduating fewer-skilled graduates, then doesn't it follow that undergrad programs are giving out diplomas not as well-earned as those in the past?

And what percentage of Americans have college degrees? Twenty-eight percent. That means that at least seven out of every ten Americans earn lower salaries. The huge push to have all students college-ready is not going to suddenly make the twenty-eight percent number double over the next several years.

In a way, public schools are doing a disservice by not properly training the vast majority of its population for the real world and the actual jobs that await them. It behooves public schools to do something with the 72 percent. Of course, offer opportunities and support for students to enter the college track. But instead of tsk-tsking at those who aren't college-bound, point them toward different pathways.

Schools need to look at the local economy, see where the demand is, and offer training for students to meet those employment opportunities. Not everyone is going to college, not everyone is going to graduate from college, not everyone will be a CEO or president of a company. It's just not possible.

Since the unemployment rate has stayed steady at 5 percent in recent years, obviously non–college-educated people are getting jobs. And that means that the vast majority of America's jobs require no college education. So why train students to believe that they can all attend college and receive high-paying jobs when those high-paying jobs don't exist?

Of course, just because a person doesn't earn as much money as someone else does not make them unhappy, correct? One doesn't have to look further than the classroom for an example. Many teachers are satisfied with their jobs and their pay. Just exactly what are schools supposed to produce? High-paid employees or decent citizens?

There are jobs in the marketplace waiting to be filled that don't require college degrees. True, some are low-paying ones that most Americans refuse to do, which is why illegal immigration is such a problem. But there is a tremendous need for skilled labor. How often have you found it difficult to find a reliable and responsible person to work on your house?

Many experts point out that the fastest-growing jobs in the country—including health technology, plumbing, and automotive repair—do not require a college degree and are the types of jobs that are least likely to be outsourced.

Each year over a quarter of a million jobs are available for truck drivers, paying $34,000 salaries. A student who knows how to build a computer network can earn $60,000 annually without any college degree. Car painters get paid $22 an hour, about the same salary as a beginning classroom teacher with five years of college.

According to the National Automobile Dealers Association, over one hundred thousand job openings in sales, clerical, and managerial categories are available at dealerships and the industry is working overtime trying to locate qualified workers.

Harlow Unger, author of *But What If I Don't Want to Go to College? A Guide to Success Through Alternative Education,* claims that there are "50 million jobs out there that don't require a bachelor's degree and pay upwards of $40,000 a year." According to the U.S. Department of Labor, by 2010 almost two-thirds of all projected job openings "will require only on-the-job training."

Here is a short list of good-paying jobs taken from Michael Farr and Laurence Shatkin's book *300 Best Jobs Without a Four-Year Degree:*

Job	Average Salary
Air traffic controller	$102,030
Transportation manager	$66,600
Real estate broker	$58,720
Elevator installer and repairer	$58,710
Dental hygienist	$58,350
Radiation therapist	$57,700

Some schools pay attention to the real world. In Irving, Texas, students take construction classes and work alongside carpenters, plumbers, and electricians actually building a house. At the end of the school year, the house is auctioned off with the proceeds helping to fund the program.

At Adlai E. Stevenson High School outside of Chicago, students who study politics in the classroom receive training as voter registrars and sign up thousands of new voters. Some of these students end up working for politicians.

The Cincinnati Public Schools recently opened a new $8.4 million building for its zoo academy where students assist zookeepers. Working in coordination with the Cincinnati Zoo and Botanical Garden, the building houses a glass-enclosed rain forest that will be used by both students and zoo visitors. The zoo academy began in 1977 and provides a rigorous curriculum of science classes including botany and anatomy.

At the Sound School Regional Vocational Aquaculture Center in New Haven, Connecticut, students learn how to build boats, sing sea chanteys, and row dories. Most students go on to college while the rest go into marine vocations.

Culinary arts programs are popular these days. There is one where I work and it is heartwarming to see young people actually run a restaurant business, from the way they seat the diners (the teachers) to the way they serve the food. Interestingly, most of these students struggle in traditional academic classes. Yet for one part of the day they are able to succeed and do well.

There are even schools that have teacher academies for future educators. The Urban Academies Program in Broward County, Florida, begins targeting these students as early as the ninth grade, offering full college scholarships. The results? Hundreds of new teachers, over 90 percent of whom have remained on the job after just a few years.

Other countries offer apprenticeships to those teens not going on to college. Germany has a machinist program with the Daimler-Chrysler automobile company for sixteen-year-olds. Japan has contracts with Toyota to train young people.

The U.S. public school system could learn a few things from Germany's, where fewer than 10 percent of students drop out of high school. More than half of teens enroll in three-year apprentice programs where most of them exit with a job in hand.

It's a benefit for companies to get involved with schools since they help train their future employee pool. That's why almost one out of every four German companies offers apprenticeships. And the interns are paid. What a wonderful way to combat outsourcing, eh? California governor Arnold Schwarzenegger himself enrolled in a sales training program in his native Austria.

A more scaled-down apprentice program exists in North Carolina, called Apprenticeship 2000. Since 1995, the consortium made of manufacturing companies has recruited eleventh graders from dozens of high schools for the four-year program. Upon graduation, the students are guaranteed jobs starting at $30,000.

The public's perception about the manufacturing sector is that jobs have been lost due to technology, automation, and outsourcing, and that the jobs that still exist are menial, assembly-line-like, dirty, and low paying. While much of that perception is accurate, the jobs that remain are fairly high paying, with salaries ranging between $50,000 and $80,000 a year. And these jobs are fairly available, too. According to an industry survey, almost 90 percent of manufacturers struggle finding machinists and technicians. There is such a need to fill these positions that manufacturing companies are offering bonuses and other financial incentives that can boost annual salaries over the six-figure mark.

American Micro Products Inc., headquartered in Ohio, covers relocation costs for qualified new employees. EJ Ajax & Sons in Minneapolis pays for apprentices' college tuition in order to get the training they need. One young person who took a job at EJ Ajax & Sons told the *Los Angeles Times* that he chose this route because it would allow him to attain the American Dream of home ownership faster than his peers who still have more college ahead of them. Plus, his salary is higher than theirs will be once they enter the job market.

When Toyota opened a plant in San Antonio, Texas, the company came up empty filling two hundred technical positions despite receiving one hundred thousand job applications. So Toyota did what other companies end up doing: recruiting from other companies or other states, sort of a stateside outsourcing.

A good way to prevent outsourcing is by making sure all students, not just voc ed ones, know how to apply what they learn in school. The United States spends the second-most money per pupil in the world (behind Switzerland) yet American fifteen-year-olds rank below most countries' students in applying math skills to real-life situations.

Instead of training students how to take multiple-choice tests (we all know how frequently we take those after graduating from school), how about providing them with more relevant coursework?

Kids may struggle with the Pythagorean theorem, but can they calculate how interest is compounded on a credit card debt? Balance a checkbook? Fill out a loan application? Figure out a gratuity in a restaurant? Know what a gratuity is? (They should. Many of them will end up in service-oriented careers.)

Maybe if young people saw the connection to real life more they would get the math more. Why not give high school students real tax forms with fake numbers and have them fill the forms out? CPAs can be guest speakers, discussing the process.

Half of high school seniors can't correctly answer questions about personal finance and economics. How important is it for young people to understand basic financial knowledge? The average credit card debt of college-aged students is $3,000. Almost half of high school seniors have a debit card, and 25 percent have bounced a check, according to a JumpStart Coalition for Financial Literacy survey. Teenagers have cell phones, car payments, auto insurance premiums.

Students need to know how to use more practical writing skills as well. If they can't write a five-paragraph essay analyzing the themes in *To Kill a Mockingbird,* can they write a single-sheet résumé? And, by the way, even though I am an English teacher and do enjoy teaching essay writing and Harper Lee's classic, which is more relevant? Has anyone besides a college professor ever gotten a job in this country based on a five-paragraph essay?

Nearly two-thirds of the public support "real-world learning," as do 70 percent of teachers.

High schools should follow the lead of colleges. A basic cooking class at Caltech in Pasadena fills up immediately. At the University of Oklahoma there's a life skills class that requires students to register to vote and write a living will before taking the final exam.

The most practical class I ever took in high school, and the one that has helped me the most in my life, was typing. How many high school kids today are able to squeeze in a typing or keyboarding class among the mass of AP classes and other courses required for college?

Students should have the option of studying Shakespeare or shop. Schools need to provide career pathways for those students not going on to college. Of course aim high. Yes, provide ways for all children to rise to the level of scholar. But after a while, if a young person is not doing well in such a system, then alternatives need to be offered; otherwise, the system fails the child, not the other way around.

And let's not forget that "high-paying" and "rewarding" are adjectives that may not necessarily coexist with one another. Ever met an unhappy attorney?

12

Put the Best Teachers in the Worst Schools

One of the shameful truths about American public education is that those children in most need end up with the worst teachers. Because of union rules, teachers with seniority can choose where in a district they wish to work and not be placed according to the needs of the schools. So what ends up happening? The newest teachers work in the most challenging environments: the lowest economic areas with high percentages of minority children.

Students in poorer areas are five times more likely to get inexperienced or incompetent teachers than more affluent students. In California, one out of every five teachers at a high-minority school has no teaching credential.

An Education Trust study assigned teachers from Illinois a quality score, which was divided into quartiles. The study found that while only 11 percent of teachers working in schools with mainly white students ranked in the lowest quartile, 88 percent of teachers working at mainly minority schools ranked that low.

In California, 85 percent of new teachers who haven't completed credential coursework end up working at schools with a majority population of minority students. These are the same type of teachers who end up teaching the worst classes at the worst schools. What's crazier is that they also tend to take on an additional early morning or late afternoon class for extra money, classes that are geared toward the most struggling students who are trying desperately to pass their state's exit exam after failing numerous times. New teachers are likely to be picked for extracurricular duties as well, such as club and class advisorships, further eliminating time for their skills to ripen. Why do educators do such dumb things?

For too long the worst schools have been like beauty colleges and dental schools where the public can receive free services but at potential risk from novices. The best chance for these young people is to have the best and brightest teachers, not the worst and dumbest.

For those who believe that minority students don't care about succeeding in school, the 2006 "Where We Learn" study released by the Council of Urban Boards of Education revealed that African-American students "were the most likely, at 92 percent, to believe that hard work in school will pay off with success."

More than half of black students think that there is a serious problem with kids not respecting teachers as well as using profane language, according to a Public Agenda poll (fewer than one-third of whites held that sentiment about their school). These kids recognize the problems but are powerless to fix them. With weaker teachers meaning weaker classroom management this finding isn't surprising. How tragic that the kids who need better schools, better teachers, and a better overall environment receive the complete opposite.

The National Bureau of Economic Research's Eric A. Hanushek, in studying Texas schools, found that "spending a year in a classroom with an experienced teacher who ranks at the 85th percentile in terms of effectiveness can translate to an average 9-percentile-point learning gain for students." In other words, quality teaching positively impacts children.

Everybody would win if districts offered more money to the most outstanding instructors to work in harder-to-staff schools. Call it combat pay if you wish. Pay teachers more money to do a harder job. That's all. It's that elemental.

However, I'm not talking about adding a paltry few thousand dollars to a teacher's annual salary; rather, a major boost. I guarantee if competent teachers were offered 25 percent more money many would do it.

Bonuses of up to $7,000 were paid to teachers who raised test scores in Tennessee's Hamilton County school district. While basing incentives on test scores should not be the way to go, such a program does prove that there are teachers out there who would like to earn more money, and there's nothing wrong with that. In addition to the extra pay, teachers in the hard-to-staff Benwood schools (so named due to support from the Benwood Foundation) receive help with their mortgages as well as a free master's degree program as incentives to stay.

Virginia has a program offering teachers $15,000 bonuses for working in a low-performing school for three years. Alabama offers bonuses for both teachers (up to $40,000) and principals (up to $60,000) who work at low-performing schools in Mobile County. The 2007 New York City schools contract created "Executive Principal" positions that pay principals $25,000 more for leading a high-needs institution.

One would think that incentives would be made to hire National Board Certified Teachers (NBCTs), discussed more fully in chapter 27, for the worst schools. Why not hire these accomplished teachers to work at these schools?

Ironically, there are fewer NBCTs at these schools, where they are needed the most. Only in California is there a higher percentage working and that is due to a $20,000 bonus for staying four years at lower-economic institutions. Again, the bonus works.

The principals must be the best as well since lack of strong leadership is the number-one reason teachers leave the poorest-performing schools. According to studies done by the Education Trust, schools that serve disadvantaged students well have principals who "are more likely to match talented teachers with students who need them most" and not just have the best teachers teach the advanced classes.

Another factor impacting the achievement gap is the salary gap. While children in a particular school district are funded equally, the money is not equally spent. Because veteran teachers earn higher salaries, suburban schools with smaller minority populations actually receive more money than urban schools whose teachers earn less money due to their inexperience. So once again, the kids who need the most experienced teachers don't get them since less money is spent on teacher talent. What's wrong with this picture?

13

Abolish Homework

One of the biggest misconceptions in education revolves around homework. Supposedly the more homework a child is given, the more learning is taking place. And the more homework a teacher gives out, the better the teacher. Not so, in both cases.

Young people are in school all day working like adults. When are they supposed to act like young people? They don't have mortgages yet. They don't have marriages yet. They aren't parents yet—well, at least most of them.

It's time to put the child back into the hood . . . his own childhood. Children should have time to play and interact with other kids, especially playing outside, considering the childhood obesity problem in this country.

Today kindergarten teachers give five-year-olds weekly packets of worksheets to take home. It seems that schoolwork spills over to the late afternoon and evening hours no matter the grade level.

Once kids enter secondary land, homework amounts jump up dramatically when each of the child's six to seven teachers assigns it. Imagine how burdensome to go through a day with more work piled up hour by hour. If each teacher gave thirty minutes of work each day, kids would have at least three hours of homework. By the time three o'clock comes and school ends, the second job, homework, begins. Understandably children feel overwhelmed and beaten. One student put it this way. "Ever since school started I have had no more than five to six hours of sleep. I have been living off caffeine and sugar just so I can make it until sixth period."

Increasingly more parents are concerned with the amount of homework their children bring home whether the grade level is first or tenth. One out of every five parents believes that their children have too much homework. Some school districts have gone as far as banning homework.

One father filed a lawsuit against his son's school district, located near Milwaukee, Wisconsin, because his child was given homework over summer vacation. While I'm not supporting what this parent did, it does prove how sensitive some people are regarding homework, and why abolishing it would at least eliminate such frivolous lawsuits. In this case, common sense prevailed when a judge threw out the complaint.

Let's face it, with two-income families the norm, parents come home exhausted. They hardly cook for their children anymore, let alone sit down together at dinnertime. On top of that they are expected to carefully monitor schoolwork, too? Who has the time anymore?

Students tell pollsters that homework makes them feel stressed and most wish they had more free time after school. Child development experts say that it is during so-called free or play time when children sharpen their creative instincts. Therefore, give them more of it.

While it can be a nice family activity for parents and older siblings to help out with younger ones' homework, isn't the teacher the best judge of how to get the work done instead of a mom or dad?

That's why making the school day longer and incorporating study time in all periods as proposed in chapter 5 is a good idea—it would eliminate the need for homework and free up more time at home for kids to be kids and parents to be parents.

Having students stay longer in school to complete work would also aid those who may not have computers or Internet access at home. Additionally, many low-income students lack proper study areas in their homes, especially if they share bedrooms with siblings or other relatives. A family's dining table in the kitchen with people walking by constantly is not the optimum setting in which to study.

No more homework also ensures that the work done by each

child is, in fact, that child's work. Have you ever helped out a little more than you should have on one of your children's assignments? Perhaps have Uncle Terry with his circular saw build the science project?

Tim Russert in his popular book *Big Russ & Me* commented on the difference between homework when he grew up in the 1950s and homework today:

> We didn't have as much homework as kids do now, and I certainly don't recall having to construct dioramas or other projects that require adult intervention, a visit to a lumber yard, or a degree in mechanical engineering. . . . Homework was something that children did all by themselves.

If parents took the time to look at the type of homework assigned, they would realize that little of it provides students with a deeper understanding of what they are studying during the school day. Usually it is more math problems, more questions at the end of chapters in a history or science text.

Homework, to paraphrase Shakespeare, is full of sound and fury, signifying nothing. Since teachers don't have a lot of time to grade homework, they tend to assign work that can be quickly evaluated. Having students write multiple sentences to answer thought-provoking questions is not something most teachers voluntarily do. Who wants to give oneself more work? So the teacher typically gives a glance as she goes up and down the rows of students, marking little checks in her gradebook. Or collects daily homework and has a student TA check it off. The students put a lot more time into it than does the teacher, and then homework isn't even worth a significant percentage of a pupil's grade.

Perhaps the biggest advantage for abolishing homework is the elimination of individual textbooks checked out to students. No longer would schools have to fork over millions of dollars to textbook publishers in order to purchase one book for each child. Instead, one set of textbooks per classroom would do the job. Or, better yet, have the students buy their own books, or have the books on a disk or available online, easily accessible via a computer.

The K–12 textbook publishing is a $6.2 billion market. The New York City Public Schools spent over $130 million on books alone in the 2004–05 school year. Think how that money could have been better spent. Plus, no longer would teachers have to check if books have covers or not. The books students would use would remain in the classroom under the care of the teacher.

Dr. Alvin Rosenfeld, author of *The Over-Scheduled Child: Avoiding the Hyper-Parenting Trap,* believes that "parents are being told that the right way to raise their kids is to involve them in every enrichment opportunity possible, even if it means leaving the entire family feeling anxious and stressed." Look at the explosion of Baby Einstein products. Playing classical music while one is pregnant will ensure your baby will be bright, right?

I can't recall how many times I've seen parents eating on the fly, feeding their children fast-food meals before or after a sports practice or game. Right after kids rush through a day of school, their parents continue the push to attend activities several days a week. I had this one student who didn't get home until after 10:00 P.M. on Mondays after orchestra practice. Then she ate dinner and began her homework. Somehow she took a break from her work to sleep.

And so homework continues, as it did last decade, as it did last century. Another sign of how little has changed in the public school system.

Can we finally put to rest the storied antagonistic battles between children and teachers and their parents?

"Sally, did you do your homework?"

"How many of you, class, did your homework?"

Even Santa Claus gets into the act. "If you're a good little girl and do your homework, Santa will pay a visit to your house."

Think about the positive aspects to abolishing homework. No more lost books, silly excuses like "my dog ate my homework" or "my printer's not working," or tedious bookkeeping by teachers to check if homework was done.

This doesn't mean that young people never, ever have anything to do outside of school hours. They can still read a book. They can still practice an instrument or sport. They can still do research. And if they need additional assistance then, yes, a few extra math problems should be assigned.

Of course kids need to be challenged. They should have to work forty hours a week, but then, like many adult workers, be able to unwind when coming home.

A superintendent in Lancaster, Texas, decided to suspend students who did not do their homework over the three-week winter vacation. Gee, isn't a winter break supposed to be a vacation, not an extension of school?

Let's retire all of this nonsense now.

14

Enough with the Testing

We are a nation of numbers. Is the stock market up? Are mortgage rates down? Which movies grossed the most money over the weekend? Give us a score, tell us who won and lost.

Educators are no different. The GPA of students. The ranking of students. SAT scores. AYP results.

Numbers give a quick glimpse about a school but that's all. Parents don't have the time to investigate everything that goes on at their children's school. They want to see the grades, and now they want to know the school's test ranking or annual yearly progress (AYP). The information needs to be short and easy to digest, and politicians are well aware of this. That's why they brilliantly came up with the idea of assigning schools numbers in a ranking system based on standardized test scores. On every district and school Web site there is a prominent link to test scores and accountability. Parents like this because it provides them with a quick glance at how the school compares with other schools.

In a blink, parents look at how high their children's school's score was. High is good, low is not. And truly this is what state and federal politicians have put all their reform efforts behind: a numbers game.

The current craze of standardized testing is just another example of how we Americans want quick fixes and simple solutions.

Politicians have provided busy parents with a "Knowing a School for Dummies" guide with the publication of test scores. They have fed right into the numbers mentality of Americans and Americans have swallowed it whole. And the testmaking companies are smiling all the way to the bank.

Mistakenly perceived as the Good Housekeeping Seal of Approval for schools, a school's good test ranking has quickly become another status symbol people brag about, like an imported luxury car, giving parents the false impression that their children attend a good school. But most parents don't understand what the numbers are all about.

I hate to break the illusion for the taxpaying public, but there are plenty of good teachers at so-called low-performing schools just as there are many incompetent ones at the high-performing schools. No matter that lower-economic schools are at a disadvantage due to their high number of non-English-speaking students who must take the English-written tests. Is it any surprise that districts with the highest test scores include the most expensive neighborhoods?

Public ed critics who have desired making public schools run more like private industry have finally gotten their wish. Schools that have for the longest time avoided playing the numbers game are now gamemasters. Children are being reduced to test scores and ethnic categories.

Testing has put education in a fog. It's unclear to many what the point of all the testing is.

No wonder that former U.S. Secretary of Labor Robert B. Reich refers to schools today as "test-taking factories."

By controlling classroom curriculum through testing, politicians have forced schools to spend an inordinate amount of classroom time on test preparation. The effort it is taking to train teachers in how to develop test prep lessons, pulling them out of the classroom (leaving students in the hands of substitutes), and the time to actually administer the tests, is wreaking a mighty blow to the skimpy 180 days of instructional time, leaving less time for teachers to do their job—teach.

Testing is crushing the morale of a teaching staff who is already overworked, underpaid, and underappreciated. With principals applying increased pressure on teachers, teachers likewise place pressure on students, putting them under so much stress that performing at their best on these tests becomes difficult.

People who look at testing as a sign of reform have it backward. Testing is actually preventing real reform from taking place.

AN NCLB PRIMER

There's an old joke about an elderly Jewish woman about to enter a closed-off pool. A perturbed attendant noticing her action tells her, "Excuse me, ma'am, but can't you read the sign? It says, 'No Swimming Allowed.' "

The old woman, going on with her business of swimming, instructs the younger man, "That's the way you read it. The way I read it is, 'No, Swimming Allowed.' "

And that is exactly the way to read the federal government's No Child Left Behind (NCLB) law of 2002: no, children left behind in a system that if housed in a building would warrant a place in the National Register of Historic Places.

Whoever came up with this title to the federal government's latest education fix-all program should receive a medal. What an emotionally charged phrase, "no child left behind." After all, what educator would leave struggling students behind without coming to their aid? What parent would leave children behind in a market? You wouldn't leave your children behind at home while you and your spouse jet away for a Las Vegas getaway. . . . Oops, one couple did do that.

In a nutshell, NCLB stipulates that schools must show that all students, meaning 100 percent, no matter the ethnicity, achieve at a certain level of proficiency by 2014 through testing of all students in grades three through eight, plus one year from high school (decided by each state), and that all children be taught by "highly qualified" instructors. Schools not meeting federal standards face consequences such as losing government funding.

NCLB is an elaborate public relations stunt. You see, NCLB requires that in each core subject every child is taught by a "highly qualified" teacher. Never mind that each state has come up with its own definition of "highly qualified," thus providing a wide array of meanings.

Last year in California a group of parents and advocates filed a lawsuit against the U.S. Department of Education for its liberal use of the label "highly qualified." In that state, over ten thousand teachers are working in the classroom at the same time they are earning their teaching credentials. From their very first day of teaching these interns are anointed as "highly qualified."

Thus, the government may be able to hold a press conference proudly proclaiming a qualified teacher in every classroom; however, it is misleading, akin to saying that we are winning the war against terror as suicide bombing after suicide bombing occurs.

Just as real estate agents rattle off their oft-repeated mantra of location, location, location being the three most important things to look for in shopping for a new house, so do politicians warble ad nauseam about what they consider the three most important ways to teach children—testing, testing, testing.

Since it became clear early on that it would be near to impossible for states to meet NCLB mandates, the federal government has continuously been in revision mode, backpedaling its requirements, allowing states loopholes to massage their definition of "proficiency," in effect giving permission to label students who are not proficient as "proficient."

In Tennessee, if there is a racial group with fewer than forty-five students representing it, then that entire minority population does not have to be counted in that school's reported scores. This means that a school can completely ignore forty African-American children who are struggling, allowing the rest of the school to appear to be meeting federal mandates. Millions of student scores have been thrown out this way. Meanwhile, the dreaded achievement gap between whites and nonwhites marches on.

What's fascinating about how the federal government has put its footprint in the classroom is that it was a Republican president of all things who pushed for more government control of schools, not less, which is contrary to one of the major tenets of conservatism, limiting government not enlarging it. Yet that is just what President George W. Bush has done.

At the same time, Democrats, who are always taking teachers unions' money and endorsements, are stepping out of their liberal box and demanding to do away with tenure, an idea you would think would come from the Republican side and their business philosophy of firing people who are not doing the job. How strange the reversal of political roles. Oh well, that's why I'm not a political science teacher.

At some schools, teachers are being evaluated on how well they prepare students for standardized testing. Yes, that's right, the forbidden "teaching to the test" is actually being encouraged by principals. A "good" teacher would be one who gives her students sample test questions every day. Is this what Washington's elected officials had in mind when they created this program?

NCLB, with its exclusive emphasis on math and reading testing, has not met its target of reshaping schools and needs to be abolished. It is inherently flawed, oversimplifies student achievement, and further damages the already low morale of teachers who are excessively overburdened with preparing students to take test after test to the detriment of the rest of the curriculum.

EXIT EXAMS

Along with NCLB and its testing mandates, nearly half the states have developed their own exit exams impacting fifteen million students, two-thirds of the country's high school students.

What is the point behind these nonchallenging exit exams? In many cases developers of exit exams earnestly desire to make earning a high school diploma more meaningful, and so they create a challenging exam that really tests the students' knowledge. What many states discovered upon piloting such tests, however, was an extremely low passage rate. So instead of holding firm to a high level of achievement, the exit exams became watered down to the point of irrelevance.

The California High School Exit Exam, or CAHSEE, had to cut its length in half and include easier material. Even then, it took several years before it was enforced. And when it was finally enforced in 2006, a group of parents, as expected, sued the state claiming that CAHSEE was unfair (the courts upheld the test). Despite eighth-grade math and tenth-grade English skills being tested, a passing threshold of 55 percent in math and 60 percent in English, plus a host of free intervention classes and one-on-one tutoring, and five chances to pass the darn thing, one out of every ten California seniors still did not pass it. But do not worry about them, as most were given a piece of paper declaring completion with some form of competency.

As you see, the whole thing is a charade. One by one districts and states have devised exit strategies by handing out certificates of completion to those students not graduating. This way students can still walk the stage while districts can avoid lawsuits. It's like making up a rule, then coming up with myriad ways to get around the rule. These certificates signify that despite failing the same test multiple times, a student really knows the material. What?! Talk about a self-defeating policy.

Utah reneged enforcement of its exit exam upon discovering the large number of students who wouldn't graduate. In New Jersey, students failing its exit exam three times have a way out with the Special Review Assessment (SRA). All a student has to do is have teachers and administrators sign a paper that says he does have the skills required for high school graduation despite failing the test three times. In 2005, 740 students passed the test but 940 received an SRA. How's that for holding the line and ensuring the integrity of the exit exam?

So, what's the message to the kids? You don't really have to pass the test now, do you? If you fail what the state has decreed an all-important test, no consequence will befall you.

It has been estimated that exit exams are weeding out—make sure you're sitting down—a whopping 0.77 percent of seniors. Ooooh! What an impact exit exams are having. Yeah, they are really making sure only qualified students earn that diploma. They are really ensuring that a high school diploma means something. Uh-huh. Like NCLB ensuring all teachers are *highly* qualified. As my nine-year-old son would say, "Yeah, right."

Not that earning a high school diploma should be as challenging as passing a state's bar exam, but ask any bright high school student and he will tell you what a joke the exit exam is. Kids are smart enough to recognize that passing one is not an achievement; it is just a requirement. To proclaim "I passed my high school exit exam" is akin to saying "I passed my driver's test." No one who does poorly on a driving test is barred from ever driving a car, just delayed; one merely retakes the driver test again and again. The same is true with exit exams.

Exit exams provide students and parents with a false sense of accomplishment. Plus, no future college or employer is ever going to ask the applicant if he passed his high school exit exam or not. It will not open any doors.

And, as with other standardized tests, days of instruction get thrown out in order to administer it.

Most damaging, it gives state education bureaucrats ammunition (really blanks) to proclaim at a news conference that the direction of the schools is sound, the programs are working.

And the uninformed public sees the twenty-second story on TV and feels good about schools. Yuck!

A more practical reason to do away with most standardized testing is the raw cost of human labor and printing. The money and effort that goes into testing children is enormous.

According to the California State Department of Education's Standards and Assessment Division, standardized testing, including the NCLB requirements and the exit exam, costs over $118 million annually.

The U.S. Government Accountability Office reports that states "will spend between $1.9 billion and $5.3 billion to develop, score, and report NCLB-required tests."

Just what was this money spent on before?

At my school each teacher receives a thirteen-page testing booklet on how to administer the tests. It's interesting to note that teachers are restricted to a limited photocopy quota, but when it comes to copying test instructions, the sky's the limit.

All facilitators of the test must watch a video on how to administer it. Since the video repeats everything that's already in the test instructions, our school, in order to be legal about it, runs the video on a monitor in the background with the sound off while administrators read over the handout.

Page 1:	agenda for the meeting to discuss the testing packet
Page 2:	cover sheet (I don't know why this is necessary but it's there)
Page 3:	table of contents
Page 4:	check-in and check-out procedures
Page 5:	day-by-day breakdown showing which tests are given on specific days
Page 6:	testing bell schedule (printed double-sided)
Pages 7–8:	general info and reminders
Page 9:	day-by-day breakdown showing the length for each test and the page number where each test is found in the test booklet
Page 10:	procedures for return of test materials
Page 11:	a sheet to be posted on each door that reads, "QUIET! Testing in progress. DO NOT DISTURB. QUIET!"
Page 12:	more reminders
Page 13:	class roster of students taking the test

Because testing devours the morning, the rest of the school day allows for only twenty-four-minute periods. That's not sufficient to get significant work accomplished.

An ancillary problem with all this testing is the strain it is placing on companies who produce and score the tests. Only a handful of companies exist to handle the whole workload. For the 2007–08 school year, states administered over fifty-six million tests, ten million more than in the 2005–06 year.

The Associated Press reported that Education Sector, a

Washington-based think tank, found that "35 percent of testing offices in [23] states had experienced 'significant' errors with scoring and 20 percent didn't get results 'in a timely fashion.'"

Education Sector codirector Thomas Toch said that "the testing industry in the U.S. is buckling under the weight of NCLB demands."

Testing company Harcourt Assessment, Inc., lost most of its $44 million contract with Illinois when the state's test scores were the last to be reported in the nation.

Scandal hit the College Board in 2006 when it was discovered that over 4,400 students had their SATs scored incorrectly, lowering their scores by more than 100 points in some cases. Meanwhile the colleges those students applied to already had the wrong numbers in their hands.

Let's not be too hard on the College Board. After all, they have been around for over one hundred years, and the SAT has been around since 1926, and this is the worst scoring mistake reported, so for the most part accuracy has ruled. However, think about this: The more standardized testing that takes place, the more pressure on the testing companies to fill orders and to score all the extra tests in a timely fashion. Trying to take on more work yet produce results in a short time span is a time bomb ready to go off.

As a parent, I want the most highly qualified instructors teaching to my children. As a teacher, I want to be treated professionally so that I can meet the needs of parents and their children. In reality, the politicians, by creating this standardized test race, have started something that is quickly getting as out of control as any wildfire does in California.

Many schools have immersed their students in test prep classes, or special tutoring, even reserving Fridays to have students take practice tests.

Let's say reports came out that doctors were not doing their jobs well enough. There were too many sick patients, too many illnesses not properly diagnosed, and incorrect medications prescribed.

As a result, state and federal governments came up with standards of medical practice, spelling out specific strategies and behaviors for dealing with patients: "patients receive adequate diagnosis of illnesses"; "patients receive proper and appropriate medication"; "patients shall receive fifteen-minute visits with physicians."

Now the accountability piece needs to be put into place: Patients fill out surveys each time they visit a doctor; patients participate in focus groups; patient charts get reviewed by the state medical examiner.

Would all of this rigmarole dramatically improve health care?

Imagine the amount of time doctors would have to put into such a system of checks and balances, plus additional training on the system itself. And the added stress upon the physicians' shoulders. How would that impact the quality of care? Would all of this produce better doctors? Think of the added cost to health care.

Thankfully, despite malpractice suits, society generally trusts doctors and believes in their high level of knowledge.

The same can't be said about teachers, unfortunately.

Many people distrust their knowledge, many question what they do on a daily basis. And that is why there is testing, to make sure the teachers are teaching.

Meanwhile, whatever happened to the weight of the final grade in a class? Does all that day-in and day-out work by the student not count toward anything anymore?

As I stated in my previous book, *The $100,000 Teacher: A Teacher's Solution to America's Declining Public School System* (Capital Books), the problem is that there doesn't exist a simple buzzword or number to demonstrate how much students learn from "assignments that probe the higher-level thinking skills of evaluation and synthesis and avoid the 'when' something happened or 'who' was involved rote type of learning" commonly used on standardized tests.

The fact of the matter is that an accountability system is and has already been in place—it's called student work. It doesn't have a catchy name, one can't make an easy acronym out of it, and no politician can claim credit for it.

Isn't it interesting how in their elementary school years students bring home completed work by the reams that parents proudly display on the refrigerator, but by the time they reach middle school, work no longer gets showcased?

Once the student products become less colorful and graphic in nature, once students begin writing, the products may not be so attractive. One can't glance at a sheet of lab notes from a chemistry class and immediately grasp the meaning of it (it takes time to examine it) compared with a Santa face with glued-on cotton balls. And that's what test scores are—single-glance things that are superficial.

The only worthwhile result of standardized testing is that it does provide a comparison of how one school does with the same test as other schools. What that tells you is that one school has trained its student population better than another. I also think it is useful to have students in America take a test and compare the results to those in other countries.

And what real information do tests provide? That kids who normally do well in school likewise do well on tests. Surprise! Therefore, schools that already have high-achieving students can boast in a hollow way how much better a job of educating young people they do than schools with lower test scores. That's crap.

Daniel Chambliss, sociology professor at Hamilton College in Clinton, New York, told *The Washington Post* that "tests measure very narrow kinds of things under very specific circumstances and real life doesn't work that way."

And when you hear what skills employers desire of their employees—coming to work on time, showing up for work, speaking in a proper way to customers—none of those traits are tested, although they easily could be.

With increased pressure to raise student scores come increased incidents of cheating—by teachers, that is. In 2005, the city of Houston, Texas, had to take action against six teachers and three administrators involved in a cheating scandal on state tests. What's funny is that one teacher who was coaching students how to answer some of the questions mistakenly fed them the wrong answers. Whoops.

In many cases, improved test results fade as students proceed through school. The National Assessment of Educational Progress in their National Report Card: Science 2005 showed that "scores improved for elementary students, remained flat for those in middle school and declined for high schoolers." This proves that as children age they get tired of learning in a school setting. The average person moves every seven years, changes jobs at least ten times, yet we expect children to stay put in a thirteen-year system and consistently do well and improve each year.

One superintendent said that "teachers look at the data in their own classroom to determine what standards their students have or have not met, how to group kids according to what they have or have not done, and to design lessons that will bring them up to the next level." Someone give that person a reality shot. Do parents actually believe that teachers have luxurious amounts of time to scrutinize test data and to tailor individual instruction for each student? If so, then they must believe that a person can eat his way to losing weight.

Deb Sigman, California's state testing director, actually told the *Los Angeles Times* without laughing, "Folks think we do nothing but testing, but it's not a huge intrusion in terms of the overall number of instructional minutes." Ha! When was the last time Ms. Sigman stepped into a classroom and spent a week observing what was happening? Testing and test results dominate faculty meeting agendas and staff development sessions.

It is remarkable when I look back at my teaching files, back to the late 1980s and early 1990s, how many wonderful lessons and assignments that highly engaged students sit unused in my filing cabinets. I still strive to fill the days with work that stimulates student thinking, but I used to do much more when there was less testing and fewer test prep materials that needed to be distributed, read through, studied, and analyzed.

People are getting rich (and believe me, it's not the teachers) creating companies that help schools analyze data and organize it into reports. Districts have had to hire or train people to knowledgeably crunch numbers.

Testing has put too much emphasis on the subjects tested, namely math and English, to the detriment of other subjects. Education writer Diane Ravitch describes the myopic focus on math and English testing as "schooling our children, not educating them." In a process called "narrowing the curriculum," more than two-thirds of schools have diminished time in history and music, among other areas. According to *The New York Times,* "at MLK Junior High in Sacramento, 150 of the school's 885 students spend five of their six class periods on math, reading, and gym, leaving only one 55-minute period for all other subjects." As Columbia University education professor Thomas Sobol put it, "That's like a violin student who's only permitted to play scales, nothing else, day after day, scales, scales, scales. They'd lose their zest for music."

Creativity has no place in today's modern classroom.

The whole system is on the verge of collapse. Public education went 150 years without much standardized testing and guess what happened? The United States became the world's superpower.

So, please, dear politicians, cut us teachers some slack. Place a moratorium on testing for one year. Allow some reflection time to take place. Let us digest all the new changes that have been legislated. For once, trust the teachers on this one and save yourselves some money in return.

Until people are willing to trust teachers' evaluation of their children's work in school, testing will continue to dominate public education, eroding teachers' critical work in the classroom.

15

A Twelve-year-old Third Grader? Yes

In the old days, if you had a lot of Fs, you got called down to the principal's office.

Nowadays, if you have a lot of Fs, you get called down to the principal's office.

What's the difference?

In the first example, the "you" refers to the student. In the second, the "you" refers to the teacher. And that's a mighty paradigm shift.

Society has its N-word. School has its F-word. Dare I say it? *Failure.*

Teachers are under tremendous pressure to pass kids. Social promotion is the policy most schools operate under. At all costs, students are not to be held back a grade, even if they are failing. The pressure is applied from the principal, the district, the state and federal governments. Those who have a lot of students earning Fs get called into the principal's office. Principals demand to know why so many students fail in a teacher's class. My question is: Do the students with the Fs ever get called down and questioned by the principal as to why they are failing?

One principal's memo from one of the largest school districts in California requested teachers to reconsider their F grades. Why the pressure? If the school had a low graduation rate it would not meet the NCLB requirements. One teacher told the *Los Angeles Times* that "we do everything we possibly can to pass them. To be asked to go beyond that is ridiculous . . . I've never seen anything like that in my forty-four years of teaching."

Two government studies released in 2007 showed that students' grades were rising even though standardized test scores didn't go up. What does that mean? Teachers feeling pressure to pass kids despite their skill level?

Parents also put the squeeze on schools to change their children's grades. Almost half of teachers report having a student or parent ask them to change a grade even when it isn't deserved.

One teacher I know buckled under intense pressure to change an Advanced Placement student's F to a D despite twenty-five absences.

A student with a 4.5 GPA sued the Kanawha school district in West Virginia because she got an F on a leaf project in her biology class after missing the assignment's deadline. According to the *Charleston Daily Mail*, "The student's parents were seeking, in addition to punitive damages, damages for 'emotional stress, [and] loss of enjoyment of life.'" The judge didn't agree and threw out the lawsuit.

I had a student who had over thirty absences in my honors class, missed the last three weeks of the semester including the final exam, and seemed shocked to discover he was getting an F. He called me up demanding a conference with both of his parents.

So, after requesting a translator since neither of his parents spoke English, I met with them. His father defended his son's academic abilities profusely and demanded to know why I wouldn't let his son make up the work that was not done. The boy lied in front of his own parents to say that all of his grades on the work that he did do were As and Bs when actually the work turned in was predominately Ds and Fs. If there ever was a student who earned an F outright it was this young man who, by the way, pulled the same stunt the previous year, bringing in his overbearing parents, accusing the teachers of conspiring against him. The evidence did not matter.

Even after I thought the whole matter was put to rest, this same student came to my room the next week acting like he was my boss, saying that he spoke to the administrators and that I had to give him make-up work and change his grade. I'm not sure if this kid is going to go into law but he would make a wonderful defense attorney for an Al-Qaeda operative.

Of course no one wants a twelve-year-old in a third-grade class. And this doesn't mean that students should just wallow in their own failure.

According to Baltimore sociologist Karl L. Alexander, 64 percent of students who repeated a grade in elementary school and 63 percent who repeated in middle school ended up without a high school diploma. No area in the achievement gap between blacks and whites is more glaring than the statistics for repeating ninth grade. Using the National Center for Education Statistics data for the 2004–05 school year, more than twice as many African-American students repeated ninth grade as white students. In New York, 44 percent of blacks repeated the grade compared to only 5 percent of whites.

A kind of checkup needs to be implemented at regular intervals to gauge student progress. And guess what? Schools already have such checkups. They're called report cards. The problem is that too often with the workload that teachers have they can barely keep their heads above water just doing grades, never mind carefully analyzing each student's performance and diagnosing the next steps to take in assisting the pupil or offering advice to the school administrator or parents on what steps should be taken.

One year my colleagues and I had to discuss ways of cutting down the failure rate in our department, which stood at an outrageous, are you ready, 17 percent. Looked at from the opposite end, that meant English teachers were passing 83 percent of their students. That's pretty damn good. Yet we still had to create a plan on how to bring the failure rate down even further. Well, what is the ultimate goal? Not have a single student get an F? Most Fs are earned by absentee students, not students who come to class every day and can't do the work at a certain level. Should teachers go to extreme measures and go to the students' homes and watch over them as they do the work?

Just as a patient whose prescribed antibiotics aren't quite

powerful enough to knock out an infection needs a stronger dose, so does a struggling student need additional assistance if what currently is being given him isn't working.

Intervention needs to happen and it needs to happen before June and before April and before December.

One documentary on education showed a school that received a large grant from a private foundation in order to purchase supplementary reading material to help struggling readers. It wasn't until April that these materials arrived, way too late to help the failing students.

Schools bend over backward trying to get students to pass their classes. Much money and effort is spent on this population. About the only thing that is not being done is having teachers do the work for the students.

After a certain point, however, students must take responsibility for their academic futures. And if parents realized that schools would strictly adhere to a no social promotion policy, then they might help motivate their children to do better.

New York City mayor Michael Bloomberg, when taking over the public school district in 2002, held firm against social promotion even though it resulted in the removal of school board members whom he helped get elected.

Schools must have teeth in their policy of not promoting failing students. If a student does not demonstrate that minimum ability has been mastered, that child needs to repeat the grade. It's that simple.

16

Bring Back the Golden Rule

"Put your right hand over your heart, ready, _____."

Did you fill in the blank with "begin"? If so, you are a product of America's public school system and the system has taught you well.

From your first memories of school you were conditioned to recite words to a hanging flag, not even knowing what the words meant, dutifully performing the ritual every day (for the longest time I kept saying "invisible" instead of "indivisible"). You probably couldn't wait for your turn to hold the flag or lead the rest of the class in the recitation.

The Pledge of Allegiance is ingrained in all of us. We have public schools to thank for that. Oh, there's nothing wrong with it. Reciting the pledge is one of the few remaining rituals of school from yesteryear still being done today. Battered by lawsuits, attacked by atheists for "under God," the pledge lingers on.

One of the most important jobs of schools is to teach all students about American customs. Part of being American is being courteous to and considerate of others. Unlike the pledge, this training has eroded over the past decades. The golden rule no longer rules. It's not a class or a course or a state standard, and it's definitely not something easily assessed on a multiple-choice test. Yet the absence of its instruction is very clear in our society.

Have you ever been the first driver to arrive at a four-way stop and watched in amazement as another driver who arrived later than you zooms through the intersection? "How rude" pops in your head.

Have you ever observed children acting up loudly in a restaurant, thinking to yourself, "Where are the parents"? Probably sitting right next to the children are big people who are commonly known as grown-ups (and I use that term loosely) but who choose not to monitor or correct such rudeness. One coffeehouse actually had to post a sign asking parents to watch their children.

How about cell phone etiquette or lack of it? At a bagel shop you're behind a man who continues talking on his cell phone while having his order taken. And he is not doing either of the tasks very well. "Inconsiderate" runs through your mind.

Perhaps if good manners were taught again we would finally have that kinder, gentler nation President Bush the elder dreamed of a while ago.

Surveys show that many problems students have with school revolve around attitudes or behaviors. Most students believe that too many kids lack respect for teachers and use bad language, cheat on assignments and tests, cut class, abuse drugs and alcohol, and fight. Parents surveyed also cite fighting and a lack of respect for teachers as areas of concern. And two out of every three teachers consider students' misbehavior as a major nuisance.

Everyone seems to recognize there is a problem at schools with the way young people act, but such behavior is ignored by school officials, whose focus remains firmly fixated on testing.

Students need to be taught from their first day of attendance that school is a special place where they need to act accordingly, with respect. Too many students treat school as nothing special. They throw trash on the ground, they talk trash in the halls, and they act as if the classroom is an extension of their home environment, continually eating and drinking and talking, putting their feet on desks, listening to their iPods, talking on their cell phones. Do children act this way in a pediatrician's office? Do they act this way in a place of worship?

Why do schools have to resemble the rest of society and its lack of decorum? One year the senior class purchased shirts with the saying WE'LL KICK YOUR CLASS emblazoned on the front. I've heard teachers on stage during pep rallies scream, "Let's kick their ass!"

Part of a teen's daily vernacular is the phrase "That's so gay," which is like the old saying "That's so retarded."

I admonished one lad about his use of expletives. "Watch your language," I told him. "What, what did I say?" he asked his friend. "You said the S-word." "Oh, I didn't even know." And that's the problem. Expletives have become so ingrained as part of natural speech for youngsters, there is no longer a line of appropriate and inappropriate language.

One female student wrote in an essay about how a certain character was a "prick." She had no idea that it was a dirty word. She must have heard it on TV or, worse, at home.

Another student wrote in his journal about a girl he liked. He used the phrase "she has nice breasts" three or four times. The immigrant kid honestly did not realize that such a description was inappropriate for a school assignment.

Many schools have recently had to deal with freak dancing or "freaking," which is when teenagers' dance moves simulate sexual acts. One student, when informed of the antifreaking policy at his school, said, "How else do you dance? I wouldn't go. It would be boring."

Go up to a teen and mention PDA, and he will know immediately what you're talking about. For us square folks, PDA stands for Public Display of Affection. We're not talking about holding hands, but mouth-to-mouth exploration, and body-to-body attachment. Young people need to view going to school as a serious endeavor. Adults know that in the workplace there is a way to behave, and students at school are in their workplace. So PDAs have no place at school.

Some teachers shy away from correcting student behaviors, fearing parents who are equally misbehaved calling them down for a conference with the principal, taking them to task, demanding in a huff and a puff, "Who are you, teaching my children how to act?"

One mother demanded a conference with me because I reprimanded her fifteen-year-old son for making fun of a classmate who was giving a speech. "You're not his parent" was her corrective tone to me.

Public libraries have had to resort to closing during after-school hours due to loud and obnoxious behavior from kids who have no place to go after school and before dinner.

According to a story in *The New York Times,* students from Maplewood Middle School in New Jersey who spend time at the local library after school "fight, urinate on the bathroom floor, scrawl graffiti on the walls, talk back to librarians, or refuse to leave when asked." As a result, after dealing with these problems for a decade, in 2007 the Maplewood Memorial Library began closing from 2:45 to 5:00 P.M. during the week. The library said that it "can no longer deal with large numbers of students who come after school and wait, sometimes into the late evening, to be picked up."

Some libraries, like one in Wickliffe, Ohio, ban kids under fourteen unless they come with an adult. Another in Euclid, Ohio, plays classical music to keep visitors sedate. With so few parents at home right after school, libraries have become the hangout for kids, serving as another child-care center.

Rude behavior is a direct result of public schools no longer teaching the golden rule curriculum.

Nowadays, marking a child's citizenship grade is optional for teachers. Remember the old ESU system, *E* is for *excellent,* *S* is for *satisfactory,* *U* is for *unsatisfactory*? It's been replaced by 1, 2, 3, 4: 4 = exceeds standards, 3 = meets standards, 2 = approaching standards, 1 = below standards. Don't be misled, however. Educators will tell you that 4 *is not* an A, 3 *is not* a B, and so on. The numbers relate to the level of competence a child has achieved on a particular standard. Got it?

My son attends the same school district I did. What a difference forty years makes in terms of how important citizenship is. As I look at my first-grade report card from the 1960s and compare it to my son's from a couple of years ago, "Qualities of Citizenship" is at the top of mine while "Social Skills" rests at the bottom of his. The downward shift of the behavior evaluation from top to bottom is symbolic of where our society's manners have gone. Good citizenship no longer merits much attention.

In fact, nearly one-third of a single side of my old report card is given over to explicit definitions of the "Qualities of Citizenship" section:

> **Works well with others:** Child has the ability to get along with others, can work and play harmoniously in a group.
> **Initiative:** Child has the ability to meet problems and attempt a solution on his own; is self-reliant and independent; is ready with new ideas and suggestions.
> **Dependability:** Child fulfills promises; follows directions well; can be counted on when working independently, as well as under supervision.
> **Self-control:** Child has the ability to adjust his actions to conform to rules set up by a group; has the ability to control his natural impulses and desires.
> **Consideration for rights of others:** Child has respect for other people's property, in seeking its use and in caring for it; has respect for rights of others in the classroom and on the playground.

Each quality would get a check for "very good" or "satisfactory" or "unsatisfactory," all three terms quite clear in meaning. Plus, even though it was first grade, children used to get real A, B, C, D, F grades, unlike today where letter grades are purposely delayed until third or fourth grade.

Especially with the large influx of immigrants and the overly PC culture we have, it seems people are afraid to correct others' behaviors. Could the lack of spelling out and modeling proper manners be one of the key factors in why our society is as mean-spirited as it is in its entertainment and its people-to-people interactions?

We have become so afraid to qualify observed behaviors that we need to assign numbers instead of grades. But come on. What parent doesn't translate a 4 meaning outstanding, a 3 meaning good, a

2 meaning average, and a 1 meaning poor? What, are we so super-sensitive that we don't want children and their parents to feel disappointment in a poor rating? So we cushion it with a 1? To me, that is not educating children properly. Educating them properly means telling them exactly how they are doing academically and socially using descriptive language.

When was the last time you saw "unsatisfactory" being used to describe a student's work? No, the PC wording today is "needs improvement." First of all, the word "need" sounds good. We all "need" something, right? And "improvement"? Wch-heh-ell, that suggests wonderful, positive things, to improve oneself. We all can use a bit of improving, now can't we? Hey, just come out and say that the child's behavior or academics are low, poor, bad, awful, terrible, horrible. Those colorful adjectives give parents more accurate information than "Johnny is between a 1 and a 2 on the standard scale. We want him to move closer to the 2 by next month."

No, today in kindergarten, first- and second-grade teachers discuss with parents if their children are "meeting the standards." Is this what society has come to? Educating children to meet standards? The word "standards" has such a clinical sound to it. We have completely bled out any whiff of subjectivity on the part of the teacher. Well, hasn't that teacher with at least five years of college earned a certain level of expertise? Shouldn't that teacher offer valid opinions on students' knowledge levels? Of course it is subjective! But subjective from someone learned (hopefully).

If an English teacher says a piece of writing deserves an A you should as a parent or a student feel confident that such a grade was decided on after careful thought and consideration. To challenge a teacher's grade is to say, "You don't have it right." I know with writing, you can write up the most detailed rubric (or grading chart) possible, with multiple columns, showing students each element that needs to be in an accomplished piece of writing—thesis statement, supporting details, topic sentences—but there will always be students who claim a teacher is not being objective in an evaluation. Well, it is impossible to be objective. The teacher must be subjective, we hope, and utilize all of her training and knowledge and experience in analyzing student writing.

When you go to a doctor and something is bothering you, you don't want him to say, "Well, your ailment could be this or that. I really don't know. You can take this or that. It's up to you." No. You want your doctor to come out and say with the complete backing of his professional education and experiences, "You have this. Take this and you will feel better." Teachers need to do more diagnosing like this, but their hands are tied by fears of hurting anyone's feelings (God forbid!) and threats of parental lawsuits.

Of course, there is a certain segment of educators who would like to do away with letter grades altogether. They think the system makes students too competitive. Well, wake up. American society is competitive. Ignoring that fact makes public education and what it does all a farce.

Educators, parents, and society as a whole have to stop soft-pedaling the real world. Look at the fantasy a couple of teachers fostered recently in an after-school child-care program in the Seattle, Washington, area. When teachers discovered that children ages five to eight were getting too possessive of the Lego town they had built, new ground rules were implemented such as all buildings were to be of the same size and were to be considered public structures to discourage students' sense of "owning" the Lego houses.

In an article published in *Rethinking Schools,* educators Ann Pelo and Kendra Pelojoaquin admit to wanting "to take part in shaping the children's understandings from a perspective of social justice" and so were disturbed when the Lego playing "mirrored those of a class-based, capitalist society—a society that we teachers believe to be unjust and oppressive." Curiously, the children attending this after-school program come from well-heeled parents who can afford the $500-a-month tuition and who obviously have benefited nicely from our "class-based, capitalist society" enough to help fund these teachers' salaries.

It's quite challenging in teaching kids today to combat many distractions that have made their way into the classrooms, namely cell phones and iPods.

You know that warning that appears before the movie in theaters and is announced before the start of theatrical performances, "Please turn off your cell phones, and refrain from talking"? A teacher today needs to say this at the start of every class.

Look at cell phone use among teens, at least two-thirds of whom have one. Many districts, such as New York City, ban the use of cell phones entirely, while others have modified bans allowing students use of phones during snack and lunch. The problem with a curtailed-use strategy is that there is no real way to police students who use phones while walking between periods to their next class. I've seen plenty of kids walking the hallways chatting on their phones while on their way to use the bathroom, making a mockery of a limited-use strategy.

New York City schools reported 2,500 cell phone incidents in one school year. And that's just the actual reported incidents. How many other times did a phone ring in a classroom and a teacher out of kindness or exasperation ignored it?

Once when I was walking my class down to the bookroom a student got out her cell phone to make a call. I told her, "Unless you're assisting a surgeon, you need to put that away."

While the ringing of a cell phone is disruptive no matter the setting—a library, a restaurant—having such a sonic disturbance while a teacher is teaching her heart out completely breaks the learning mood that has been carefully nurtured.

One time when a student was delivering an oral report, a student's cell phone went off. Have you ever heard the ringtone on a teenager's cell phone? The loudest music imaginable blasts from the device, obliterating the quiet atmosphere that student needed to do her presentation.

After the phone was taken away, it rang again as it sat on my desk (she forgot to turn it off). When class concluded, she actually had the nerve to ask for it back. Didn't she understand the problem her ringing phone caused? And who's calling her anyway during class time? I followed school policy and handed it over to the assistant principal's office. The fact that she didn't seem to understand the problem the ringing of her phone caused is a much deeper issue than the phone ringing in the first place.

Unless you've been in this situation it is hard to imagine how damaging a phone ringing and ringing and ringing is. The teacher has to figure out whose phone rang. Then the teacher has to take the phone away from the student. Then the teacher has to put the phone in a sealed envelope with the student's name on it. Then the teacher has to take the envelope down to the administration office. That's an awful waste of a teacher's time.

Worse than that, however, students often cheat using cell phones, by either texting friends about what questions are on a test or taking photos of the test. I have caught crafty students texting while apparently sitting in their seats looking attentive as I spoke. What gave one student away to me was the awkward movement of one of her arms. Sure enough, I quickly went to her and she was texting a friend while pretending to listen to the lesson. Another student told me that the only reason she had her phone out was because she thought it was her mother calling her. Now, why would a parent call a child knowing that she is in class? Students and adults just don't get it.

During one observation of another teacher, I sat a couple of desks behind a student who used his cell phone twice within a ten-minute period, first to text message a friend, second to play a video game, all right in front of the teacher, who hadn't a clue what the kid was doing.

With the phones becoming increasingly miniature, students can easily shield them. Once while I observed another teacher teaching I sat behind this one young lady with hair down her back. She had discreetly placed a handheld phone near her ear but completely concealed it with her Rapunzel locks.

Cell phone use is largely a societal problem. People have convinced themselves that they *need* to have a cell phone. Parents are some of the loudest critics of schools with strict bans on cell phones, claiming that the phone is a lifeline to their child.

Hmm, well let's see now. How did parents keep in contact with their children before 1995? I can't recall there being a problem before in contacting the school office.

People have created false needs about having and using cells, and that warped perception gets passed down to their children. If their own parents drive and talk at the same time, then why shouldn't they?

It's not uncommon for even college students to sit in lecture halls roaming the Internet on their laptops as the professor speaks, working more on their Facebook page than the textbook page.

One can rant against Apple and other companies who have put out the iPods and the cell phones and other devices for making a teacher's job that much harder. However, just as with gun violence, it is not the gun that kills a person and it is not the phone that ruins a lesson. It all boils down to etiquette and manners, something many young people desperately need a year-long course in, as well as some of their parents.

I had a journalism student who refused to remove his iPod earbud from his ear (a school policy by the way) because "I draw better if I listen to music." Well, he may draw even better if he drinks but I'm not going to allow it. I told him, "Then you're going to have to draw twice as better without it."

Not too long ago legendary golfer Jack Nicklaus made an appearance in front of a congressional committee about how important sports are to building character in young people. Affiliated with a character education program called First Tee, Nicklaus told the committee, "My father focused on aspects of the game that would make me a better person, not just a better golfer. . . . The first time I threw the ball my father said he hoped it would be the last. And it was. . . . We need to do everything we can to promote positive values in our children."

What passes as character education these days is that a word may be displayed in a room for the month or a good habit might be mentioned on the PA system. But no true ongoing character lessons are part of the required curriculum children receive today, except what individual teachers may happen to do on their own. There should be lessons on manners, everything from how to address your elders to how to eat with the proper utensils.

One of the exceptions can be found at Integrity Charter School in National City, California, where students "get daily lessons in responsibility, respect, ethics, and morals."

One student who transferred to Integrity told *The San Diego Union-Tribune* that "If someone asks me what I'm doing, I won't say, 'None of your business.' Now, I'll answer politely."

Perhaps with students learning virtues, acts of cheating will drop.

When everything is peeled away, don't we all want kids to grow up and become decent people who have skills to survive on their own? It doesn't really matter if they go to college and make six-figure salaries. How does making a large amount of middle-class money help out one's country? How does owning a huge house and leasing new vehicles help one's fellow man?

My neighbor recently built a two-story addition to his house that impacted me in the following ways: (1) my filtered view quickly turned into a full-filtered view, (2) I now feel boxed in with houses built over our backyard from all three sides, (3) I no longer feel comfortable taking the trash out in my boxer shorts (which may be the biggest negative of them all). Did my neighbor (who we've been friendly with over the years) make a point to come to our house and explain what they would be doing? No. Did my neighbor consider how our privacy would no longer exist? No. For him, he now has a master suite with a wonderful view (the view I once had), a suite that is nearly half the size of my entire house. He and his wife are physically away from the kids, who remain on the ground floor. In other words, through his addition, he has isolated himself from his neighbors and from his own family, all for more space. Is this "consideration for rights of others"? No.

Not to sound high and mighty, but my wife and I are the type of people who if we were to add on to our house (and believe me, we could use the extra space) we would take into consideration how it would impact our neighbors. In fact, my wife, having the larger heart of the two of us, would limit the amount of construction we would do in order to lessen the impact on others. This world needs more people like my wife. Now it may be argued that she was born with this thoughtful disposition. But what harm can come from teaching young people about how the actions they take, even ones that appear positive, may hurt or harm or affect others, and so, even for a second, they should think about what they do before acting on it? One neighbor's paradise can become another's prison.

Proper societal behavior should be part of a strong education. Billy Harper, the president of Harper Industries headquartered in Kentucky, told *Education Week* that the skills he seeks in future employees have nothing to do with subject matter and college readiness. No, he wants prospective workers to "show up on time, look presentable, and communicate well with customers." Aha, the golden rule. If started early enough, as it used to be, ingrained in the curriculum and continued throughout the system, we'll have better people and a better country for it.

17

Require Community Service

One of the best ways for young people to show consideration for others is by doing something for others.

The Corporation for National and Community Services estimates that over ten million students nationwide did some form of volunteering in 2004. That's a volunteer rate close to 20 percent, probably better than the volunteer rate of grown-ups. However, think how much more could be accomplished, not just for other people but for the experience of the student doing the volunteering, if such service were mandatory.

Of course students aren't born natural givers. Many fluff their college application with hours of volunteer work just to look good, not out of the goodness of their hearts. And wealthy parents spruce up their children's community service résumé by spending thousands of dollars making sure their children go to an impoverished country to build housing.

If every single student did one hundred hours, totaling five billion hours of assistance, that would be a tremendous help to those in need, not to mention an opportunity for opening up the eyes of young people to those less fortunate than themselves.

And they can start with their own community where they go every day: their school campus.

Put kids in charge of cleaning up their own campus. I don't know why school administrators continue to bang their heads against the wall with student littering issues. Can't we get past this? Let the kids take turns cleaning up after lunch or after a school activity or sports event. Even have them clean up the restrooms. Students need to see how some of their peers treat their facilities; it might modify their bad habits. It would be a deterrent to those who create messes and take part in vandalistic acts if they knew they would have to be the ones cleaning up. I'm sure the custodial staff would enjoy some free help.

At High Tech High on the Birmingham High campus in Van Nuys, California, students are in charge of cleaning up graffiti. Students are shown a video that shows how ugly a campus is when marked with tagging, and how that brings down the morale of the school community. Once kids see that connection, they protect their campus.

Having students pick up trash around the school is not the same thing as having them feed meals to the homeless. Long-term projects involving community service should be favored over short-term events like food drives. Also, imbedding a service requirement into the curriculum connects the work students do with learning about history and science.

The only state that requires community service in order to graduate from high school is Maryland, where students clock in seventy-five hours. And some of the work students do is quite worthwhile. Through fund-raising efforts, students helped preserve Civil War cannons at Antietam. Others built "Adirondack chairs at a nature center and nesting boxes for wood ducks," according to *Edutopia*. Students studying ecology planted chestnut tree seedlings to combat infections killing trees. They also learned how the trees are used in building things, plus ended up writing poems about the trees.

Young people have to be pushed into doing service for others. Once they do, many find that they like it. You know why? Because it is yet another avenue for them to break away from the enclosed classroom as later mentioned in chapter 20.

Some studies show that quality service programs "can improve academic performance and attendance." Students performing community service utilize relevant life skills such as critical thinking, working with others, and problem solving. These are traits that are frequently printed on posters in classrooms but are actually rarely practiced and never tested. Why can't students examine their community, identify areas of need, then work on solutions? That's what students did at Maryland's Decatur High School when they established a student-run volunteer center called Connections that links students to volunteer opportunities. They now have eighty people working there. This is real learning.

By getting involved, students take a higher interest in what goes on in their community, more of a civic awareness. Schools used to teach civics and how to become informed members of the citizenry. What's happened to all of that? Education and youth-development consultant Jeffery J. Miller wrote in *Education Week* that "well-designed service-learning experiences that incorporate discussion of the political dimensions of an issue selected by the students themselves can increase young people's interest in politics and can make continued civic participation more likely later in life."

A requirement to perform community service should be part of everyone's education experience.

18

Mandatory Classes in the Arts

All studies on the effects of arts education show the same results: It's not only good for the kids but it makes them succeed at a higher level in their academic core classes. Nowhere can evidence to the contrary be found. It's a slam dunk, no-brainer, bet-your-farm-on-it type of strategy. So what happened to the arts in public schools?

Three things: budget cuts, pushing more students down the college path, and exclusive focus on math and English due to testing demands.

Remember shop classes? Print, wood, electric, homemaking? Students were able to take electives each year in high school. Nowadays, with so many university requirements of four years of English, four years of math, and three years of science, students have little room in their schedules to explore other interests. A Public Agenda poll found that "57 percent of the parents surveyed think their children are already learning enough math and science."

Whatever happened to the philosophy of allowing young people to find themselves in school? What, by age fifteen are they supposed to cement their future career plans?

Ever since the near demise of art classes, especially at the elementary school level, over the past couple of decades, fee-based companies have surfaced offering children dance and music classes before or after school. Many parents gladly pay the nominal seventy- to eighty-dollar fee for ten weekly sessions that are held on school campuses. Such classes extend the learning time for young people as well as the child-care time; more parents are able to pick up children after four o'clock instead of after three o'clock.

Has anybody on the school board noticed this? Doesn't this mean that parents want this and will pay for this?

The opposition to fee-based classes rests with one of the biggest legal issues facing schools: equity. How can the district ensure all students have access to such extras? God forbid a parent sues the district because they cannot afford to pay for such programs.

I remember a department chair meeting about summer school funding and how that year due to budget cuts fewer classes were going to be offered. This meant that only students who failed classes would be able to take summer school, and that those students who desired to continue their education through enrichment classes would not be able to do so. One teacher told the principal that she knew many parents who would be more than willing to pay for these soon-to-be-cut enrichment classes. The response? It was an equity issue. If even one parent cannot afford to pay, then all students are denied the opportunity. Now that's equity for you.

Why not survey the parents? Maybe only a small percentage can't or won't pay for it. Why should that mean then that all parents would be prevented from furthering the education of their children? Can't the district provide financial aid as other educational institutions do?

Educators are so focused on the minds of young people we are starving their hearts.

Melissa Hart, a teacher and author, wrote in an *Education Week* piece about a three-day young writers retreat up in the mountains that transformed her life. Such opportunities have become rarer with the decline in art classes. As she says, "I balanced creative writing, theater, track, and cross-country in high school, and came out the better for the workout of both mind and body." Students need to learn "the power of the pen, the paintbrush, an impassioned monologue, a Mozart symphony." Noted speaker on creativity Sir Ken Robinson wrote in *Edutopia* that people "get educated out of [creativity]. . . . The whole system of public education around the world is a protracted process of university entrance . . . [resulting in] many highly talented, creative people think[ing] they're not, because the thing they were good at was not valued in school."

Smart people have made up a system that is for smart people. And when not everyone is like them, disaster ensues.

The Boston Arts Academy is a rare cross-section of strong academics and arts. Students study sound using musical instruments in the science classes. Ninety-seven percent of the student body goes on to college and they do much better on state tests than students in regular high schools. And the best news of all is that several of the students come from low-economic neighborhoods. One teacher told *Edutopia*, "For at least half the school day, students feel successful."

The American Attitudes Toward Music poll conducted by the Gallup Organization showed that over 90 percent of Americans believe that: (1) schools should offer instrumental music as part of the regular curriculum, (2) music is part of a well-rounded education, and (3) music brings families together.

I have fond memories of learning and singing songs in elementary school that my own children will never form despite attending the same school district as I did. No longer will they have a hum of "The Erie Canal" or "Hot Cross Buns" buried in their subconscious. How many children today are familiar with the great American folk song book with such classics as "Oh! Susanna" and "The Battle Hymn of the Republic"?

Nowadays, few schools dare to put on Christmas (yes, it was called Christmas way back when I was a lad) programs for fear of offending non-Christians. My district issues a two-page memo explaining how to celebrate the so-called "December holidays": "Religious music may be included in school events, but the reason for including that music must be to advance a secular educational goal." Gee, as a kid I just thought "Hark! The Herald Angels Sing" and "The First Noel" were beautiful songs, that's all. I honestly never paid attention to what the lyrics were describing.

Even though I'm not Christian, I love Christmas music and can thank public schools for exposing me to the carols. Every December our school put on a Christmas assembly for parents. Each class was assigned either a particular song or particular part to learn in whatever drama was to be put on stage.

The teaching of this music is like sharing a piece of American history. And teaching a common core of knowledge in music unites children from various backgrounds. A cliché though it may be, music brings people together in a way that Scantron multiple-choice tests can never do.

Instead of forcing struggling students to do more math and more reading, schools should give them a class that they would really enjoy. And in having that class that they really enjoy, those kids would do better with their other classes.

Researchers like Nick Rabkin and Robin Redmond of the Center for Arts Policy at Columbia College Chicago have found "when the arts are an interdisciplinary partner with other subjects, they generate the conditions that cognitive scientists and education researchers say are ideal for learning. The curriculum becomes more hands-on and project-based. . . . [And] the best programs . . . can help close the achievement gap and make schools happier places." Imagine that. When was the last time you heard the two words "happy" and "schools" mentioned in the same sentence?

Why not use "fun" classes as an incentive for doing better all-around? Use the classes kids like as a carrot, similar to holding student athletes accountable in maintaining a 2.0 GPA or C average; otherwise, they get kicked off the team. If they don't pass their math class, then there goes the yearbook, marching band, computer animation class that they really like.

No one questions the importance of English, math, science, and history. However, how did we ever decide that everybody needs all of these subjects every year for thirteen years, to the exclusion of other subjects? Retired educator Marion Brady wrote in *Education Week* that the core curriculum is so taken for granted "that reform movements don't question their centrality."

I've had several journalism students whose only reason they

still came to school was to work on the school newspaper. The academic classes no longer interested them. How much more could these young people have contributed if the school had offered more nonacademic courses?

Oh, by the way, of the $65 billion the U.S. government spends on education, only $35 million is on arts education while over $23 billion is spent on NCLB and its testing philosophy.

19

Put the A Back in Advanced Placement Classes

Smart kids are this country's most valuable resource. And how does the U.S. government reward such talent? By continuing to under-fund and cut gifted programs, rewarding these bright young people with two cents out of every dollar spent on education.

Public education ignores the plight of the gifted, solely focusing its resources on the low- and middle-skilled students. What a shame that the most able and capable are left to fend for themselves. Some believe that giving money or having programs for truly smart students is a waste. The thinking goes, "They don't need it. Why should they get anything? They are already smart. Give the money and attention to those who are struggling." No one thinks twice about allowing a child who already knows the material to just quietly go read a book in the corner or do a reading self-test on a computer. And that, ladies and gentlemen, is what's called your gifted program in public schools.

Originally, gifted programs were part of the special education legislation in the 1970s. The Jacob K. Javits Gifted and Talented Students Education Program faces elimination from the federal budget each year. An astronomical sum of $9.5 million was allocated to it in 2006.

These bright children consistently get the short end of the stick when it comes to being treated fairly: Gifted education is the worst-funded part of the education budget (why doesn't the issue of equity apply to the bright kids?); academics rarely get recognized at a school; skipping grades, an easy, no-cost way of assisting the gifted, is highly discouraged; A students are often ridiculed by their peers. Now, their one haven, Advanced Placement (AP) classes, where they have felt safe to be among other kids like themselves, is being attacked. How lousy is that?

There is a troubling trend in public schools to enroll more students in AP classes, a rush to rigor if you will. The thinking is that by having average and below-average students enroll in harder classes, schools will help them learn more and be better prepared for college. The College Board's push to expand its once exclusive AP programs has succeeded in terms of numbers: They have more than doubled in the past decade.

Labeling a course "advanced" assumes that the course is a harder version than the regular class, right? So if all students took AP, then wouldn't it be more accurate to drop the AP name? After all, if everyone has been placed at that level and no one is below anyone else intellectually, then AP Physics should just be called Physics, correct? It sort of defeats the whole purpose of having advanced or honors classes. Why not just wave a magic wand, place all students in AP classes, from AP math to AP PE, and, presto, everyone will be getting a terrific education. And if you believe that, then you must also believe that the world is taking global warming seriously.

One of the main arguments for pushing more students into AP classes is that these courses are more rigorous. Sure, AP classes tend to be more rigorous. But it isn't the curriculum all by itself that makes it so. It is the demands of the teacher. Simply handing out AP materials does not get the job done.

Ask any parent and she will tell you that AP teachers tend to be the best instructors at a high school. Why? Because the rigor of the course is such that any average instructor would shy away from it. There are plenty of teachers who don't want to take home hordes of papers to grade, hold study sessions after school, and sacrifice Saturdays and summer vacations to attend AP workshops.

The proverbial elephant in the middle of the room that no one wishes to discuss is the incompetent instructor. This strategy of creating more sections of AP classes is a smokescreen for principals who wish to avoid discussing inadequacies with certain teachers.

By saying that students need more rigor, administrators are in effect raising two hot-button issues. One, that non-AP courses are not rigorous enough. Two, that teachers of AP classes are superior instructors. Of course, administrators never dare publicly acknowledge that one teacher is better than another. Unions oppose celebrating the superior skills of an instructor. Whenever a teacher is chosen for some kind of award, the award itself is meaningless; commendations are rotated to ensure that all instructors receive recognition so as not to offend those who don't deserve it. At one department chair meeting, a teacher shot down a principal's proposal to spotlight a teacher of note each month, reasoning that such recognition would be unfair to those teachers not honored. The recognition program never materialized. Coming out and admitting that certain teachers are better than others is not part of the education culture.

Schools today are putting all their eggs in one basket, directing all children to four-year universities. Ladies and gentlemen, such an approach is bound to fail. Of course, give students the opportunity to succeed; yes, provide additional assistance (tutoring); but do not force students who hate school into AP classes. Just sitting there isn't going to make them brilliant. AP classes don't have a special scent to them that makes one's IQ and test scores increase just by being there.

Shoehorning students into AP classes is actually limiting their choices. If they are struggling in regular English classes you shouldn't decide that the solution is an advanced version of the same class.

I have seen impressive dedication from non-AP students whose only class they look forward to every day is journalism. Working on the newspaper versus reading a textbook hooks them into the school.

These poor young people who patiently wait all day for their journalism class or their dance class or their auto shop class or their music class will not be allowed to have that one hour when they thrive, when they are at equal footing with their peers, when they succeed, which they look forward to going to every day. The one class that most probably *keeps* them in school so they do *not* drop out.

When the L.A. Unified School Board debated whether to make it mandatory that all students beginning with the class of 2012 take courses that fulfill the University of California and State University systems' A through G requirements, ultimately transforming it into a college preparatory school district, protesting students wore T-shirts that read LET ME CHOOSE MY FUTURE. So, in the second-largest school district in the country, where fewer than half of all students graduate from high school, the solution from then-superindendent Roy Romer was to make school even tougher. That's what struggling kids need—you fail at math and English? Well, here, take more math and English. That will help you. How ludicrous!

The end result of this recent education trend is that AP teachers have had to make compromises and dumb down their lessons in order to not lose those students unable to keep up with the pace. In the process, they are losing the smart students, who easily get bored and frustrated. In a way, doesn't an inclusion result in an exclusion? If all students take advanced classes, then the truly smart kids are being excluded from getting the education that they deserve and that's geared for them. To fix one problem you don't create another one.

Adolescents are given the false sense of entitlement that they belong in advanced classes. Oh, does that sound elitist? Good. It should be. Certain things in life should be harder to do so that those who do them have a true sense of accomplishment, not so they feel superior to those who can't. What sense of accomplishment can there possibly be for a student who gets Ds in an AP class?

If all students take AP classes, that sense of accomplishment vanishes. Once students know that no one is denied access, that there are no longer any prerequisites, why work that hard to get into them? In other words, the exact thing that makes AP so special will no longer exist.

Schools labeled as a "distinguished" or "blue ribbon" institutions have no problem boasting of their accomplishment, as well they should. However, would they brag about their achievement if *every* school received the same honors?

Well, the same philosophy should apply to student achievement.

As J. Martin Rochester put it in his book *Class Warfare,* how is it "possible for a course to be at once the most challenging academic experience a school has to offer, yet at the same time is doable by every last kid in the school"?

The least educrats can do is leave the bright kids alone. "Instead of raising the floor, the trend is toward lowering the ceiling," said Charles J. Sykes, author of *Dumbing Down Our Kids.*

The reason why tracking, the system of placing students in classes with other students of similar ability level, is no longer popular is because it supposedly makes the lower-ability children feel inferior and makes the higher-ability children feel superior. Well, doesn't that provide children who are not in the challenging classes a major incentive to work harder in order to get into those classes? Life is competitive and students need to face this fact early on. Besides, surveys show that parents favor ability grouping. And smart kids themselves like being placed in gifted, honors, and advanced classes. They like feeling special. Is that so terrible? Is the concept of the individual doing all he is capable of doing without boundaries wrong?

Picture a group of youngsters on a nature hike. The more athletic or rambunctious or energetic kids get ahead of the group and are reprimanded for not waiting for everyone else. Instead of harnessing the kids' energy, it is stifled. The same is true when it comes to the learning process.

Why should everyone have to wait until the very last person "gets it"? This is what is occurring in advanced classes today, a kind of No Child Gets Ahead direction.

One of the more revealing commentaries about how talented children are viewed in our society comes from the Disney/Pixar computer-animated film *The Incredibles:* The character Dash, a young boy gifted with incredible speed, is held back by his parents so as not to offend the other children without that special talent. Dash was denied showcasing his ability and had to deliberately not excel as well as he could in order to better fit in with the rest of his peers. Of course this is fiction, right? Well, actually, a private school in the Chicago area was barred from competing in the statewide science fair after winning its fourth straight title. The Illinois Junior Academy of Science felt it was unfair for one school to always win it; in other words, not equitable for those schools who did not prepare their students as well.

In Alexandria, Virginia, the district abolished its ninth-grade world civilization honors classes. After intense protests by parents, the district reversed its decision but demanded that students enrolled in the classes attend after-school and Saturday sessions. So the bright kids got punished. How nice.

How often have you heard people (or at least educators) say, "All children are gifted—some just open their packages up later"? Naturally parents want to believe that their children are gifted. Haven't we all been behind cars with bumper stickers reading PROUD PARENT OF AN HONOR STUDENT or MY CHILD WAS STUDENT OF THE MONTH?

Why can't people acknowledge the obvious: Some children are smarter or more talented than others. Let's not say everyone is gifted when we all know it isn't true. All it does is dilute the accomplishments of the truly gifted kids.

It's like how society throws around the label of "hero" these days. If all soldiers are heroes, then a new term needs to be created to refer to service personnel who truly have gone beyond the call of duty.

Isn't it okay to cheer on a Tiger Woods? No one is trying to hold him back by saying, "Tiger, why don't you play to double the par so that you will be on a more equal footing with everyone else?"

The only people benefiting significantly from increased participation in AP programs is the College Board. Lowering standards for AP works in their financial best interest. The more students enrolled in AP courses, the more AP tests ordered, the more AP conferences, the more money for the College Board.

Since it calls itself a not-for-profit organization, one wonders where all this additional revenue is going to. After all, each AP test costs nearly ninety dollars.

Because so many students are taking AP classes and tests, colleges have had to reevaluate how they accept that work as college credit. For example, Harvard no longer awards students credit for AP test scores less than a perfect 5.

It used to be that earning credit for an undergrad class was reason enough to enroll in an Advanced Placement course in high school, getting one required class out of the way before starting a single day in college.

Then, a quarter of a century ago, students in AP classes were given an extra point averaged into their grade point average (GPA). No longer was a 4.0 GPA the ultimate. That's why today's valedictorians typically have GPAs higher than 4.0.

This means that some students enroll in more AP classes than they would otherwise take just to raise their GPA, since a B in an AP class is like an A in a non-AP class.

Eliminating the extra grade point for AP classes would go a long way toward decreasing the stress level of young people who feel the need to pile the APs high on their academic plates. It would also rein in the escalating issue of grade inflation. Kids are getting higher grades yet their national test scores continue to decline.

I remember first teaching advanced students in tenth-grade English. Was there any special training given to me in order to better teach the more motivated kids? No. Were there any special books used to stretch the boundaries of their knowledge? No. Was there any special curriculum or course of study that clearly differentiated the advanced section of tenth-grade English from the regular section of tenth-grade English? No.

People might be surprised to learn how often teachers of advanced classes give their students more work at a faster rate than their nonadvanced counterparts and call it a day. As if the amount of work and how fast you do it determines how smart you are. And this is how we nurture what could be our country's future leaders?

I have never used this approach and can credit no one in my credential program or my district staff development with teaching me that. It is something that I just thought about and observed. Smart kids crave more independence, and they think about things at a much deeper level than other kids.

Unfortunately, there are plenty of instructors who use the same lesson for both advanced and nonadvanced classes. And who can blame them? It's less work. Come on, they're not going to get fired for not differentiating the curriculum. And are the honor students going to file formal complaints against a teacher who is working them less than they should be? Of course not.

How backward that we reward and give a standing O to students with perfect attendance but for truly remarkable results of bright children nary an acknowledgment occurs.

Schools like to boast about the increased numbers of students enrolling in AP classes. But you won't hear them boast about the proportionate number of students who passed the AP tests. Many fail, while others don't take the AP test at all.

Some say that it doesn't matter; what matters is that the students were exposed to the rigorous curriculum. However, UC Berkeley researchers found that unless students take the AP test, taking an AP course will not help them in college. This is similar to allowing people to rent a beach house at Martha's Vineyard in order for them to feel super-wealthy. One of the little pleasures in life for myself is to splurge on a five-star hotel and be pampered. It offers a glimpse of how it is to live a privileged lifestyle. But after the one-night stay (remember, I'm on a teacher's salary here) I get back to my middle-class reality of making my own meals, cleaning my own house, and wiping my own son's bottom. Just staying at the upper-class establishment doesn't put one in the upper class.

Readiness programs need to be made available, not necessarily to force every student to take an AP class, but for those students who are at a disadvantage for whatever reason, from never having taken an advanced class before to socioeconomic factors. However, all students entering an AP class should come with a common base of knowledge. Otherwise the class becomes a sham and will turn into shambles when the teacher can't cover the material or can't cover the material at a deeper level.

Remediation or scaffolding, both terms that have a positive connotation in education circles but really mean "dumbed down," harms the brighter students. If a kid doesn't know how to write a thesis in an essay or even what one is, the ones in class who are already "there" get punished by having to go through extensive reviews. Struggling students need to get assistance, but not during the teaching of the course. Otherwise, the rigor of the class, supposedly the whole reason behind shoveling everyone into AP classes, no longer remains.

One study on giftedness discovered that 15 to 20 percent of gifted kids drop out of school, mainly due to boredom.

And what is so magical about the AP curriculum anyway? Some prestigious private schools have begun to dump AP classes and replace them with their own college prep courses because they find the material too constricting. Santa Monica's Crossroad School's headmaster told parents in a letter that the school "prefers students to be reflective, analytical, and ongoing learners. Classes geared to a specific, externally designed test do not best achieve this objective." The common phrase used to criticize the AP approach is that its courses are "a mile wide and an inch deep." These schools prefer more hands-on assignments that are teacher-driven, not test-driven.

What would happen to the College Board's AP program if all colleges stopped giving students college credit for the courses? Would students still take them?

Educators do a disservice by assigning value to minor accomplishments such as preschool "graduations" and perfect attendance. What's next? You raise your hand once a day and you get a commendation mailed home?

Soon it seems like everyone is a winner. It's like the habit of handing out goody bags at children's birthday parties so that a guest doesn't feel bad that another child receives presents because it is his birthday. My wife and I have felt the pressure of goody bags since my first son was three years old. How much stuff should you put in a goody bag? Should you fill it with lots of cheap junky toys? Or should you give each child one special toy? Why can't a polite "thank you for coming to my party" suffice? The whole point of goody bags is to make all children feel special . . . on someone else's birthday? Huh? And if that is the only way to get Mikey to go to Joey's party, forget Mikey. What about the cake and ice cream? What about the bad cardboard pizza? That should be enough of a treat for attending.

I witnessed an English class full of juniors studying the same words as my son had in the first grade. The lack of rigor was mind-numbing. The solution isn't for all students to take hard classes. The solution is for all teachers to be hard, and demanding, with high expectations.

While we need to provide the majority of America's youth with opportunities that ensure America's economic strength, we should be doubling our efforts for the young people who truly shine in the atrophied public school system. These young people should be lifted high on the shoulders of school personnel, be feted at every chance, and have cafeteria menu items named after them (okay, maybe not that one).

If the smarter kids who make up the bulk of the college population are short-changed, America's future will be, too. As Frances R. Spielhagen and Bruce S. Cooper put it, "Neglecting the capabilities of our brightest students is a form of economic and political suicide."

Fostering programs for the best and the brightest must be a priority. Period.

20

Leave School as Often as Possible

Have you ever noticed that the more years kids are in school, the less fun it becomes? The increased pressure for students to perform on standardized tests certainly hasn't helped. Unfortunately, "fun" is not in the standards.

Look at the joyful activities that occur in elementary schools: visits from guest speakers (many of whom are parents), special dress-up days for PJs or clothes from the 1950s, schoolwide assemblies or festivals that include all grades singing and dancing. There is greater parent involvement—you can't find an empty seat during one of those assemblies with video cameras all around (the only time you will see such huge interest after elementary school is at the twelfth-grade graduation).

And then there is that other special aspect to elementary school, one that makes many memories—school field trips.

Why do these fun things dry up? I'm not sure. I am sure, however, that there is a connection between older kids becoming less interested in school as they march through the K–12 system and their decreased involvement. Shouldn't the older kids get some perks as well, and might that not help them do better?

Opportunities must be made to ensure that students of all grade levels explore and discover things outside of the classroom.

After so many years, students get tired of attending school and sitting in classrooms. That is why test scores show their biggest gains during elementary school, no gains during middle school, and losses during high school. Fatigue sets in.

I remember my mom going with me on my first-grade field trip to Exposition Park's Rose Garden. But I don't remember the day I learned how to add.

I remember the first time I ever went to the Los Angeles International Airport, learning that it is referred to as LAX. No, it wasn't to go on an airplane trip; it was my fourth-grade field trip. But I don't remember the day I learned about personal pronouns.

The point is that as much as teachers want to believe that the textbook-based lessons they carefully craft make a difference in the lives of their young charges, they really don't.

Think back on your education experience, and the most vivid memories you have probably revolve around either a specific teacher with whom a bond was formed, or some special event that took place, such as a field trip.

I usually schedule two to three field trips in one year. Now some folks think it odd that an English teacher would take his students on field trips compared to, say, a music teacher or science teacher. But one of the fun things about being an English teacher is that your subject covers many areas—art, music, literature. I take students to the Getty Museum to study artwork, the Disney Concert Hall to hear the L.A. Philharmonic, and the Dorothy Chandler Pavilion to see an L.A. Opera production.

Many touchy teachers are quick to criticize instructors who wish to break out of the four-walled classroom and take their students elsewhere to learn, since it means the kids will miss their classes.

A couple of teachers have actually asked me if it would be all right for my students to miss a future day in my class because the students would be missing a day in their rooms due to my field trip. Does that make any sense? One teacher, without even asking me, told her students to have me read over their homework from her class and sign my name to it. What's that all about? Why punish the kids for learning beyond the four walls?

I also know of teachers who purposely, almost maliciously, schedule quizzes on days when they know students will be out of school on a field trip, despite education codes stipulating that no student can be penalized for an off-campus activity.

You'd think an educator would wish to limit the number of days that young people have to sit in uncomfortable plastic seats.

Field trips are positive, memorable events for kids. They give children a sense of responsibility. I know that when I take my students to the opera, I have them get dressed up, often better dressed than I've seen grown-ups at evening performances. It makes them feel good about themselves that they are doing something that usually only adults get to do.

Several of my students live in apartments, sharing bedrooms with siblings, so spending a hundred dollars on an opera ticket isn't feasible. That's why programs like the L.A. Opera's free student matinees are so important, opening doors to a world that is usually closed to these young people and their families. Immigrant families especially may not know an area's special historical sights or museums, so field trips to these places broaden a child's knowledge. And, as I said earlier regarding the arts, having all children visit similar cultural institutions bonds them, makes them feel a part of the community. Plus, field trips are a way of involving the parents as chaperones. Often parents who come along to the opera or to the Getty Museum tell me that this is the first time for them to see these things as well.

Of all the positive aspects to field trips, the most important one is that it gets the kids out of the classroom they live in all day long for thirteen straight years. It gives them a break from the system's routine.

I know that as a teacher whenever I have a day off that's not a holiday I come back to work refreshed, with more vigor. And students feel the same way when they can get away from school for even a few hours. It provides a balance in their lives and gives them perspective on life.

One reason why students don't go on more field trips is the amount of paperwork it takes for a teacher to take her class on one.

Where I work the teacher must follow nine steps in order for a field trip to happen:

1. Fill out an application form, which has to be signed by the principal.
2. Have every student fill out a field trip permission form to be signed by both student and parent.
3. Notify all of the students' teachers of the field trip and have them sign off on it.
4. Handle transportation needs; i.e., reserve a bus, fill out that company's forms, and arrange for payment.
5. Ensure enough adult supervision by asking parents to serve as chaperones.
6. Make arrangements for a substitute and fill out a form.
7. Determine if any student needs medication and, if so, complete a form.
8. Submit an alphabetical list of those students going on the field trip to both the attendance office and the switchboard operator.
9. Leave a contact cell phone number where the teacher can be reached.

Since schools typically don't pay for buses for field trips, the teacher must divide the total transportation cost by the number of students going. Then the teacher has to collect the money from each student and write out a receipt. The money then needs to either go directly to the bus driver on the day of the event, or be deposited into a school account in order for a check to be cut.

No argument that any of these items are not important or should not be done. The problem is that all the work has to be performed by the teacher. Teachers have no secretaries to assist them with this work. It seems that surely the school could simplify the process for the teacher who was kind enough to give up much time in preparing for an out-of-the-ordinary educational experience.

For example, a teacher needs to develop two lesson plans and have them be judged on several criteria before being accepted into the L.A. Opera's program. Then the teacher has to agree to attend a Saturday teacher in-service workshop. This is true with many major museum visits as well. I'm not complaining because the time I went to the Getty Museum workshop I was fed with better food than I ever received at a meeting at work. There were platters of buttery croissants, bagels and lox and cream cheese, along with freshly squeezed orange juice. I'm used to getting those sticky things individually wrapped in plastic and shot with plenty of preservatives (in fact, some of them look strangely familiar from earlier, much earlier meetings), and no-name bottled water.

So the paperwork alone is enough to discourage some teachers from attempting field trips. What a shame. Districts should streamline the process as much as possible for their teachers, provide them secretarial support, provide them with a mini-handbook encouraging them to enchant children with wonderful worldly experiences.

There are schools scattered around the country that have programs that foster extensive learning beyond single-day field trips outside the four-walled classroom. Programs in Arizona, Connecticut, and Montana allow students to research local history by conducting interviews with citizens and using those oral histories to create multimedia presentations that are then displayed in local museums.

The Walden Project, part of Vergennes Union High School in Vermont, goes further than most by taking a couple of dozen teenagers and a couple of teachers three days a week into the outdoors all day where, as one student put it, they don't read about science but actually do it.

Attending professional theatrical productions, visiting museums, going to places of employment as part of a job shadowing program, studying history firsthand—all these activities add tremendously to the learning experience of young people in a way that reading a textbook does not.

Thinking outside the box is literally what students need to do. Plus, it's fun.

PART THREE

The Way Teachers Need to Be Treated,
Trained, and Rewarded

21

The Sweatshop Schoolhouse

"We're here for the kids." "We do what's best for kids." Often have these words been proclaimed from atop school district offices. However, has anyone thought that by doing what's best for teachers you are doing what's best for kids? North Carolina governor Michael F. Easley put it well: "Teacher working conditions are student learning conditions."

If teachers were treated better, if they felt they got the respect they deserved, if they felt their worth was duly noted, then it would benefit students as well. They would have adults working with them who felt supported, felt that what they did for the kids not only mattered but was valued by those adults they work for, and, feeling this way, would work even harder for the kids.

Imagine if teachers came to work with their heads held high, with the confidence that they had the full backing of their superiors, how such higher morale would translate to higher aspirations.

Teachers rarely leave the profession because of a bad class or bad students. In fact, it's not even the lack of money that causes teachers to walk out of the classroom. It's because of the system and its horrendous working conditions, as well as lack of support from one's superiors. A teacher's workplace can make or break that instructor's longevity. Rarely a day goes by without interruptions, meetings, or other annoyances that erode the energy needed to do the most important part of the job: working with young people.

A 2007 study done by California State University found that nearly one-quarter of that state's new teachers exit the profession in four years or less. Why? More than half left teaching because of "inadequate supports, such as a lack of time for planning . . . and bureaucratic impediments such as classroom interruptions, unnecessary meetings, and too little say over the way their schools are run." Undisciplined students and rude parents also made the list of reasons for departing the schoolhouse (both topics are examined further in this book). As education professor Ken Futernick phrased it in a *Los Angeles Times* article, "We have a high-school dropout problem in large part because we have a teacher dropout problem."

Outside of the military there is no other occupation that is so programmed, regimented, and factory-like. Be ready by 8:00 A.M. or earlier to teach at full alertness and brainpower to a group of twenty or more young people. Train your body to go to the restroom only during a predetermined ten-minute morning break and a thirty-minute lunch.

Thirty minutes in which to both help students and swallow one's food is not appealing to many people. Fighting for photocopies and supplies also doesn't exactly flag down a lot of folks. And don't forget the ungrateful parents who think they can do a better job than an M.A.–educated person.

Given the slipshod situation teachers are in, it is amazing that good work does occur despite the gaping holes of support.

It sounds corny and all too American, but the adage of "work hard and you will prosper" does not apply to teachers. A teacher can work as hard as she can and, frankly, it doesn't pay off. That's why the teachers who have high satisfaction in their work are those who either don't need the money from their jobs in the first place (a spouse does that for them) or are good-hearted, missionary types who really, really believe in doing this for kids and don't mind being treated like dirt. Frankly, these are low expectations to have for one's self. And since people entering teaching have tacitly agreed to these conditions, little will change.

Everybody knows that if you become a teacher you will not make a lot of money, you will not garner a lot of respect, but that you are probably a pretty decent person. Well, why can't a decent person be treated and compensated well? It is quite astounding how society just assumes that good-hearted people, willing to work with young people the rest of their working lives, are out there in America in abundance. And to a certain extent that assumption is true. However, you can't also assume that all good-hearted people are highly qualified. And that other good-hearted people, perhaps higher-qualified good-hearted people, are also out there not willing to sign the unwritten contract to subservient working conditions.

Much of the public school system runs counter to quality and to providing teachers with the optimum environment to teach at a high level.

Teachers are the day laborers in the professional world and their classrooms are the sweatshops. They might as well all huddle together outside district headquarters ready to be picked up and taken to the next teaching job.

Educators have so little real power that when they rise (to use the term weakly) to the position of a counselor or an administrator, many salivate at the chance to be above the others, namely the teachers, even though many are only earning a few thousand dollars more than the most experienced instructors. There is some psychological dynamic to the wielding of power over those who are powerless. If a group of people are weak, like teachers, then it is easy to use them and mistreat them. Knowing that they have a job for life and have few options in their career, that they are stuck there (to put it in a negative way), administrators abuse them. Teacher morale means nothing.

Besides, where is a teacher going to go if she doesn't like where she works? While it's easy to transfer to another school as long as it is within that teacher's district, once leaving the district's confines for another, teachers can only be paid seven years' worth of their experience. In other words, a fifteen-year veteran earns the same salary as a seven-year teacher when jumping districts. So, what ends up happening? Nothing. Teachers who are not happy where they work stay unhappy since they don't want a severe pay cut. Administrators, knowing this, take advantage of it. What's in it for them to make a pleasing workplace?

How rare to find administrators spending any time thinking about how they can make life easier for teachers. It would be curious to scan through the agendas at monthly principals' meetings to see how often the subject of improving teacher morale surfaces. How much time in district offices is devoted to thinking about how to make things easier for those in the most important positions in the entire district? Instead of an afterthought, shouldn't that be the prime area of focus?

Here's a potpourri of issues teachers across America deal with and live with.

WHAT OFFICE?

Teachers don't have offices. It is disconcerting when a teacher has to scrounge around for office space in order to hold a conference with a parent. Talking to parents in a classroom, especially at an elementary school where parents are forced to sit in tiny chairs, is not a good way to conduct a discussion.

Also, teachers are not informed if their room is to be used at night or on weekends. So imagine coming back to work on a Monday to find your desk a mess, office supplies missing, strange things written on the board, desks arranged differently, and so on. It is quite an unsettling feeling, not knowing that your office space is secure.

WHAT COPIES?

Ask any teacher and she will tell you that the single most important supply item is photocopies. So any time there is a ceiling put on access to a copier or the number of copies that can be made, it is a major hindrance to the teacher. It is like limiting syringes in a doctor's office.

At my school there is one copier available to nearly one hundred teachers. Every time they need to make a copy, teachers must bring their own paper, punch in a special code, open the copier drawer, insert the paper, make the copies, then open the copier drawer again to retrieve any unused paper, and finally clear the code. With so many people constantly opening and closing it to put in and retrieve paper, it's no wonder that the copier's downtime has gone up. Why can't a clerk keep the machine fully loaded?

I once asked the principal—if he is so concerned about copier use, why doesn't he offer an incentive for those teachers who do conserve? Another teacher shot that idea down because it would not be right to reward one teacher over another. Huh?

Just as teachers prefer obedient students, administrators prefer obedient teachers, teachers who don't challenge or question edicts from above, teachers who don't complain about conditions.

Independent thinking is not accepted. School administrators do not want to hear from teachers. They fear their power of ideas, so their voices are squelched.

And guess what? Teachers obey. For example, one year, with no formal announcement, the photocopy allotment for teachers was cut in half. This item was communicated to teachers via e-mail, a deliberate act to stifle any open discussion about it.

Except for a few e-mail replies, most teachers accepted it without protest. This type of passivity emboldens administrators to rule at will with little challenge to their policies.

Ironically, the workshops teachers had to attend that year focused heavily on photocopied material. At each session, handouts were distributed to teachers with the intent for them to photocopy the packets for their students. Yet teachers now had half as many copies available to them. So, how could they possibly implement these strategies *and* make fewer copies?

LIMITED PERSONAL ITEMS

In St. Paul, Minnesota, Interim Superintendent Lou Kanavati found a way to decrease energy bills by initiating a twenty-five-dollar fee for each appliance a teacher had in her classroom, i.e., twenty-five dollars for a coffeemaker, twenty-five for a microwave, etc. The teachers union president Mary Cathryn Ricker responded, "We bring papers home to grade and we don't charge the district for electricity at home." Could you imagine a company in any other industry getting away with this?

Actually this policy isn't as bad as the one in Kenosha, Wisconsin, which bans small appliances in the classroom altogether. What people fail to realize is that teachers, unlike most other workers, can rarely leave the confines of their workspace. They spend nearly every working minute in the classroom, and so having a microwave is quite practical, not at all a luxury item. Teachers who sacrifice breaks and lunches in order to work with students should be rewarded with free appliances, not charged for using them.

SIMON SAYS

More and more districts are mandating rigid teach-by-the-numbers curricula that handcuff teachers' creativity. Programs like Open Court provide teachers with an actual script to read to students, and all teachers of the same grade level need to literally be on the same page. Teachers have been told specifically what to put up on a bulletin board, and how to arrange classroom furniture. Some teachers are instructed to sit in rocking chairs when reading to students.

New York City has a "balanced literacy" curriculum where "children sit on rugs, desks [are] arranged into clusters of students with varying abilities (not in rows), a 'word wall' serves as a vocabulary reference, lessons last five minutes," according to *The New York Times*. Principals visit classes without warning to make sure that the rugs are being used. To avoid getting into trouble, teachers give signals to their students so that when administrators walk in they automatically go on to the next part of the lesson.

One teacher told *The New York Times* that "in many classrooms, the word walls have the same words at the end of the year that were there at the beginning."

YOU WANT WHAT?

Once I became National Board Certified (further explained in chapter 27) I asked my principal if I could get business cards printed with my new title on them. He said he would try to fulfill my request but doubted it would go through.

My, you would have thought I had asked for something completely ridiculous like a raise. How dare I ask for a business card! What, a teacher doesn't need a business card? The funny thing is many teachers would agree. It's this low expectation that so many teachers have of themselves that has put them in a deep ravine of low respect they may never climb out of. For one thing, how about handing out business cards to parents on Back to School Night? How about handing them out at conferences and workshops to promote the school, the district?

A business card is an inexpensive passport of professionalism, and teachers don't know how to act professional. Many dress like slobs, several act like students, and, voila, they are treated that way by secretaries and administrators. How can you demand respect when you come dressed for the beach? How can you expect to be called a professional when you talk in the back during meetings?

After a couple of months went by without any cards I asked the district directly for the same thing. The reply I got from a secretary was, "Do you suppose you could get some cards made from your school's print shop?" I didn't know how to break it to the secretary that, one, business cards were quite inexpensive, especially since there were only seventeen National Board Certified Teachers in the entire district (even though I appeared to be the only one requesting cards), and, two, the school I work at hadn't had a print shop for over twenty-five years.

I then took my business card request to the superintendent. At the beginning of the school year he proclaimed in front of the entire district's faculty that if any of us needed support and weren't getting it, to pick up the phone and call him directly. Well, I contacted the superintendent three times. Not only did he not give me business cards, he never responded to my e-mails and phone calls.

I ended up paying for my own business cards, omitting the school district's name and logo. After all, I wouldn't want to embarrass them. Price: $40 for 250 cards. The cost to the district: zero. In respect, that is.

They just don't get it. To pay for little things like business cards would pay off immeasurably in respect for the district.

LACK OF TRUST

Where I work, at the end of the school year, the teachers have to turn in their keys. It's degrading as you go from secretary to secretary, having them sign off on a form that you turned in your grades, turned in your gradebook, turned in your keys. It's as if you are a crook, or you're fired and you aren't guaranteed a job in the fall. It's not a very warm way to end the work year.

It also gives out a peculiar message that the teacher is not expected to pop in during the summer to work on anything. If you are a principal, is this what you want to encourage? Is this the message you want to communicate? Discouraging teachers from going to work when they aren't getting paid?

KEEP THE TEACHERS OUT OF THE LOOP

One year my school changed the back-to-school assembly. For years when we had these assemblies, the school would be on a special bell schedule, meaning that each class was slightly shorter to accommodate the two assemblies. Without input from teachers, the administration decided to keep a regular bell schedule and hold the assemblies during whole periods; in other words, complete classes would be cut for the assembly. Remember, these assemblies are scheduled during the first few weeks of the school year when teachers are in overdrive trying to get their classes in a rhythm. Now which is best for students and teachers: to shorten all classes a little bit or to completely eliminate one class? When you are a teacher and have two or more sections of the same course, you make a concerted effort to keep the classes in the same place in the curriculum. It's less confusing than to have one period in one chapter and the other period of the same course in another. This is what happens, however, when a class is canceled for whatever reason.

As is usual, those not working in the classroom quickly forget that teachers tend to make lesson plans. It may not be deliberate, but administrators do things that fit their timetable, not the teachers'; ideally, it should work the other way around. Why not ask teachers when a good time would be to hold an assembly or a meeting? Teachers need to be included.

Sometimes teachers receive no advance warning about emergency drills under the rationale that administrators don't want to tip off the students that a drill will take place at a certain time. What, they don't trust teachers to keep it to themselves rather than blabbing it to their classes? One teacher who was off campus during an unannounced lockdown drill came to work perplexed upon finding no one walking around the school. Not telling teachers that there is going to be a schoolwide emergency drill is purely a "gotcha" exercise, to catch teachers who are not following procedures. It does absolutely nothing to make the school safer. All it does is erode the trust between administrators and teachers.

YOU MAY *NOT* MOVE ABOUT THE CABIN

It's easy to see why some view teachers as students. Both have to be there during specific times of the day. Both stay in classrooms all day long. Both follow the same bell schedule. Both share the same lunch breaks. Both have limited access to computers. Both cannot leave campus.

As a teacher you feel like you're in a straightjacket when it comes to the freedom of moving about. You can't go to the bathroom anytime you wish. You can't make a quick personal call anytime you wish. You can't get up from your workspace and take a walk, even a few yards away, anytime you wish.

What those in charge fail to understand is how refreshing it is to walk away from the prison-like atmosphere and how it benefits the students when adult workers feel like normal human beings who on a brisk morning can walk about the school grounds, or go to a nearby coffeehouse, grab a cup of java, and come back to work, clearheaded and energized. There are real benefits to allowing people the freedom to do such simple things. Instead, teachers are under penalty of admonishment if they but walk one step outside the gate.

The rare times when I leave work during the day to run an errand I feel like a criminal, as if I'm escaping (there's the prison terminology again).

I was commiserating with a couple of secretaries about how restrictive our jobs seem in terms of not being able to leave the premises all day long. "If you ask permission to take a fifteen-minute break you won't get it," one said. "So it's better not to be honest." All adult workers are treated as the students, confined to campus from 8:00 A.M. until 3:00 P.M.

The school structure is geared toward socializing both the student and the teacher. And the teacher has taken it and accepted it like a zombie for too long.

Where I work there is an eight-foot-high gate that secures the parking lot. This gate is locked most of the school day with a padlock looped through a chain. So if a teacher needs to run an errand during her prep period, say to the post office, here is what she is expected to do:

1. Get out of her car to unlock the gate.
2. Push the twenty-pound gate open.
3. Get into her car and drive past the gate.
4. Get out of the car again and pull the twenty-pound gate closed.
5. Lock the gate and get back into her car.

BIG BROTHER

At one meeting the principal told the teachers that he had noticed many of them not arriving at work on time on the one day a week when students arrive later due to teacher meetings. Therefore, he was introducing a new form that teachers had to fill out that showed what was being discussed at the meetings and who was present.

Not surprisingly, the principal had support for his ideas—from teachers no less. "We all know those who don't show up, but I don't want to be the police," said one teacher. "I don't want you to rat on your colleagues," the principal said with a straight face. No, that's exactly what he wanted teachers to do and why the form had to be filled out.

Another administrator had the chutzpah to actually preface her comments this way: "Not that we are saying you are like kids, but, like kids, when given a certain amount of freedom sometimes you don't make the right choices." In other words, if some teachers came to work ten or twenty minutes late on the days that teachers held meetings, that was completely unacceptable, not to mention *not in the contract.* How dare a teacher stop by Starbucks and not be at the meeting at the exact starting time! Why are those in charge so anal-retentive? Is a teacher who arrives five minutes late to a meeting a *bad* teacher, while someone always punctual is a *good* teacher? It would be interesting to poll administrators on what makes a good teacher. No doubt a good teacher is someone who attends all meetings and is never late to them, follows every syllable of the teacher contract (except when it benefits the principal, such as working for free in the evening or on weekends), never questions authority, fills out all required paperwork with barely a peep of protest, never sends disruptive kids down to the dean's office, has no student's parent calling about some issue. How does having some teachers not at work all at the same exact minute negatively impact the students who arrive at school one hour later?

By the way, the administrators who were assigned specific meetings to attend were frequently absent. But, remember, they are administrators.

The whole point behind the meeting attendance form was nothing for students, nothing to promote a better learning environment. It actually worked to poison the work environment for the teacher, reinforcing the lack of trust administrators have in spades toward teachers. One teacher did mildly protest that filling out such a form would take some time. But you see, not even the principal was going to read the forms. It was just his way of controlling what teachers did. How dare a teacher arrive at work a minute late! Yep, it is just like a factory environment.

What, can't teachers be entrusted with unsupervised time? Does it occur to anyone here that maybe, just maybe, because teachers' work lives are so carefully monitored, whenever they are given even a second of unsupervised time they stretch it into a minute? Well, it's to be expected and should actually be encouraged. Why not let them hold their meeting at Starbucks? What is so magical about holding a meeting in a four-walled classroom? It's healthier to tell teachers, "Go somewhere, anywhere but here, and have a meeting. Bring back some notes on it as your accountability piece. Just don't be late when the kids start class." Why can't there be school leaders who do things like that?

BIG BROTHER: HOME EDITION

During a Passover seder, my phone rang and I picked it up to hear the recorded voice of the district's superintendent telling me that tomorrow was election day and I should go out and vote. First of all, I don't live in the city where I teach so I didn't have an election to vote in. Second, *it was Passover*. How insensitive was that? Boy, do I need a Do Not Call Registry for my own district.

NO TIME TO BREATHE

Faculty meetings frequently start ten minutes after the end of school, giving teachers little time to go to restrooms, finish answering questions from students, or catch their breath after the assembly line of classes.

Well, for the administrator or counselor who has no classes and no students, getting to a 3:10 meeting isn't a problem. But if you teach until 3:00, it is unreasonable to expect promptness. Yet they do.

In those ten minutes, many things need to happen:

- Students need to leave the room.
- Questions from students need to be answered.
- The teacher needs to ready the room for tomorrow (e.g., write the agenda on the board, get handouts ready, etc.), especially since the meeting ends at 4:30. If a teacher were to do all of this afterward, she would be at work past 5:00.
- The teacher must take attendance or input it into the computer.
- The teacher may need to use the restroom.
- The teacher must walk to the meeting room, which may be very far from her own room.

Stern PA announcements during class time reminding teachers to "be there at 3:10 sharp" reinforce the condescending treatment teachers receive. Such warnings erode teacher morale, and I feel embarrassed that students have to hear this, that their own teachers, many of whom they look up to, are looked down upon by the school's administrators.

If teacher input were so valued, then administrators would be more accommodating to ensure a full house for a meeting.

REFRESHMENTS?

At the very least teachers should be given refreshments at afterschool meetings. Some schools provide none, others provide the cheapest thing they can get their hands on such as donated day-old pastries, or Costco-size, industrial-strength tins of something that passes as edible. I was at one meeting where the only things given to teachers were those crackers with cheese and a little red spoon. I wasn't surprised to see teachers gobbling that down. We were all sitting in a circle and it was quite embarrassing watching this one grossly overweight person scrape every bit of cheese out of the plastic compartment, then lick the spoon as if it were the most delicious delicacy she had ever eaten. You see, the mentality is, you treat teachers like crap, so feed them crap and they will eat it.

A principal hosted an all-day meeting and provided coffee. When I got a cup I asked where the cream or milk was, and she said, "Oh, I don't use cream myself so I didn't get any." Whaaa?

As a way to boost morale, the principal suggested that each month a different department host a snack for the entire school staff. And who was going to pay for all of this? The teachers themselves, of course.

WHY WOULD ANYONE LISTEN TO A TEACHER?

Typically if a student wishes to drop a class, it is an easy thing to do. If a parent wishes a child to drop a class, it is an easy thing to do. If a teacher wishes for a child to go to an easier or harder class, it is a much harder thing to do. The teacher must prove why the student should be moved, even though of all three individuals it is the teacher who would know best, after an entire half year with a young person, what is best for that child.

Whenever I recommend a student not to take an advanced English class, the counselors are very suspicious of my motives, as if all I'm trying to do is make my classes smaller.

I had a difficult time removing a student with twenty-nine absences in one semester. That is about six weeks out of an eighteen-week semester; the kid wasn't there one-third of the time. Yet the counselors refused to move the child to another class because the other teacher had four more students than I did. I offered to take a handful from the other teacher in exchange for this one. It's not that I didn't personally want the student. It was my professional opinion that she would have a better chance of success with another teacher, if she was determined to remain in a rigorous class (her parents signed a waiver for the whole year, sentencing her to honors English despite her performance). Plus, sometimes a female student does better with a female teacher. It's funny how the administrators and counselors will stand at attention when a parent makes a comment like "I want my child in this class" but when the teacher gives a reasoned opinion based on data that vote doesn't seem to count.

Surprisingly, one administrator, upon hearing of the twenty-nine absences, didn't wait for me to say anything else but shook her head and said, "The honors class is not a good match for her." Exactly. Thank you for listening to me. I felt like Kevin McCarthy's character near the end of the science fiction classic *Invasion of the Body Snatchers* when the authorities finally believe his incredible story about aliens taking over human bodies. A huge relief that someone, somebody, believed what I was saying. Instead of screaming, "You're next!" I was screaming, "Twenty-nine absences!"

CHASTISE THE TEACHER

"You will be asked to 'get out of line' and return later if your materials are not properly prepared." Is this a counselor speaking harshly to a queue of students waiting to register for classes? Far from it. It is a counselor's e-mail to all teachers about returning standardized testing materials.

Sometimes the admonishment is more subtle. Where I work administrators came up with a good idea of posting homework assignments on a school Web site. However, who is supposed to be the individual who dutifully goes to the computer each day to type in each night's assignments? Teachers don't have secretaries or clerks who can do this for them. And student TAs are not allowed access to teacher computers.

When you are an excellent teacher who works beyond your salary, an extra ten minutes of work each day is something you can't commit to. The teachers who did post homework were mentioned by name in a schoolwide e-mail. Of course, doing it this way ensured that it was the names *not* mentioned that got people's attention.

WHO'S TO BLAME? WHY, THE TEACHER, OF COURSE!

A major part of any teacher's evaluation focuses on her classroom management skills, especially from the point of view of an administrator who is in behavior modification mode all day long. Notice the emphasis is not on the individual unruly students but on the class as a whole. Depersonalizing bad behavior gets the mischievous kids off the hook easily. The kids really don't have to be accountable for their individual actions.

If a principal walks into a classroom and finds that several students aren't on task, the teacher is the only one to blame. "Ms. So-and-So, why can't you control your class?"

Ms. So-and-So will then be placed on an improvement plan and be asked to attend hours of staff development training in classroom management. Sounds like a prison term handed down to a celebrity on a DUI charge.

Sure the teacher can write a referral and send the student to the administration office. But if a teacher is unlucky enough to have too many of the rapscallions, the teacher is the one who will be called down to the principal's office and interrogated as to why she is writing up so many referrals.

TEACHER AS CRIMINAL

A memo went out to all teachers regarding their signing off on weekly attendance sheets. Here is part of what was e-mailed; the entire text was in bold print.

> Staff who do not return the sign off sheets by Friday afternoon will immediately be notified by administration to return signed and dated attendance signing off sheets. In addition we will remind repeat offenders that completing their attendance is part of the teacher's bargaining agreement.

Was it necessary to refer to teachers as "repeat offenders," terminology normally associated with criminals? I didn't think that this was appropriate, so I e-mailed my principal this concern. His response?

> Professionals would not have to be reminded over a dozen times to do what is required by law, contract, and common sense.

Okay, but exactly how many teachers out of a hundred are we talking about? Five? Ten? Probably not twenty or thirty, right? So if you're going to send out a harshly worded message, why not target it to the "repeat offenders"? Why taint the whole teaching staff?

Such blanket generalizations worsen teacher morale; however, they do make administrators' jobs easier, avoiding direct confrontations with individual teachers. Any time administrators have to have a frank discussion with a teacher about something sensitive, it is called a "courageous conversation" among those in the know. How silly to call a principal "courageous" for basically doing his job.

DO YOUR DUTY

Since most school districts do not pay teachers to go on jury duty, and the government doesn't allow that to be an excuse, teachers must serve during their vacation periods. Once again, teachers get the shaft.

Some teachers still do yard duty (another prison reference), supervising recess or lunch. How humiliating. Picture a CPA patrolling a parking lot twenty minutes a day. It would never happen.

YOU CAN'T JUST CALL IN SICK

When most people call in sick, it requires a mere phone call. When teachers miss a day of work, however, it's a major project. That's why teachers tend to go to work ill; it's easier than having to write up detailed instructions for a substitute. Plus, a teacher has to cross her fingers that a sub shows up, number one, and if one does, that she follows the instructions. Often there is collateral damage when a teacher returns to her classroom after an absence, including missing office supplies and grade books.

Whenever I am sick I need to write up lesson plans late at night or early in the morning before class begins, often driving to work at dawn to put together the substitute teacher packet despite feeling awful.

It can also be quite stressful knowing that during critical

moments you can't leave work immediately. When my mother was literally on her deathbed and I received an urgent call from my sister to rush to the nursing facility, I couldn't just drop everything and get over there. I had to call down to the office and wait for someone to take over my class.

When I told the secretary that my mother's health was failing, she asked for me to wait until the end of class before leaving, since only fifteen minutes remained in the period. Never mind that my mother was coming to the end of her life.

Finally, ten minutes later a sub came in so that I could leave.

> Two [elements in a great place to work] have never
> changed and never will . . . trust and recognition.
> Employees treasure the freedom to do their job as they
> think best, and great employers trust them . . . telling
> employees they're doing a great job costs nothing but
> counts big. And it's so easy to do more. Give them free
> bagels and doughnuts twice a week. Wash their cars. Take
> them to a movie on Friday. The cost is insignificant.
>
> —Geoff Colvin, "The 100 Best Companies to Work For in 2006,"
>
> *Fortune* magazine

If there were a company called Teaching it would fail to make *Fortune*'s 100 Best Companies to Work For list every time.

Just like the Peter Finch character from the 1976 film *Network,* teachers need to open the doors to their classrooms, run out, and shout at the top of their lungs, "I'm mad as hell and I'm not going to take it anymore!"

22

Father Knows Best? Fuhgeddaboutit!

Lower pay, lack of career advancement, abysmal working conditions, and overly patronizing treatment—all trademarks of the teaching profession, a profession dominated by women. This is the biggest reason why teaching is a Single A team in the major league world of professions.

Historically women have been treated unequally in terms of pay, position, and prestige. Three out of every four teachers in grades kindergarten through twelve are female. However, men dominate the power positions: The majority of high school principals and superintendents in America's 14,000 school districts are male; fewer than 20 percent of supers are women.

This disparity has fostered a male authority/female subordinate relationship similar to a parent/child dynamic that permeates public education, where there is intimidation on the part of administrators and docility on the part of teachers.

A few years ago, upon hearing that our next principal was to be a woman, I had a female teacher tell me that she did not want a woman in charge of a high school; she was only comfortable working for a man.

Sexually tainted jokes and comments are part of the public school flotsam and jetsam. One time I was in charge of ordering a chicken lunch for a meeting. I asked an administrator for his menu selection and he said, "I like breasts. And I'm not talking the chicken kind, if you know what I mean," adding a devilish smile.

During my first year of teaching, even though I was much

younger and less prudish, I complained to an administrator about a female student who was wearing an outfit that was too revealing. He told me, "Oh, come on, Brian, enjoy the show!"

Women tend to be more nurturing and giving individuals and therefore have for decades been willing to dedicate themselves beyond the call of duty—a perfect fit for working with young people. This, unfortunately, has damaged the profession.

These teachers are the darlings of the administrators, who typically point to them as models of the teaching profession. Why? Because these teachers will work day and night and not demand anything in return. Some of these women are married to men who make enough money for both of them and so, in a way, they view teaching as paid volunteerism; it's nothing to them to do work without compensation. However, administrators shouldn't assume that all teachers can be as "giving" of time. They don't seem to get why others, whose teaching careers provide the main household income, wish to be compensated properly.

I have often heard from principals how proud they are of teachers who volunteer to advise a club or chair a department. Yet these slave laborers are inadvertently harming the rest of the teachers. Their reticence in speaking out against policies that are unjust makes those who do voice criticisms pariahs in the eyes of the administration.

Many teachers, partly due to their strong Judeo-Christian ethics, sincerely believe in the "I'm there for the kids" credo and view their jobs as missionary-like, a "calling" if you will, with money, working conditions, and respect all running a distant second to *the kids*. What parent wouldn't want such good-hearted souls teaching to their children? The problem is that the wonderful qualities that make them wonderful teachers, warm and giving and patient, are the same traits that administrators take advantage of.

One time a principal asked for teachers to give up three of their five days off during spring break to attend a conference. When the teachers inquired as to compensation, here was the reply: "There is *no* money to pay you for this trip." You guessed it—a few teachers went anyway.

These instructors sacrifice, sacrifice, sacrifice, but what they are really sacrificing is their own profession.

Teachers are the doormats of the professional world. They allow themselves to be used, abused, and misused. Truly, much of their misery is caused by their own inaction and silence. A hopelessness that nothing ever will change in terms of the way they are treated and the working conditions they are given blankets a school's teaching troops.

As educators graciously accept free PTA lunches, key chains, and pens in celebration of National Teacher Day and Teacher Appreciation Week, gestures designed to make up for the major inadequacies in their profession, teachers need to look no further than their own collective mirror to find, as Cassius told Brutus in Shakespeare's *Julius Caesar,* "The fault is not in our stars but in ourselves that we are underlings."

Personally I do not find it cute when teachers participate in fundraisers for their schools by working at ice cream shops for free, dishing out scoops behind the counter. It's degrading, quite frankly. How would you react if you walked into a McDonald's and saw your accountant behind the counter trying to raise money for his office?

Or at school carnivals a "hit your teacher in the face with a pie" booth or "dunk the principal" tank—are these stunts supposed to make the educators more human, more "with it" with students?

It is teachers' urge to please and their desire to help others that reinforces subservient behavior, this bending over backward to please their superiors.

At one meeting there was an activity teachers were to do in groups. On the handout it stated for the larger groups to "divide into four smaller ones, each containing two to three people." The facilitator at our table, a fellow teacher, was a bit flustered because we only had seven in our larger group. "Gee, we're going to have to have a group of one, I suppose." Well, golly, who says we have to divide into four groups? The piece of paper? Why not three groups or two groups? But her approach was very similar to many in education. Obedient, following the rules, strictly by the book. That is the structure they were schooled in and that is the structure they now work in, and to veer away from that is unfathomable.

A teacher who talks to an administrator sometimes has to grovel, sometimes has to pretend, always must second an administrator's idea, never second-guess it. The teacher has to relate in a subservient way, and if ever asking for a favor, look down, avoid eye contact, like asking Dad for the keys to the car.

It's easy to abuse people who are complacent. Here's the way one male teacher worded an e-mail to the entire school about three missing folding tables (keep in mind this is a teacher speaking to other teachers):

> The school purchased five folding tables. Now three of them have vanished. I have waited two weeks for these tables to reappear, to no avail. Please do not let this come down to a room by room search.

He probably felt he could get away with such brusqueness because, well, he was speaking to mainly female teachers.

The worst enemy to the teaching profession isn't the overbearing principal, the litigious parent, or the bratty student. It is the docile teacher. The teacher who does what she is told.

Even the teachers unions, which one would think would do more for women politically, haven't been immune to the Good Ol' Boy Network. Since 1858, the National Education Association (NEA) has only had a female president for about 20 percent of its existence— for a mainly female profession. The last female president was back in 1989. The only reason the percentage is even that high is because for a period of fifty years it appears that the NEA was deliberately alternating male and female presidents. Regarding the American Federation of Teachers (AFT), only three presidents have been women since 1916. That's incredibly low considering the AFT also represents another predominantly female field, nursing. Only two females have been president of the American Association of School Administrators (AASA) since its inception in 1865. If one looks at the AASA Web site, however, there is a parade of female and minority faces flashing on it.

Teachers, put a little backbone in it. If more women became high school principals and superintendents it's very possible that teachers would be treated with more respect and no longer be the Rodney Dangerfields of the professional world.

23

Edutainers—the Way to Teach Teachers

Employees of the Container Store go through two hundred hours of training, enabling them to speak intelligently about plastic boxes.

There are teachers in classrooms in America right now who have had zero hours of training before the very first day of impacting young minds. And their product happens to be our kids.

That's the situation children across America go through year after year with new teachers. The teaching profession needs to do a better job of training its own.

Why is so little actual practice required when it comes to the most important job in this country (outside of life-saving occupations)?

The reason why students aren't achieving at high levels is that their teachers aren't achieving at high levels.

Parents by the millions allow their own children to be with teachers all day for most of their youth. Isn't it prudent to ensure that those adults are of the highest caliber?

With nearly one-fourth of teachers teaching subjects outside of their college majors, how realistic is the federal government's pledge of not leaving one child behind? You know what the definition of a quality teacher is? One who can fill out an application form.

Teachers as a group typically have low SAT scores, ranked below agriculture majors. And those teachers leaving the profession earliest tend to have higher SAT scores. Wonderful!

Where will all the new teachers come from? Each day one thousand teachers leave the profession, costing $5 billion a year.

Enrollment is declining in teacher credentialing courses, yet job demand is up. Barnett Berry, the president of the Center for Teaching Quality, equates the challenge of improving teacher training and quality to that of the Marshall Plan that rebuilt Europe after World War II.

What happens, then, is a number of teachers earn their credentials on the job on emergency permits, taking courses after work. In other words, a teacher during the day, a student again at night.

Finding fully credentialed teachers has become almost as hard as finding help at home improvement stores. School districts in cities like Baltimore and New York recruit teachers from other countries to fill job vacancies.

Teaching is no longer your mom's occupation. More and more the state and federal governments are dictating what is taught, how it's taught, and sometimes the way it is said to the students.

Is it any surprise there is a lack of interest? Who in their right mind would voluntarily enter a profession that:

- Doesn't pay you what you're worth.
- Ignores how well you do your job.
- Provides no bonus or incentives for working harder.
- Deprives you of any authority over your profession.
- Counts to the minute when you work and the length of the breaks you get.
- Provides no office space and no office support.
- Entitles everyone to tell you how to do your job.

How many reforms in the past twenty years have made teaching *more* appealing? All of the so-called reforms such as more testing, more standards, more federal intervention, have made teaching less attractive. If anything, teaching is more pressure-filled than ever before. Do people perform better under pressure?

It is difficult to explain to a person who has never been in front of young people how stressful it can be to put forth a tremendous effort in teaching them something, only to have many of them ignore you, berate you, harass you, embarrass you, tune you out, talk to others. Teachers put up with a lot of crap.

It is a stroke of incredible luck that many of the three million teachers in the United States are good. Nothing in the system supports quality.

What disturbed me about one teacher in training who observed my classes was how frightened she appeared when I suggested she talk to my class for a few minutes. You would have thought I asked her to jump off a building. "Oh no, I don't want to do that." Well, then, *why are you studying to become a teacher?!*

Somewhere there needs to be an entrance exam for student teacher candidates, an audition that can quickly determine if an individual has the goods or not before entrance into a teaching program is allowed. Hold them twice a year and have a group of retired teachers with distinguished reputations sit in on the auditions à la the *American Idol* threesome.

An opening question might be, "Are you afraid of speaking in front of people?" That would weed a lot of people out from the get-go.

The traditional way of training teachers has been for candidates to begin taking credential classes while undergraduates, then to finish the coursework during a fifth year of college when the all-important practice teaching, pejoratively referred to as student teaching, occurs. Why can't they be called teacher interns like their medical student counterparts? You don't hear them being called student doctors.

The student teacher typically teaches in the morning and takes classes in the late afternoon and/or evening. What commonly happens is that certain courses are only offered at certain times, leaving a student no time for a job for an entire year. Student teaching pays no salary, so one has to either live with one's parents or have a spouse who works. What a sacrifice for these people to make, as if they don't sacrifice enough throughout their entire working lives as teachers.

That is why so many people are attracted to fast-track licensing programs. New York City Schools has a New York City Teaching

Fellows program as a way to attract midcareer professionals into teaching. From 2001 to 2004, the number of participants grew from 383 to 2,441, a sixfold increase.

It isn't easy going through a crash course on how to become a teacher, especially after working in another field and feeling a sense of confidence in knowing what one was doing. Samantha Cleaver, a special education teacher in Washington, wrote a revealing piece for *Education Week*. In it she describes her experience as a member of the District of Columbia Teaching Fellows: "Before we were teachers . . . we were lawyers, PR specialists, computer programmers, government workers. Then we moved to the bottom of a very tall ladder, with only eight weeks to train. No wonder we find it hard to navigate, to fit in, and are easily overwhelmed."

One of the pitfalls of sink-or-swim programs is that the period of time for student teaching is significantly shortened. Usually those who survive already had certain attributes suited for teaching. But to have people actually teaching young people all day, then taking evening classes to finish a credential is the worst way to go about it, even though surveys show that such a practice is a big draw for those who do it this way.

Much attention has been paid to certain companies that take people and put them through a boot camp–like training, then ship them out to schools, the most famous one called Teach for America. The problem with these groups is that their approach to teaching is to treat new teachers like paratroopers who magically drop down out of the sky and run in and fix problems in schools. However, their stay is only temporary. Like soldiers serving a stint in the army, these candidates are not in it for the long haul.

The Hoover Institution discovered that in New York City schools "three-fourths of the Teach for America recruits and half of the other uncertified teachers had already left" by the third year. And this just adds to the revolving door of teacher attrition seen in this country's worst schools where kids deserve stable, experienced instructors.

A study of fourth and fifth graders in Houston by Stanford University indicated that those students taught by certified teachers had higher test scores than students taught by noncertified teachers.

The best solution is for student teachers to get paid as medical interns do, not much money but some, so that they can continue learning their field.

At California State University, Northridge (CSUN), teacher candidates are assigned to one class period daily at a school. That equates to five hours a week in a sixteen-week semester for a grand total of (drumroll, please) eighty hours of training. During the second semester of student teaching candidates are assigned three teaching periods, amounting to 240 hours. Added all together, a student teacher actually teaches 320 hours before exiting the program. That's equivalent to eight weeks of full-time work. That is two months of training that is supposed to well equip them to be in front of a live classroom audience.

Thankfully attorneys and architects have more than eight weeks of training before they try cases and build buildings. I guess building young minds is not as important. Children are taken advantage of in so many other ways, they might as well be used as guinea pigs in the hands of freshly minted instructors.

Keep in mind that CSUN has one of the most intensive training programs available. Other programs only require *one* semester of student teaching.

Many times student teachers are asked to put in dozens of hours of observation. Go to a school, find a teacher, and sit there watching her teach. Nothing else is required. I had one young lady give me this form that had to be filled out and turned in to her professor. She wanted me to sign my name to a forged document that showed several hours that she was supposedly in my class observing me teach. She looked surprised when I told her that I couldn't lie and sign the paper. So if professors of training courses think that their students are really doing the observing, they are quite naïve.

The bigger questions in all of this, however, are: Haven't college students already done a lifetime of observing teachers? How does quietly sitting in the back of the room help you become an effective teacher? These students don't have to participate in the lessons. What, just by sitting there, through osmosis, they will come out of the observations better instructors? Come on! The whole thing is a waste. Would you want to find out that your surgeon learned his craft by watching and not doing several operations?

Much of what makes a great teacher cannot be taught. That doesn't mean that teachers can't collectively learn a body of knowledge that enhances their innate instincts. But today's and yesterday's colleges of education fail at just that. Ask former president of Columbia University's Teachers College Arthur Levine, who wrote a scathing report in 2006 that was issued by the Education Schools Project.

"Educating School Teachers" took four years to complete, with no fewer than twenty-eight institutions examined. In it, Levine blasts most of the country's schools of education for being incapable of producing outstanding instructors. The schools have "the least accomplished professors" with "coursework . . . in disarray," and the lowest admissions standards (some schools don't turn anyone away), which is why he describes them as "cash cows." "Aspiring teachers [are] woefully unprepared for their jobs."

Levine, who is now in charge of the Woodrow Wilson National Fellowship Foundation, goes on to say that "teacher education right now is the Dodge City of education: unruly and chaotic. . . . There is a chasm between what goes on in the university and what goes on in the classroom." The report calls for more practical preparation and for a five-year training program, a bachelor's degree, and one year of credential work to be the norm.

Another critical report on teacher training that came out in 2006, called "What Education Schools Aren't Teaching About Reading and What Elementary Teachers Aren't Learning," by the National Council on Teacher Quality, gave failing marks to nearly all of the seventy-two teacher colleges it studied, due to the lack of teaching sound reading practices.

Louis V. Gerstner, former IBM CEO and head of the Teaching

Commission, said in the group's final report in 2006 that "most education schools are vast wastelands of academic inferiority." Boy, 2006 was not a very good year for teaching colleges.

In order to reach young people today, teachers need to be edutainers. They have to engage their audience on a daily basis, keep them riveted to the material, then excited about doing work. You can push student teachers through a kaleidoscope of courses on learning theories and standards strategies all you want. But when that instructor goes out on stage, most of that coursework proves irrelevant. And if that new teacher didn't get training in how to get the attention of the class and hold on to it, that teacher and those students will suffer.

So how should teachers be trained?

Raise entrance requirements. Make sure applicants have a 3.0 GPA before acceptance into a teacher training program. At CSUN, which produces the largest number of teaching credentials in the state of California, 35 percent of students studying to become elementary school teachers got Ds or Fs in a college math course.

Insist they major in the subject they will teach. There is only a 40 percent chance that students will have a chemistry teacher who majored in the subject.

Teach them how to design lessons with rigor and to have high expectations for all students regardless of ability level. Too often teachers get easily frustrated when a class is not performing at a particular level, resulting in the lessons slowing down and expectations dropping.

Give training in voice inflection and projection. In other words, acting lessons. It's important for teachers to speak up and have fluctuations in their voice. A teacher may know her pedagogy and develop wonderful lesson plans, but frankly she doesn't belong in a classroom if students can't hear her or are not interested in what she has to tell them. Better to have the teacher who, although weak in methodology, doesn't speak in a monotone voice, whose volume is loud and not soft, who gesticulates and moves around the room. That teacher will connect more with students than the former one. Taking an acting class is required of all student teachers at Western Washington University in Bellingham.

An ideal professional development experience for middle and high school science teachers exists at the Exploratorium museum in San Francisco where a TV show is produced, modeled after the *Iron Chef* show on the Food Network. Not only do the teachers get ideas in terms of lessons but also in terms of presentation, since the show is Webcast live several times during the summer. As a plus, it showcases teachers on TV so students can cheer them on.

Get them in the classroom teaching to youngsters as soon as possible, at least for two years. Don't wait until the last semester of the program.

Once they get a job, restrict their teaching day to three hours during their first year and make sure they don't teach the hardest classes. Ideally, a new teacher should be paired up with a master teacher such as a National Board Certified one for her first year. This master teacher's job is to observe her teach, say, in the morning, then sit down with her in the afternoon and carefully go over videotape and other material. New teachers need immediate feedback on their practice, which is why it is preferable to have them teach and learn on the same day. Too often the way new teachers are mentored entails a dizzying number of after-school meetings. Well, after a new teacher works all day it is not the best time to sit down and analyze everything in a quick hour. Yes, it costs more money to have two teachers on staff working only half days, but it costs more to lose that new teacher within a few years.

How interesting it would be if the new teacher and the mentor teacher shared the same students. While not possible at the secondary level, it is doable in the elementary grades. The new teacher can watch what the mentor teacher does with the same students. Discussions between the teachers would produce helpful lessons for the students.

One of the best things that can be done for new teachers is giving them plenty of time off to visit other teachers' classrooms from all grade levels and subjects. These "days off" are helpful in two ways: One, the new teacher can be exposed to different teaching styles and take away fresh ideas. Two, the teacher will return the next day with recharged batteries which, in turn, benefits the students, who will get a refreshed teacher.

Ensure they have the ability to convey to students passion for the material being delivered. As soon as students get a sniff that their teacher doesn't really have a buy-in with what she is teaching, that their teacher seems lackadaisical, whether or not the material is being understood you might as well close the class.

It doesn't matter if the subject is geometry, biology, drama, art history, or track and field. Students pick up immediately which of their teachers have it or don't have it.

What is depressing is how many teachers don't care about the kids. All it takes is a few loudmouth misbehaving cretins and whatever drive to help others that teacher had within herself back in the early beginnings of her teaching days vanishes. Since that teacher has no place to go in her career and is "stuck" teaching to students, and since the way teachers get compensated cements that teacher's position in the district for her working lifetime, that room is now a room of despair. And every student entering that door each fall will suffocate from the poisoned air. The strong ones will have the resiliency to overcome it, but too many will not.

And how do you teach passion? You can't.

Perhaps one reason teaching just hangs out there in the purgatory of professionalism is because a great deal of being a successful instructor comes from the individual and not from a textbook. The perennial chicken or the egg question in education circles remains: How much is teaching an art form versus a science? Is there a body of work, a course of study, that makes a student teacher ready for the classroom? Obviously a good teacher must have the inborn personality traits as well as training in educational theories and pedagogy.

One of the most intensive teacher training programs is at Baylor University in partnership with the Waco Independent School District. Teacher interns get immersed in the classroom culture early. They begin teaching lessons to small groups of children during the junior year. By the time the teacher interns are seniors, they are doing their student teaching, unlike the normal routine of doing it during the fifth year. After the candidates do their student teaching during the day, they have their "classes" with their professors onsite in the evening, a nice convenience.

What's contradictory about much of the student teaching experience is that often candidates do their work at more middle-class schools, schools where they are least likely to get a job upon completing their credentials. Why not have them work at some of the toughest schools with some of the best master teachers? After all, this is where most of them will end up. How well prepared can they be if they receive all their training at easier schools? That might be one reason for the high attrition rate.

But at Waco this is not the case—80 percent of the children taught to by student teachers receive free or reduced-price lunches.

It is long overdue for high schools to have teacher academies. It is odd that educators overlook their own profession whenever there is a career day or a job shadowing program. It's as if we all just assume that young people want to become anything but a classroom teacher. Treat schools as baseball farm teams, places where future teachers are born.

Exceptions to this are the Teacher Cadets program in South Carolina and a teaching academy in Los Angeles. The one in L.A. actually offers jobs to those completing the program. The problem is that students need to maintain only a 2.7 GPA. Yes, that's right, a C+ average. Is that who we want teaching to our children? Average students themselves?

Even after teachers earn their credentials they are forever bombarded with more and more workshops, better known as staff development. Most of it is garbage. A workshop that would be worthwhile, though I've never seen it, is one that focuses on "what's hot" with kids. Inform teachers of what kids are plugged into, what stuff ruminates in their heads: the music, the movies, the technology, the slang. Throwing in topical references is an excellent way to connect with students. It puts smiles on the faces of the kids, and it shows them that teachers care enough to at least be conscious of stuff the students like.

Based on all my years of observing teachers and seeing engagement among students, if I had to choose between a person who knows all the theories and strategies but lacks connecting with kids versus a person who immediately has a captive audience but may be wobbly in terms of how the mind works scientifically, I would have my own sons be in the room of the latter instructor without blinking an eye.

24

The 99¢ Teacher or the $150,000 Teacher—
Who Do You Want Teaching Your Child?

Currently forty-seven million children are enrolled in public schools. That number is expected to increase by two million by 2014, which means more classrooms and more teachers.

Where are these teachers going to come from? What qualities will these teachers have?

If in Las Vegas's Clark County School District there is a shortage of four hundred teachers right before the start of school, who will the district end up hiring in such a pinch? Outstanding, highly qualified people? Or anyone who walks through district headquarters with a Social Security number and is not a registered sex offender?

Remember, these people are teaching to your children. And these children will be servicing the American economy years from now.

Isn't it funny how the quality of the teacher, her pay, her working conditions, and her status are rarely discussed, even more rarely included in reform forums. Everybody takes it for granted that the teachers will be there; the good ones, the average ones, and the awful ones. The teachers will just take care of themselves. It's the same attitude public education has about gifted kids as discussed in chapter 19. No need to put any energy or thought into how to teach this special group of youngsters who contribute so much to society later on. They can fend for themselves.

And teachers go along with this junk, that's what is the most astonishing thing about it. They are told in meeting after meeting that if only they made more calls home to parents, if only they tutored more students after school, if only they examined test data more carefully, if only they used more technology, if only they used one more strategy, did one more thing, sacrificed one more hour, then all would be right with the world and all children would rise to the maximum level of their potential.

You know what teachers as a group remind me of? That old Coca-Cola commercial from 1971 where all kinds of people, every race, creed, religion, are standing next to each other on a hillside singing "I'd Like to Buy the World a Coke": "I'd like to teach the world to sing in perfect harmony, I'd like to hold it in my arms and keep it company."

It is easy to make fun of people who go along with this but the sad part of it is that many, many teachers really, really believe in this. As a parent, you gotta love it.

If your child is fortunate enough to be with a gifted instructor at the wholesale salary that she earns, feel blessed for the luck.

The increasing pressure that is put upon teachers to perform at an optimum level is not proportional to the financial rewards and incentives in place (which are few).

How much is a good teacher worth?

Would you think it a bargain to pay thirty-eight dollars an hour for an outstanding educator to teach your child? That is the going hourly rate for the average-salaried teacher in America.*

Let me ask you. Who else could you hire at thirty-eight dollars an hour? Certainly not an attorney, whose rate is in the three-figure range. How about an electrician or plumber for thirty-eight dollars an hour?

Now here's the bad news. Beginning teachers earn twenty-four dollars an hour. That's right, twenty-four dollars an hour for one of the most highly demanding and important jobs in this country.

---

* The average salary is about $48,000; $30,000 for beginning teachers and $70,000 for veteran teachers. Divide that number by 1,260 hours of work based on 7-hour workdays and 180 days a year.

Even teachers at the high end of the salary scale earn only fifty-six dollars an hour—and that is after twenty-five years on the job with a master's degree.

How outrageous that we demand that teachers know what they teach and be able to teach that knowledge to others, yet we will pay them no more than others who don't know what they're doing.

Among eleven jobs in education from superintendent to custodian, teachers are ranked eighth in salary, fourth from the bottom, right below school librarians and just above school nurses. If we looked at a salary chart showing average salaries in the medical field, where do you think doctors would rank? If we looked at salaries in the legal field, where do you think lawyers would rank? It's no surprise, then, that such a low salary ranking carries over to low authority ranking. This must change.

Who's going to apply for a job that can only offer $70,000 at the end of one's career even if one holds a doctorate degree?

An outstanding teacher who motivates children to learn and be curious about life deserves $100,000 or more. There are a few districts that do pay teachers six figures, but usually that's only the very top salary after decades of experience and specialization.

In order to revamp the way teachers get paid, four things need to happen: (1) truly evaluate teachers on their performance, (2) offer high salaries for those who perform well, (3) offer bonuses and other incentives, (4) develop different types of teaching positions, in other words, a career ladder.

Here are some questions that still puzzle me after almost twenty years of teaching.

Why are elementary school teachers paid the same amount of money as high school teachers? Now I'll be the first to say that elementary school teachers have a critical job of laying the learning foundation that future educators in higher grades build on. However, the stress level is not comparable to that of a secondary teacher who has to deal with over one hundred kids daily. Look at the differences.

Elementary	Secondary
shorter workday	longer workday
one class	at least five classes
as few as fifteen students	as many as two hundred students

A kindergarten teacher has twenty students a day for three and a half hours. A high school math teacher could have as many as two hundred kids a day for five hours. Why do both get paid the same amount of money? How can these two jobs possibly be viewed as equal? There's the difference in the number of hours, the difference in the number of clients, the difference in the level of expertise.

Before the 1970s the norm was to pay secondary teachers and administrators more money. Due to the unions and collective bargaining, all salaries were evened out to eliminate any distinction between a kindergarten teacher and an AP physics teacher.

Currently, secondary administrators still earn more than elementary ones, which is the way it should be. Walk into the office of an elementary school and compare the sedate nature of that environment to the helter-skelter vibe of a high school office. It's a completely different place to work. The more stressful the job, the higher the pay should be.

Why shouldn't certain fields pay more than others? A person should be paid based on performance and difficulty of work. No health teacher can look in the eyes of an English teacher and say that she works nearly as hard. Any time a district offers a workshop called "How to Handle the Paperload" it is peopled with English teachers, not coaches. Coaches, by the way, earn stipends for coaching teams. Shouldn't a teacher teaching an Advanced Placement course also be provided a stipend? If math and science teachers are hard to find because of better-paying job opportunities, then why don't teaching positions in those fields pay more?

Why not pay a math teacher at a middle school more money than a physical education teacher? It's a harder subject for students to grasp, plus it's harder to persuade smart people in that field to choose teaching over more lucrative job opportunities. From a basic supply-and-demand Economics 101 standpoint, how can you not pay the math teacher more money? It is only logical.

Why are teachers paid more money in the suburbs where there are fewer problems compared to teachers in urban areas that require more talent for a more challenging clientele? As mentioned earlier in chapter 12, America's neediest students get the worst service. The best schools tend to have the easiest teaching environment, which appeals to veterans. If significant bonuses were available, better teachers would go where they are most needed.

Why doesn't salary reflect effort? In other words, why does a teacher who engages students, gets them thinking, and makes them look forward to attending class get paid the exact same amount of money as another teacher who couldn't care less about the students, mumbles incoherently all day long, and races against the students for the exits at three o'clock?

Why can't people admit what makes a great program at a school great?

Look at high schools with winning basketball teams. Is it the program that's great or is it the coach who has built the program?

How many drama, journalism, and music departments depend on strong, passionate teachers for their success?

And how often does a great program falter after its teacher leaves or retires?

Yet strong teachers receive the same pay and often the same treatment from principals and counselors as the worst teachers. Why is that? Fear of calling out that one teacher is superior to another?

How much longer must this insanity continue? It will continue as long as people think like Associate Superintendent of Pinellas County Schools Ron Stone who proclaimed that "it is very difficult to discriminate between an average teacher and an outstanding teacher." Huh? He's got to be kidding.

All the principal playmakers in the game of educating children play by some common rules, and rule number one has been around since the invention of the pencil. That rule says that you cannot distinguish one teacher from the next, nor should you. All teachers get paid the same. All teachers get treated the same. Any honor given to a teacher (and there are only a few) needs to be done on a rotation basis in order to ensure that all teachers get recognized. And if that happens, where's the honor in that?

Quality is not acknowledged, applauded, spotlighted, or rewarded.

Teachers have low expectations of themselves as workers and this translates to the low expectations they have of their students. Much of this attitude derives from the fact that the majority of educators have never worked in the private sector. They attend school as students for thirteen years, go for another five years of college, receive their teaching credentials, and go right back into the classroom as a working teacher. They have never left school.

Since the bulk of their lives are spent in the public sector, the idea that quality matters or that an individual can be singled out for specific achievements is a foreign concept. A teacher is expected to be all-giving, continuously selfless, a total sacrificer. And if a teacher veers away from this image one iota, suspicions arise and the teacher's dedication is challenged: "Aren't you here for the children?"

During one opening day district-wide meeting, the superintendent showcased a teacher whose work with average-ability students led to an appearance at the G-8 summit. How wonderful for the students and the teacher, right? The superintendent was correct to put a spotlight on this teacher. Yet he profusely apologized to the large group of teachers: "I rarely do this, I rarely do this."

Why should the superintendent be so shy to publicly praise a dynamic teacher? Because it goes against the teacher culture—do not single out the achievements of one teacher over others. This is a cancer in the profession that needs to be removed as soon as possible if public schools ever hope to attract a higher caliber of talent, people who pride themselves on working hard and being recognized for it.

Such a system deters many bright people from ever entering the teaching profession, one bereft of money and prestige.

Should the best teachers earn six-figure salaries? Yes.

Should all teachers be paid six-figure salaries? No.

By paying teachers a qualitative salary, i.e., a salary based on how well they teach, public schools can begin to have a major mind-shift toward rewarding quality. Maybe they can even use it in slogans like "quality your child can trust."

Interesting how teachers are assigned the classes they teach— at random. All a principal cares about is to fill a seat with a person who is credentialed in that field. But other factors need to be looked at. Some teachers do well with higher-achieving students, while others do better with lower-achieving students.

One would think some conscious connection between the qualities of the instructor and the characteristics of the class would be made. Nope. The teacher is hired to teach the courses that have been left over. There is no conscious decision on why a particular teacher ends up with a particular group of students or a particular course. Imagine if a bunch of doctors opened an office, then realized there was a demand for an in-house radiologist, yet not a single one of the doctors had studied radiology. And so they drew straws to find out who'd be the radiologist for the office. Scary, isn't it? Thankfully that isn't happening in medical offices, but it is happening in school classrooms.

Here's what happened when a decision had to be made as to who would teach an advanced class for the second semester. The choice was between one teacher who had years of experience teaching the class before and currently had two sections of it, and a teacher who had never taught it before. The administrators chose the inexperienced teacher. Why? Because she had fewer years on the job and so it was cheaper to pay her for the extra class. Was that the best decision for the students who were going to have a new teacher in the middle of the year?

During a trip through the office, the principal called me over and asked if I would be willing to take over the yearbook since the teacher who had been doing it was retiring. It made me feel good to know that the principal was making a conscious decision to choose me because she liked what I had done with the student newspaper. I told her I wanted a little time to think about it. So that night I mulled it over and decided to go ahead and accept the assignment. The next day when I went back to tell her that I'd do it, I found out that she went ahead and hired a new teacher to do it. In other words, I was just a warm body to her who happened to be passing by her office. My talent had nothing to do with her initial interest. As soon as the first person said "yes" the issue was resolved, the position filled, the class assigned to an instructor. Quality is a foreign concept in public schools.

Typically, firefighters and police officers earn more money than teachers, even though college degrees are not required for those jobs. And they are allowed to retire early with a full pension. Why can't teachers be treated in a similar fashion? While each of those jobs has adrenaline-rush moments, teachers have continuous stress every day they work. I've lived through a fire and a handful of homicides at my school.

Now, no one is denying the importance of these fields. It's just that teaching should likewise be viewed as essential to society.

As I mentioned in my first book, *The $100,000 Teacher,* "When done well, teaching is a highly demanding, mentally exhausting, stamina-draining, energy-depleting activity. Teachers are performers working to engage their audience every minute of every day. It's all 'live' with no TelePrompTers and hardly any time for rehearsal."

Everybody knows that teachers don't get paid what they deserve. But then teachers have never been paid based on how well they teach. Never. A teacher's salary depends on the number of years on the job plus the number of college credits earned. Former Florida State commissioner of education John L. Winn refers to the way teachers get paid as "a failed relic of the past." That's why an accurate way of gauging and rewarding superior teaching with financial rewards must be put into place.

Thankfully, a few forward-thinking districts and states around the country have thrown out this relic and replaced it with what's called a performance-pay system, often overriding unions' objections.

The concept may sound familiar. Pay people for how well they do their job. How innovative is that?

The Houston School Board is the largest school district in the nation (seventh-largest in the United States) to pay teachers based on performance. After its first year of using performance pay, the Houston Independent School District handed out bonuses to eight thousand teachers, the most totaling over $7,000, which equated to twice the monthly salary of the teacher. Now that's a bonus. Not surprisingly, the local teachers union opposed this plan.

The main problem with this program is that it focuses entirely on students' test scores. An excellent instructor might have a classroom of poor testers while an average one has a classroom of valedictorians. Standardized test results should not be part of evaluating teachers.

Florida has the Special Teachers Are Rewarded program, known as STAR, which pays the top 10 percent of teachers bonuses equal to 5 percent of their annual salary. Half of a teacher's evaluation is based on test scores, the other half on other factors.

And who stands in the way of this program? Yep, the Florida Education Association is fighting it in the courts.

The most progressive pay plan exists in Denver, Colorado; it's named ProComp, which is short for professional compensation. Voters passed a property tax increase of $24 per year on every $100,000 of a home's value to pay for the joint district-union plan, which was six years in the making. It's been estimated that over twenty-five years, a teacher's salary could be boosted up to 40 percent.

And, unlike most other unions considering performance-pay plans, the Denver Classroom Teachers Association not only supports it but helped develop it. You can imagine why the NEA views this union as a pariah. Nearly half of the district's teachers choose to participate.

While ProComp does use test scores, that factor is but one of four main ways for teachers to earn higher salaries. The others are enrolling in professional development workshops or earning National Board certification, working in hard-to-serve schools or in hard-to-staff positions, and receiving good performance evaluations. It is this last one that is most intriguing because each teacher gets evaluated in five different areas—instruction, assessment, curriculum and planning, learning environment, professional responsibilities— based on a four-point scale. This proves that there is a way to evaluate a teacher for quality.

Other states with districts that either have implemented or are considering alternative ways of paying teachers are Tennessee, Mississippi, Alaska, Massachusetts, Iowa, New Mexico, and Arizona.

There are several union arguments against performance pay. "It is unhealthy for teachers to compete with one another." Well, it is unhealthy for good teachers to continue not being acknowledged and applauded for the terrific work they do.

"It is impossible to quantify good teaching." No it's not! I can take someone off the street and show them a classroom with an effective teacher and one with an ineffective teacher. That stranger could easily distinguish the difference.

"It allows management to play favorites." Management already plays favorites with teachers' schedules and other things. As long as human beings are in charge, subjectivity will play a role. However, there would be less of a chance of a single administrator playing games if teachers were evaluated by a panel of master teachers and administrators from different schools.

"The benefit to students is not proven." Lawrence W. Kenny, economics professor at the University of Florida, studied links between performance-pay plans and higher student achievement and concluded that "incentive programs can and do work." Another study found that when teachers get paid according to their performance, their students' performance increases. In other words, money does motivate people to work harder. Who would have thought?

The big question that needs answering when it comes to paying teachers more money is "Where is the money going to come from?"

Let's say 10 percent of the three million teachers in America are worth $100,000 or more, and that such compensation would in effect double their current salaries of $50,000. Multiply 300,000 times

$50,000 and that equals $15 billion. Remember, the annual education bill is $500 billion, so $15 billion more is not so outrageous.
Still, where is this money? It's actually already there in the system.

As analyzed more in-depth later on, money can be taken from
current grant programs, and special education and Title I funds.
Additionally, lowering the top salaries of the *Night of the Living
Dead* veteran teachers who do little but show up and collect pay-
checks will free up money to pay higher salaries for those excelling.
Plus, having fewer teachers, as mentioned in chapter 2, would do it.

If we look at hiring a group of people for their expertise as an insurance policy to protect this country from economic disaster, $15
billion is not that much money.

Besides, it really isn't that pricey considering the cost of the
Iraq war—$100,000 per minute.

There were people who gave up weeks of their lives to sleep on
filthy sidewalks outside movie theaters to wait for the opening of the
final *Star Wars* installment.

There were people who camped out in front of electronics stores
days ahead of the release of Playstation 3, with violence erupting in
many parts of the country for the four-hundred-dollar product.

There are people in this world who think nothing of paying
$75,000 for a single bottle of wine, $100,000 for a backyard swimming pool, $100,000 for a used Mickey Mouse toy.

This country has a warped sense of importance and value.

Could you imagine if teaching actually became an attractive job?
Think of the possibilities.

Don't we want graduates from the Ivy Leagues teaching third
graders? Don't we want some of the future scientists to teach kids
rather than forever work in a laboratory?

Imagine the job applicants swarming district offices across the
country if the starting salary for a teacher was $50,000 and the
highest was $150,000? How inspiring it would be to see a line of can-
didates snake around a school district office like a line of aspiring
contestants on a reality TV show, all with the proper credentials,
applying for the limited number of teaching positions available.

Some say that if teachers were paid six-figure salaries it would bring in the wrong kind of people who'd be in it only for the money. Well, I've got news for you. The wrong kind of people are already attracted to the profession as it is. With several holidays and summers off, work ending at three o'clock, and little supervision, teaching has pulled in many minimum-work workers. With a performance-pay system in place, anyone who truly is in teaching only for the money would be weeded out. With the current 150-year-old system, no one is weeded out—ever.

Perhaps with a high caliber of people entering the teaching profession, the quality of substitute teachers will also increase. One substitute teacher in Ohio was fired after putting clothespins on the lips of kindergarten boys in order to keep them quiet.

I know that a teacher asking for more money is as foreign as your own mother asking to be paid to babysit your children. Your reaction is, "What? Aren't they supposed to be doing this out of love for children, not love for money?"

The old "teachers are there for the kids" saw doesn't work anymore because teaching is much more stressful today. More is being asked of teachers. The stakes are raised, so the salaries and working conditions should be as well.

You can have a group of professionals who do care about their clientele yet at the same time believe that there is no conflict in desiring proper compensation for services rendered. The group that comes to mind which has lived with this so-called duality for some time are doctors. While sometimes you'll hear people gripe about greedy doctors (and when it comes to cosmetic surgery many would agree), how many of us feel that when doctors examine us the only reason they are probing our orifices is to have a more expensive car?

There is nothing wrong with believing that the more money is offered the better quality of people will vie for those jobs. Nothing whatsoever.

A popular story teachers enjoy sharing with one another (or commiserating over is more like it) revolves around people at a party who are discussing how much each earns at their respective jobs. Among the group is a CEO who asks a teacher what she makes. Her response is, "I make a difference. What do you make?" This is supposed to give teachers comfort about their situation?

Better-quality teachers are the best chance any child has in a classroom. The NCLB law, the AP curriculum, the way students are grouped, the classes they take, all are second-class, superfluous details that distract from the key to transforming schools: the classroom teacher.

Polls all across America show that people believe the best way to improve student learning is through improved teacher quality.

When teachers start getting paid professional salaries you will see the level of candidates and respect rise significantly.

You can't expect top-notch K–12 instruction without paying for it. Nothing less than our country's economic future is at stake.

25

No More Tenure

A group of kids are trapped in a room with an adult who doesn't like them. The adult is supposed to take care of these kids, prepare them for life, but instead is damaging their futures.

What sounds like a scenario for a B horror movie is a reality for hundreds of thousands of young people in America who are trapped with ineffectual instructors.

Envision working at a place where no matter whether you did a good job or not you were guaranteed employment; where no matter what the boss told you to do, you really didn't have to do it; where your boss was the one who could actually get fired, not you. Sounds like nirvana, huh? If you are a public school teacher, this is not your imagination—it is reality and it is one of the major reasons why education is in critical condition today.

The seasoned teachers have the least financial incentive to work harder, and since they are tenured have no fear of being fired.

What is going to happen to a teacher if her students don't understand the material? Absolutely nothing.

What is going to happen to a teacher if her students' test scores don't increase? Absolutely nothing.

What is going to happen to a teacher if she shows up late every day, doesn't assign work, couldn't care less about children? That's right. Absolutely nothing.

You can't even use the incentive of getting fired with tenured teachers. Though it could be seen as a threat, at least it would wake some people up and give them a reason to change or become better.

Good teachers are never rewarded, but bad teachers are, through the tenure system. And teachers unions are the knights in shining armor to rescue those teachers from the unemployment line. The teachers who call in the union cavalry are usually weak instructors. Why do teachers unions continue to defend incompetents?

The only reason teachers have job security is because both the unions and the districts feel that teachers don't get paid what they deserve, so they try to make it up by giving them lifetime protection. Well, teachers need to trade job security for professional integrity. There needs to be a real threat to teachers that they may lose their jobs if they don't meet minimum standards.

Because of the low likelihood of successfully removing a tenured teacher, many principals opt instead to transfer or "bump" bad teachers to another school within the district. Over the past ten years, Los Angeles Unified administrators have attempted to dismiss 112 permanent teachers, a small sliver of the district's roughly 37,000 instructors. Some were fired, some resigned, but many were bumped, with principals forced to take another school's damaged goods. Recently, some districts such as in New York have implemented safety measures to prevent this "bumping" from occurring. Of course, such safeguards need the blessing of the teachers unions.

Teaching is the type of profession that attracts people who want job security and who understand the system. Basically if a new teacher gets acceptable (not excellent, mind you) evaluations from the principal for three years, that teacher has a job for life; barring some heinous crime being committed, tenure will protect that teacher until retirement. On the evaluation form there are two boxes for an administrator to check off: "Meets standards" and "Does not meet standards." Notice the absence of a third option, "Exceeds standards." So why should a teacher even desire to get higher-than-average marks when they are not expected to be that good? Teachers are constantly being told to have high expectations and standards for their students, so why shouldn't districts demand the same from their teacher workforce? This is just another example of how quality doesn't matter a twit in public schools. Since quality is not a valued commodity, an outstanding teacher can easily get by in her career by giving 70 or 80 percent and still be considered a star instructor.

Except for when conducting mandatory evaluations, administrators try their best not to enter classrooms unless absolutely necessary. This is fine for teachers who don't need oversight, quite risky for those who don't know what they're doing. It's difficult to know for sure why administrators rarely make unannounced appearances. Is it due to their being uncomfortable, or their being overloaded with other tasks? All I know is that whenever they do schedule what are called "walk-throughs," short, unannounced visits, they try to ease teachers' concerns by making a big deal to convince them that such visits are *not* evaluations.

First of all, I don't quite get how walking into a classroom and observing someone teach can be construed as not being an evaluation. It is. Second, so what? Why wouldn't any good teacher want feedback, especially when so little is given? Don't make it into this giant endeavor; just send administrators into classrooms on a regular basis.

Teachers are partly to blame for this anxious climate since many feel insecure about what they do, fearing any adult walking into their rooms without prior notification. What are teachers afraid of? What, are they asleep? Are they showing porno? Are students smoking dope? No, teachers are simply insecure—big time.

Teachers too easily feel threatened due to extreme low self-esteem and lack of confidence. This stems from not getting regular feedback. If no one sees them perform their job, naturally they will be reluctant to have anyone observe them teaching.

Having teachers be part of an administrative team that evaluates teachers for real would be a huge step toward professionalizing teaching. Such a step, however, requires an enormous amount of trust on everyone's part. The principals must trust the teachers doing the evaluating, and the teachers being evaluated also need to trust those teachers. It is wise to have the team of administrators and teachers evaluate teachers at a school site other than their own.

This would eliminate one of the primal fears that teachers have of being authentically evaluated: principal politics. If the principal and teacher are unfamiliar with a teacher at another school, then that lends more credibility and objectivity to the process.

Today's public schools demand more of everyone working there. However, teachers know that they don't really have to work any harder. If your boss tells you the company numbers aren't where they should be, you know you better do something to improve them or you're on the street. Teachers are being told that their numbers, in this case student test scores, aren't where they should be, but without the threat of losing their jobs.

Teaching provides no financial incentives, so why should they care? What's in it for them? It's actually the principals who could lose their jobs if a school fails to meet its testing goals. This translates into irritating administrators belittling their teaching staffs for the poor results. And teachers are becoming numb to this attitude. It has no muscle, no teeth.

The fire has been lit under teachers' feet, all right, except that burned-out teachers are wearing fire-retardant shoes that no flame can penetrate.

Researcher Charles J. Sykes stated in his book *Dumbing Down Our Kids:* "There is probably no word used more frequently by educrats than *excellence.* They pledge it, trumpet it, include it in mission statements, press releases, curriculum guides, and endless presentations to parents, school boards, and local businesses." Yet the punch line is that excellence in public schools is a random occurrence. There's nothing in the system to guarantee powerful instructors. If your child comes across a brilliant teacher, consider it serendipitous. In this era of accountability there is none where it really counts and that is with the teacher in the classroom.

Give principals the power to fire bad teachers. Each day an incompetent teacher is allowed to be in the same room with young people is another day of learning permanently lost.

At least in New York City teachers accused of wrongdoing can be removed from the classroom, if not outright fired. These folks are sent to one of thirteen reassignment centers or "rubber rooms" where they await hearings. According to *The Village Voice,* over the past seven years, the number of teachers assigned to these centers has nearly doubled. While only a tiny fraction of teachers go through this process—just under 700 out of 80,000—it costs $33 million a year since teachers still receive their full salary. Some teachers stay in rubber rooms for weeks and months, even years before finding out if they still have classroom jobs. Fewer than half of the cases end up being substantiated.

Bad teaching breeds bad students, which breeds bad workers, which breeds a bad workforce, which breeds a bad economy.

Guess what? The solution to many of public education's problems is not a new reading program, not a new computer, not bilingual this or collaborative that. It's—tada—the teacher, or to paraphrase Bill Clinton campaign strategist James Carville's slogan, it's the teacher, stupid. The highly trained, highly motivated (think money), highly supported (picture a photocopy machine), and mostly autonomous (are you listening, Washington?) instructor. And when you think back on the most gifted teachers you had in school, chances are those teachers were mavericks, the ones who no matter what was said in faculty meetings, at school board hearings, or in state capitol buildings metaphorically shut the door, rolled up their sleeves, and got on with the gritty job of teaching. If it weren't for those independent-minded teachers, education would be in an even worse rut than it is today.

David L. Brewer III, a retired U.S. Navy vice admiral who in 2006 took over as superintendent of Los Angeles Unified School District, had this to say about incompetent teachers, as reported in the *Los Angeles Times:*

> You need to go in there and coach and work and train and do all the professional development you can. . . . But there's an old saying: There are two kinds of birds: chickens and eagles. If you throw an eagle up, eventually it's going to fly. If you throw a chicken up in the air, all it's going to do is poop on you. Eventually, you got to understand it's a chicken and leave 'em in the yard.

People will work harder if their jobs are on the line. Tenured teachers' jobs are not on the line.

Teachers should join the rest of the American workforce and embrace with open arms the right to be fired—as long as everything else vastly improves.

26

What Perks?

There is a feeling among a lot of people that teaching isn't real work. This is because teachers work at schools, places full of children.

Anyone who views teaching as an easy job has no idea of what it's like to teach today, from encroaching government mandates to students posting clandestine videos on YouTube of teachers they don't like.

And for all this work, teachers are getting bonuses and huge salary increases, right? Of course not. What decent business owner would demand so much extra work from his employees without offering the slightest of incentives?

Hard work is not rewarded, innovation is not applauded. Work without rewards produces low teacher morale and deep-seated resentment. And I'm not talking about company cars or retreats in exotic locales.

Through your job, have you ever gotten free tickets to a sporting event or concert, a free CD or DVD, had a company Christmas party, gone out to lunch with colleagues?

Not if you're a teacher.

Teachers are recognition-starved professionals who are the professional world's slave laborers.

There is something to the act of tangibly showing how much employees are valued instead of merely paying lip service. Nowhere is this more true than with public schools showing how much they value their teachers.

Lip balm companies should hire administrators as their spokespeople because I can't think of any other group of workers who have used words more than actions in praising teachers. All teachers should have bumper stickers that say: YOU MATTER. REALLY. NO FOOLIN' (NO MONEY EITHER), YOU REALLY MATTER.

You know how some companies, maybe even the one you work for, have an annual employee recognition lunch or dinner, a place where people's names are mentioned along with the number of years of service they have provided the company? Such events do not occur in schools. A district will host an elaborate fete for a school board member after serving for four years or a principal after five, but a teacher of thirty years might get her name mentioned in the district's in-house newsletter—if she's lucky. Big freakin' deal. And just how much would it put a district's budget back to honor employees once a year?

In 2006 Georgia governor Sonny Perdue gave each teacher in his state a one-hundred-dollar gift card to help pay for classroom supplies. Isn't that nice? How would you respond if your boss gave you a one-hundred-dollar gift card for paper for your printer at work, pens for your desk, coffee for the break room?

While a thoughtful gesture, it doesn't come close to paying the average six hundred dollars it is estimated that teachers spend on their classrooms each year out of their own pockets.

During one teacher appreciation week the PTA placed business cards in teacher mailboxes, a different one each day with different sayings and little items attached to the cards. For example, one day the saying on the card read, "We think you're simply marble-lous," with a glued-on marble. Another day the saying was "We are the lucky ones," with a penny attached.

Now I don't mean to demean the efforts of parents whose thoughts were in the right places; however, it reminds me of how insulting it is for a waiter in a restaurant to receive coins from a patron as a gratuity for an expensive bill. It's better not to tip at all.

That's how I feel about the "gifts" given to teachers during these phony-baloney Hallmark-fabricated days and weeks. Take all the doughnuts, free lunches, pens with the school name on them and save your money. If people truly wish to show appreciation, then they need to work at getting good teachers the salaries they deserve. It's not necessary to have the apple on the desk.

Oh, and by the way, just as Secretary's Day has been altered into Administrative Assistant's Day, many schools have changed Teacher Appreciation Day into Staff Appreciation Day so as not to offend the other workers at a school. They can't even allow teachers this one measly day for themselves, huh? Just another example of watering down what little attention teachers already receive, and more political correctness.

During the first year my wife started working at her new job, she was taken out for lunch and given a present on her birthday, received several commendations (in other words, was singled out for her contributions to the company), and was given a Treo phone, a laptop, and a bonus. I've worked at the same school for two decades and have never received any of these things. Except for the technology and bonus, all the rest cost little, but show much in terms of how a company values its employees. This ingredient is nonexistent in public education.

The best a teacher can expect is to get an administrator to write exemplary comments based on a lesson observation once every couple of years. She needs to put that in the recognition bank for the next two years until the next evaluation comes along because that's all that is going to happen. But then it really doesn't matter how good the teacher is. There will be no salary increase, no bonus, no promotion.

Bonuses do exist in a few places. Virginia piloted a program giving teachers $15,000 bonuses for relocating while the teachers already there got a $3,000 retention bonus. The districts reported a higher caliber of teacher applying for these positions, proving that bonuses had a positive impact on attracting better talent.

North Carolina's Guilford County School District recently began a program called Mission Possible that is geared to attracting math teachers to eight low-performing high schools with a $10,000 signing bonus.

Even Harvard Medical School began offering bonuses for doctors to teach at its school instead of going into private practice. Doctors teaching interns typically earn thirty dollars an hour, compared to a hundred dollars an hour the average practitioner earns.

Frequently, the teachers who perform magical things with students cannot earn enough money to live in the school district where they work. Teaching is a noble profession? Maybe. But with $500,000 as the median price for a house in Los Angeles County, trade nobility for affordability.

One way of enticing teachers to certain districts where the cost of living is exorbitant is by providing them affordable housing through down payments, subsidies, or delaying the payment of loans. New York, Chicago, and San Jose are three districts that do so.

In order to attract math, science, and special education teachers to its harder-to-staff schools, New York City offers housing subsidies of up to $14,000. The cost of the program is around $1.5 million, a small price out of the $15-billion annual budget.

Offering bonuses would greatly enhance the teaching profession, making it more appealing to others, especially ambitious people who enjoy working hard but also receiving just compensation.

27

A Career Ladder

Teachers have the strongest bulletproof glass ceiling of any college-educated workers in America.

How many people would go into a career where their very first position remains their last position from which they retire? That's the lot of the teacher.

There is no motivation in the teaching field to work harder and continuously improve oneself. Once tenure sets in, you have a job for life. How miraculous it is then that this country has as many talented teachers as it does. How frightening that it all hinges on an intangible—pure luck.

Nothing in the system provides incentives for anyone good to get better, work harder, or stay longer in the profession.

They might as well hang a sign outside the district's door: AMBITIOUS PEOPLE NEED NOT APPLY.

Career ladders need to be established to motivate teachers to better themselves, thereby bettering student learning, and to give them opportunities to pursue higher salaries and prestige. Rochester, New York, is one of only a few districts that actually have such a system. New York City recently created a master teacher position that pays an additional $10,000.

In my first book, I designed a sample career ladder with defined teaching positions and accompanying salaries. The main idea behind any career ladder is that with each step higher on the ladder the teacher increases not only her salary but her responsibilities outside the classroom. The teacher would teach less to students but more to other teachers, having her expertise reach further.

Teachers don't ever make more than double their low beginning salary and often yearly increases dry up as the teachers stay longer on the job. Why should a fifteen-year veteran teacher who can only earn a few more thousand dollars for the next fifteen years work any harder than she already does? Where's the carrot? Isn't it obvious why veteran teachers end up coasting to retirement? Why should they push themselves to work harder since their salary is frozen?

I have only one more raise in my future, coming on my twenty-second year in the district. And I know that I will get that raise no matter how hard I work, whether students learn in my classroom or not. I have a guaranteed salary for life, albeit not that much money.

The uppermost rung of the ladder should be reserved for those teachers earning National Board certification. While working with both new and veteran teachers should be at the heart of this position, it is important that the teacher still teach for a small part of her day to retain up-to-date classroom experience and relevance. These teachers would also be the ones who would serve on evaluation teams with administrators to observe other teachers.

In 1994 the National Board for Professional Teaching Standards (NBPTS) set out on a journey to elevate the teaching profession. Its mission was to offer teachers a way to get recognition for their talents in teaching young people.

The NBPTS developed a rigorous national certification program that surpassed the demands of state licensing requirements. The organization wanted to create a certificate that would mean something if earned. Such an achievement would establish teaching as a more authentic profession where a person learns a particular body of knowledge.

Like passing the bar exam, earning national certification is not easy. Unlike the bar, the process is voluntary. After paying a $2,500 fee, which many states help subsidize, candidates submit a portfolio consisting of dozens of pages of self-reflective writing that analyzes how they teach, supported by student samples, and take a battery of timed, written tests about their subject matter, lasting half a day. Videotaped lessons also need to be included.

Over half of candidates going through the national certification process for the first time do not achieve it. That's good. It should be tough, unlike the if-you-have-a-pulse-you-pass teacher tests that states administer. Those tests do as good of a job weeding out bad teachers as driving tests do weeding out bad drivers. An attorney who passes a bar exam feels a great sense of achievement and the same should be true of teachers earning certification.

An attractive piece of becoming national certified is that several states offer bonuses for that distinction without stepping on the teachers unions' toes. But bonuses to become national certified remain paltry, with only eight states paying $5,000 or more. It's not surprising that the states that offer the highest bonuses are the ones with more NBCTs.

Four of the last seven National Teachers of the Year, including the 2007 recipient, are National Board Certified. Forty percent of the honorees in the National Teachers Hall of Fame are NBCTs.

So, you would think that with such an accomplishment to offer, NBCTs would be the most sought-out educators in America, offered salary increases and bonuses, and wined and dined by other schools. In other words, be a commodity people would seek out.

Not so.

Despite studies showing that students of NBCTs perform at a higher level than those who are taught by non-NBCTs, the promise of a better profession for teachers has not materialized.

While some NBCTs have found pathways to leadership roles, many others remain in the classroom in the same capacity as before, their careers unaltered. Their knowledge is not being maximized or being passed on to other teachers and therefore other students.

The NBPTS has a major image problem. Only a minority of teachers are fully aware of the program, few school principals and district administrators have a clue how to utilize National Board Certified Teacher talent to better the education of this country's children, and even fewer members of the general public know what this is all about. When I achieved certification, one administrator congratulated me on becoming National Teacher of the Year. Huh?

Those in the upper echelon of the education bureaucracy may enjoy proclaiming at a parent meeting that X number of teachers are NBCTs; however, those same folks don't maximize the talent that exists within their own schools.

As of the winter of 2007, over sixty-three thousand of America's three million schoolteachers have earned National Board certification. That's 2 percent of the teacher workforce. This is a far cry from the NBPTS's goal of having one hundred thousand teachers certified by 2003.

For this to occur, the NBPTS needs to do a more effective job of brand-name recognition. Get corporate sponsors to advertise on TV and radio about NBCTs.

Why doesn't the president, as a way to tout the No Child Left Behind Act, host an annual Rose Garden ceremony honoring NBCTs? After all, the backbone of the act is the stipulation that each American classroom have a highly qualified teacher. You can't get more highly qualified than a National Board Certified Teacher.

Many NBCTs do not even receive the simplest of celebrations when they become certified. How about the school board acknowledging the NBCT personally at a meeting? How about inviting the NBCT to high-level meetings to seek out her input?

Plenty of teachers are uncomfortable recognizing the achievement of their NBCT colleagues. Why don't they embrace their peers as people who serve the profession well instead of envying their accomplishments?

Celebrating NBCTs is the best commercial for recruiting future candidates. If a teacher is not properly recognized when she has earned national certification, then the message is clear: It's no big deal.

I happen to work for one of only five districts in California that do not pay NBCTs a bonus. In place of extra money an NBCT can do fifty hours of extra work to earn a $2,500 stipend. (But I thought

I had already performed extra work by going through the certification process!) What's additionally humiliating is that teachers have to document the hours, account for every minute they work outside of their workday, record what they did, which teachers they worked with, and those teachers must initial the worksheet to verify that the NBCT did the work. And this is what's called treating someone as a professional.

The person in charge of staff development in my district invited all NBCTs to a meeting to discuss our plans on how we were going to work the extra fifty hours. Only three of the seventeen NBCTs showed up. I later understood why. Not even the superintendent bothered coming by to say hello to the "stellar" teachers, the term this administrator used.

The district requires that to earn the stipend, the NBCT needs to work with new teachers or do grunt work for the administrators at the school site. I learned quickly that the plan I had submitted, to research how NBCTs can best be utilized for the district, was a "no go," to borrow her words. I told her then it was a "no go" for me as well.

The two other NBCTs in attendance stopped me from leaving the meeting. One, a sixth-grade teacher, told me that even though she had only just met me, she felt it would be a shame to lose such a passionate teacher, that there must be some role for me to play in order to inspire others. Too bad the administrator in charge didn't see it that way.

After my proposal to earn the princely sum of $2,500 was turned down, I sent off a letter to each member of the school board expressing how important it is for them to use NBCTs in a unique way, that these few teachers could play a vital role in the district's duty of educating young people.

The only person who responded back to me was the assistant superintendent, who had some choice things to say. "Leadership opportunities . . . are not reserved for NBCT, rather to any teacher who is capable and willing." In other words, NBCTs aren't any more special than anybody else. "Alternate options for this work do not exist; however, I appreciate your thinking about how NBCTs can be used." In other words, we, the district, think in one specific way and cannot perceive thinking outside of the proverbial box. Those in charge are depriving America's children of wonderful opportunities by not thinking progressively, clinging on to the power they hold.

He did send me a note congratulating me on my achievement. So what if it was mistakenly addressed to "Norm" Crosby. At least he got the last name right. Doesn't say much about his taste in old comedians though.

On a more trivial note, the snacks provided for the meeting were Reese's Peanut Butter Cups and Hershey's Miniatures decorated in Easter colors. One problem with this: The meeting took place in September. I didn't dare touch them despite my weakness for chocolate.

People often gripe about bad teachers. Okay, well, here are sixty-three thousand people who voluntarily put themselves through a grueling process to show how well they teach. NBCTs give this country's education system what it sorely lacks: dynamic, visionary people to lead students toward a stronger America. Give them the authority to rule their roost. Otherwise, National Board teachers will remain national bored teachers.

28

Fridays Off for Good Behavior

Teachers are asked to give a live performance in front of an audience for at least five hours a day without any time to finesse, alter, or modify the performance. That's crazy. Even Sinatra in his heyday took time off.

Ideally a teacher evaluates each lesson after it has been tried with students. Add something here, throw something else out. But with teachers working from hour to hour with no rest except for a single hour of preparation time, the structure allows for no reflection, no time to think about another approach to open young people's minds to the lessons at hand.

What most teachers end up doing is teaching the same things in the same ways year after year because they have no time to revise their work. The one hour of preparation gets quickly sucked away by going through one's mail, e-mail, voice mail, inputting attendance, rearranging desks, wiping boards, picking up trash from the floor. Who has time to grade papers or work on lessons?

The solution is to have teachers work with students four days of the week, Monday through Thursday. On Fridays, paraeducators, retrained adult instructional aides, would be with the students. True, more of them would have to be hired in order to place one in every classroom. But the money is in the education pot, it just has to be rearranged.

It's not uncommon to reward people in stressful occupations with flexible work schedules. Some police departments have three-day workweeks. With this concept, teachers would still work five days a week, four with students and one with other teachers.

A four-day work schedule opens up many possibilities. If each classroom had a paraeducator, teachers would no longer have to take attendance, check off work, answer the phone during class. That second adult body in the room would help with classroom management; there would be fewer students acting up. The paraeducator would also provide coverage for the teacher when she leaves after the period to go to her next class (as mentioned in chapter 6), or even if she needs to quickly step out of the room during class. The paraeducator can take breaks when the teacher is in the room.

What happens on Fridays? Since students tend to be more antsy at the end of the week, assemblies, field trips, and guest speakers can be scheduled.

What do the teachers do on Fridays? They do something they only rarely get a chance to do—share ideas with other teachers. All day long teachers can examine student work, discuss particular students and their needs, contact and conference with parents. The way it is now, teachers are lucky to get a couple of hours in working with each other per month, which provides no systematic change. What other job can someone have where there is practically no interaction with another adult during the workday?

One of the best advantages to a four-day workweek is that it frees up one day a week for teachers to attend conferences (which typically are three-day affairs that begin on Fridays) without having to miss teaching to their students. It also would put an end to student-free days, those days when teachers have meetings that kids love but parents loathe as they scramble trying to figure out what to do with their children.

The term "staff development" should be buried in the education lexicon graveyard along with "new math," "whole-language reading," "holistic" (boy, what a "hole" in that approach), and "cooperative learning groups." It has been estimated that districts spend 5 percent of their expenditures, for a total of up to $12 billion each year, on staff development, which includes costs for paying substitutes. This is another chunk of money that could pay for higher teacher salaries.

Ask any teacher privately what she thinks of staff development and the frequent response will be a nonverbal rolling of the eyes. Common workshops include how to draw two concentric intersecting circles (someone made a lot of money labeling such a picture a Venn diagram) or an open mind (an outline of a head that a student fills in with words and drawings—we all know how often we use this in real life).

Nearly all staff development is mind-numbingly pointless. It's amazing to look around in a room of college-educated people and just watch them take the abuse of being spoken down to for several hours. A few gripe but all end up going along with it as if the material presented is illuminating, something that we can't live without. It gives the false impression to the public that a district's teaching force is up-to-date and current with the latest education trends. How comforting. Hardly ever is the time given over to teachers to share with their colleagues, the best staff development with a total cost of zero.

Just to prove how starved teachers are to work with one another, here is a sampling of teacher responses after a rare teacher-directed workshop that had teachers sharing their ideas with one another:

"With so much focus on SAT and AP testing . . . I'd like to have more time to plan."

"Giving us time to create activities and share them collectively was a tremendous help."

"Today was great. We never get the chance to share ideas that work with other schools. We hardly have the chance to do it with our own school; this was very valuable. I hope we will have other opportunities in the future to discuss ideas and share lessons. We spend too much time re-creating, rather than discussing, working together, and sharing."

"Why can't teachers have time to work in their own rooms to assess, plan, and feel they are 'keeping up' with all they should do?"

"It helps the creative juices [flow,] talking and planning with other teachers."

"Much district-wide staff development isn't particularly helpful. This experience was."

"Continue to provide time for teachers to collaborate."

"This was probably the most useful staff development session I have attended in years. We need time to brainstorm."

"This was wonderful! Sharing lesson ideas was the most helpful thing you could offer!"

"Give us time! We will plan!!"

With feedback like that, why would district officials ever waste money on outside people to conduct workshops?

It's important to make sure that the Fridays aren't structured to death. The way it is now, whenever there are a couple of staff development days in the year, they typically mirror the educator's normal workday: completely controlled, assembly line–like, every minute accounted for, with no time to catch a breath, and without the one hour of prep time teachers normally get. The sessions go by so quickly it's like someone standing in front of you shuffling a deck of cards and expecting you to be familiar with all the cards immediately and then use them effectively in lessons.

Here's an actual agenda from my work:

7:45–8:00 A.M.	coffee and muffins outside of library
8:00 sharp–8:30	activity
8:30–8:35	explain the breakout sessions
8:35–9:30	break out into focus groups to discuss the action plans
9:30–9:40	mini-break
9:40–10:50	continue focus group discussions
10:50–11:00	mini-break
11:00–12:00	focus groups
12:00–1:00	lunch on your own

1:00–2:00	discussion in focus groups
2:00–3:00	debrief from focus group discussion
3:00–3:15	district survey

As you can see, teachers just don't get a break away from the highly structured and controlled environment in which they work every day.

Notice the emphasis on the "mini" in the breaks. What, teachers need to be told when they can leave a meeting to use the bathroom? They are treated just like schoolchildren.

Incredibly we are allowed an actual lunch hour, double the norm. This is the only part of the day I look forward to because I can actually go out for lunch like regular workers can.

Administrators will have to trust that teachers will know how best to organize their Fridays. If some teachers decide to use part of the day to get their room together, make photocopies, pick up supplies or books, then let them.

Teachers are given too much work and not enough time to properly do the work. For this to change, teachers need time. The only way to provide them with time is to take them out of the classrooms.

29

Outlaw Teachers Unions

Carson High School, a troubled institution in the L.A. district, received a $1.5-million grant from the Bill and Melinda Gates Foundation in 2006. But because of the teachers union objections, the grant was refused, leaving the kids as they were before: struggling.

Frequently unions stand in the way of true reform. They adamantly oppose any idea that rocks their self-interest boat, including performance pay and charter schools. Rarely do they come up with an original idea; always do they shoot down others' visions. That's why former secretary of education Rod Paige referred to the NEA as "a terrorist organization," holding the school system hostage to real reform.

Mandating that all members be treated equally in terms of salary—the one-size-fits-all approach, with every teacher getting paid the same as any other teacher who has the same number of years on the job and college credits—unions stand for mediocrity, not quality.

The public has positive views of teachers yet negative views of teachers unions. A recent survey showed that 72 percent of Americans think unions too often stand in the way of removing incompetent teachers.

Increasingly the message of the teachers unions is becoming clearer to the general population: They protect their own no matter if their own are rotten or not.

The NEA is out of touch with the rest of the country. While most teachers are union members, only 11 percent of American workers are unionized.

The NEA, with its 2.7 million members, and its poor stepsister union the American Federation of Teachers (AFT), with 1.3 million, rake in more than $1 billion in annual dues.

The unions should be lauded for raising teacher salaries through robust collective bargaining agreements in the 1970s and 1980s. Many of the job protections for teachers, however, were already in place before unions were established, several backed by the U.S. Supreme Court.

Now that teacher salaries are tolerable instead of horrible, unions should reinvent themselves by leading instead of blocking the way to transforming the profession.

Teaching has increasingly become a more stressful job, partly due to the lack of incentives given to teachers to work harder than ever before. And all the unions can do is gain a 3 percent raise here, a 1.5 percent raise there—nothing in line with how much more difficult the task of teaching is now.

The actual salary differential between union and nonunion teacher contracts amounts to about $4,800 more for union members. That equates to an 8 percent raise in annual salary. Not that much. Certainly not worth the grief that takes place in drawn-out negotiations between labor and management.

When conducting contract negotiations, instead of acting as a professional group like the American Medical Association, many teachers associations resemble trade unions. The number of allowable hours worked, to the minute, is part of the contractual language, further establishing teaching as more a factory job than a professional one. The New York City teacher contract is longer than a thousand pages.

Unions like to stir it up and rally the troops. They prefer controversy. How else could they justify extracting extra dues from their members as the California Teachers Association (CTA) did during the 2005 special election, assessing each teacher an additional sixty dollars to help defeat the education reform propositions, adding up to a whopping $55 million? In fact, after the election they were left with nearly $11 million remaining in their war chest.

Reacting to the propositions losing, my local union had the following headline on the front page of its newsletter: "We Won!" It was as if the neighborhood football team had brought home a championship.

Teachers unions and their infantile tactics are an embarrassment to all hard-working teachers who regard what they do as a professional service.

One local union paid for substitutes so that ten teachers could attend ten monthly union meetings throughout the year. At a cost of a hundred dollars a day per teacher, that meant that ten thousand dollars of union dues went toward teachers meeting during the school day to discuss union issues. Is that a smart way to spend other people's money?

Whenever negotiations between a union and a district reach an impasse, it can become quite comical as teachers' work mailboxes get stuffed with flyers with each side's propaganda. The union actually labeled its contract negotiations as "Round 1," as if the district and union are opponents in a fighting match. How childish.

One particular flyer instructed teachers how to respond to a student if asked why the teacher is wearing green once a week as a symbol of the union's demands for more money (get it, green equals money?). Here's the actual dialogue teachers were to use with students:

STUDENT: Mr. Smith, why are you wearing a green
                  T-shirt/button?
UNION MEMBER: Johnny, I can't discuss this topic at this time. Ask
                  me again before school, at lunch, or after school.

During a gubernatorial election, California teachers wore buttons with WE KICK A*S emblazoned on them, the "AS" standing for Governor Arnold Schwarzenegger. Nice way for a bunch of educators to act. A union newsletter printed, "[We need to] elect people who are going to be fair and good to the working class of the State of California." See, teachers view themselves as down and dirty laborers, not white-collar professionals.

By the way, would any Republican fit such a "fair and good" description? I decided to ask NEA president Reg Weaver what it would take for his union to back a Republican candidate. After repeated attempts through letters and e-mails, I received no response. Case closed.

The stereotype of Republicans is that they are wealthy folks who generally send their children to private schools. But how many Democrats do likewise?

When Governor Schwarzenegger proposed merit pay for teachers in his 2005 State of the State address—"teacher employment [should] be tied to performance, not to just showing up"—the president of United Teachers of Los Angeles (UTLA), the strong union of Los Angeles Unified School teachers, responded that attracting people to teaching via such a concept was "la-la land." At least the governor came up with an idea, though it killed any invitation to speak at CTA's annual convention.

Did teachers unions revoke their support of Democratic senator John Kerry during his failed presidential bid in 2004 when he proposed something similar to the proposal of the Republican governor? No. As far back as 1998 Kerry said, "We must end teacher tenure as we know it." Where were the boo birds then? You know that if Kerry were a Republican the NEA would be all over him with LET'S KICK KERRY'S KEISTER bumper stickers.

Even though all teachers are not liberals and Democrats, that is the view of the union brass, and it is toward liberal and Democrat causes and candidates that teachers union dues go. Shame on those teachers who, though they disapprove of their union's politics, positions, and platitudes, acquiesce anyway by allowing dues to automatically be deducted from their paychecks, which amounts to the totality of their activism.

One of the rare times a teachers union opposed a Democrat was when Los Angeles mayor Antonio Villaraigosa wanted to take over the school district, something that would have taken away much of UTLA's power.

UTLA has an impeccable record, by the way, of high standards. During a recent school board race, one candidate was found to have been convicted of shoplifting not once but twice in the 1990s. Yet UTLA, which had given him nearly a quarter of a million dollars for his campaign (he was an employee of the union), stood by its man. Soon it was disclosed that he falsely claimed he earned dual master's degrees from USC. Even though the county's Democratic party dropped its support, UTLA remained steadfast behind him. Yep, this is the guy whom I would want to represent the best in educating young people. A shoplifter and a liar. I guess once you're a union man, you'll always get supported no matter what you do. This is why bad teachers have lifetime jobs. P.S.: That candidate did not get elected. Thank goodness for the public's good sense.

Not too long ago the Human Rights Committee of UTLA was going to host an anti-Israel rally at its headquarters, even though UTLA's own president, A. J. Duffy, is, you guessed it, Jewish. It reminds me of the Jewish lawyers working for the ACLU who defend the right of Nazi sympathizers to march through Jewish neighborhoods. What's up with that? Some kind of self-hatred syndrome? Upon hearing about the rally, one union member echoed many others' concerns about UTLA getting involved with international politics when she told the *Los Angeles Times*, "What am I spending my union dues for? For this?" Incidentally, this woman was the daughter of two Holocaust survivors. Ultimately, the rally did not occur.

Not all teachers unions oppose change. Adam Urbanski, president of the Rochester, New York, union, formed TURN (Teachers Union Reform Network), allowing forward-thinking teacher associations to discuss progressive ideas. He gives his own organization a C+ so far after over a decade in existence with over thirty local teachers unions involved. He believes that "unions must start doing what they are 'un-supposed' to do."

I do have to thank my local teachers association for making me more philanthropic. You see, I am very lucky that in the district where I work I can claim the status of a principled objector. While I still have to pay the nearly one-thousand-dollar annual union fees, I can have the entire amount submitted to a reputable charity. Each year I gladly write out a check payable to the American Red Cross, knowing that the money will be spent on something worthwhile.

Teachers cannot keep demanding to be treated as professionals while clutching on to the old way of doing things.

Therefore, in order to accomplish the goal of having teachers control their own profession as well as ensuring public support, the best teachers in the country need to unite in a nonpolitical way.

Imagine if the sixty-three thousand National Board Certified Teachers were to unite as a group to call for major reforms in the educational system. These teachers would become lobbyists and be the ones politicians look to for advice. These teachers would truly become leaders.

A nationwide professional organization of teachers is long overdue. I'm currently getting off the ground the American Education Association (AEA), which strives to become as well known and highly regarded as the American Medical Association and the American Bar Association. Its mission is to move teachers to the forefront of education decision-making in this country by developing plans on how children should best be educated and presenting these plans to policymakers at the local, state, and federal levels as well as to the public.

The AEA is not interested in counting the number of minutes a teacher is to work each school day. The AEA is above petty factory-like issues. The AEA's main objective is to raise the professional level of teaching.

Teachers need to act together in order to raise the bar for the profession. Until this is done, until teachers are the masters of their own domain, little progress will be made in the teaching of young people in America.

30

Teachers as Education Czars

Who should be in charge of medicine?
Answer: Doctors

Who should be in charge of legal questions?
Answer: Attorneys

Who should be in charge of teaching kids?
Answer: Politicians?

When forty-six of the nation's governors held a groundbreaking meeting on high school reform in February of 2005, no teachers were present. This is like holding hearings on tort reform without a single attorney there. Why would anybody intelligent do that?

Many of the profession's maladies can be traced to one perennial problem: Teachers have little control over what they do. They are subservient to principals, superintendents, and, above all else, politicians.

What's utterly frustrating for exemplary teachers is that there is a glass ceiling above their heads. No matter how hard they work, when it comes down to it, they are kept off the top floor of decision-making. Just when teachers feel they have reached a certain level of respectability in their profession—they sit on committees, chair departments, mentor other teachers—they are quickly slapped silly back to reality: They wield no authority. Despite their achievements, in the eyes of those in charge, they remain teachers. Nothing more.

They don't get paid well, they don't have any power, and they are public employees. All of this contributes to the image of a teacher who does the grunt work but is not needed for establishing education policy and reform.

Year after year the good teacher gets beaten down and either leaves the profession or retreats into her classroom cell.

How tragic that so many bright teachers are in this country's classrooms right now but rarely does anyone besides the students realize the brilliance of these people. These teachers could do wonders in transforming public schools if given the opportunity. Why won't anyone listen to them when it comes to how schools should be run?

California State University found that "having meaningful input in the decision-making process" increases teacher retention. Teachers who don't feel that their input is valued end up exiting the profession.

Whenever a state is going to adopt a new textbook or when politicians talk about what needs to be done in education, they always seem to forget to invite the people who have the most direct connection to the students—the teachers. So here you have a group of politicians, most of whom send their kids to private schools and have never spent a single day teaching a class, dictating the educational policies and procedures without the representation and advice of the people who do the teaching. It makes about as much sense as having these same politicians declare that they are going to discuss a new surgical procedure and not have a single surgeon in the room. That would never happen in the medical community, but it happens every day in education.

The best teachers are fiercely independent, self-motivating mavericks who disdain the regimental, controlling structure, rigid to the point of rigor mortis, that holds their drive in neutral. Such bureaucratic suffocation extinguishes the flames of so many creative minds.

It is difficult to work in a system where the teacher is accustomed to being the leader in the classroom, getting the respect of her students, yet by her principal and other upper-echelon school officials is perceived as a drone, whose voice and vision is stifled and stamped out, the worker bee who is not allowed to be a queen.

School districts will shell out big bucks for education experts, consultants, and specialists to come to their schools to discuss important topics, but pay nothing for their own in-house talent. What's the implication? That having your own teachers conduct workshops is not as meaningful or worth any money compared to listening to people who never taught a day of school in their lives yet believe they have all the answers?

Sheryl Boris-Schacter, former professor of educational leadership at Lesley University and currently an elementary school principal, succinctly described the limited role teachers traditionally play in an editorial for *Education Week:*

> Teachers rarely consider policymaking to be an integral part of their work; policymakers do not think of consulting teachers because of the history and tradition of task division; and few teachers would suggest that the best way to address educational issues is through increased student testing. Their input, therefore, could undermine the current political agenda. These conclusions are the result of several assumptions: teachers are poised to know the most effective instructional strategies to be used with students in their community; the American teaching force is overwhelmingly female, and there are lingering stereotypes regarding women, women who teach, and what constitutes "women's work"; the structure of schools and the school day prevents teachers from having the time to work effectively with colleagues on issues of policy; schools of education reinforce the teaching role as one that is classroom-based and substantially separate from engagement in policymaking; the profession is unnecessarily rigid regarding the roles people play. For example, principals rarely teach, teachers rarely engage in administrative work, and school board members do not often consult teachers or principals about setting policy.

Has anyone thought that by empowering teachers they are actually empowering students? The better teachers feel about the control they have over the job they do, the better job they will do. It's common sense.

It is hypocritical that teachers are expected to teach students how to be independent thinkers but when teachers exhibit their own independent thinking it is not solicited or desired.

However, a very curious thing happened in Chicago during the summer of 2006. Eighteen teachers were invited by the Center for Teaching Quality and the Joyce Foundation to discuss the issue of how best to compensate teachers. Barnett Berry, president of the center, envisions expanding this expert group of teachers, fourteen of whom are NBCTs, six being named Teachers of the Year, in order to give teachers a voice in forming education policy.

Jennifer Morrison, one of the teachers at the meeting, told *Education Week* that "teachers aren't expected to think beyond their own students or buildings—in fact, leading or contributing to the profession as a whole is discouraged because it takes teachers out of the classroom."

Another teacher said, "All teachers are not doing the same job, [but] I can't say that in a faculty meeting," and that the teacher group "would be fighting 'a culture and a mind-set' that mistrusts any behavior that distinguishes one teacher from another."

The group endorsed a form of performance pay but felt compelled to incorporate using test scores as a measure because, as one teacher put it, "No plan will fly if we don't say we'll use standardized tests."

Interesting that in two of America's three largest cities, New York and Chicago, mayors have taken control of the school districts, and in the second-largest city, Los Angeles, the process is under judicial review. Mayors Bloomberg, Daley, and Villaraigosa seemingly feel qualified to run schools, and thus far the results have been mixed. A couple of positive programs during Bloomberg's reign have been opening smaller high schools and stopping social promotion. On the other hand, many teachers feel that their voices have been stifled with the implementation of teacher-proof programs. One veteran teacher told the *Los Angeles Times* that "the creative spontaneity and the joy of teaching have been completely hijacked."

What a shame that they are all missing the boat. Education will not be improved by having mayors run schools.

Without an overhaul of the teaching profession, all other ideas mentioned in this book will do little to improve things. If teachers came first, the students would also come first.

As I was doing research for this book, I came across a report from the College Board, the folks who bring us the SAT and AP tests. The report, entitled "Teachers and the Uncertain American Future," from July 2006, demanded that all teachers receive a 15 percent boost in salary. So, of course, I was curious to see the whole report.

Looking over the names of the thirteen people listed as members of the Center for Innovative Thought, the subgroup responsible for the report, I found that not a single one was a classroom teacher; they were practically all from the university sphere. Below that list was one for the National Advisory Panel on Teacher Recruitment. None of those eight people were public school teachers, either.

On the very first page at the top there was a quote three times the size of the other text, attributed to (and I quote) the Teaching Commission (a blue-ribbon group led by former IBM CEO Louis V. Gerstner, Jr.), 2004. As I was reading the quote a sinking feeling came over me—hey, that quote is mine, from my first book! I jumped to a copy of the book and, sure enough, on the very first page of the preface, third paragraph, twelfth line, there it was:

> Many of the best and brightest college graduates continue to choose careers such as engineering and computer animation, where 22-year-olds can earn starting salaries of $40,000—a salary teachers in large metropolitan areas earn only after 10 years of work. Until the applicant pool is enlarged to attract more talented individuals from more lucrative fields, the most critical job in America will remain in critical condition.

Not a word altered, moved, or deleted. Verbatim. And I understood why I wasn't credited. I'm not a CEO of a major corporation. I'm just a classroom teacher, one of three million. Who am I? How dare I say something significant about the teaching profession? However, the person in charge of a Fortune 500 company, now there's someone we all need to stop what we're doing and listen intently to. If he can run a company like IBM then surely he knows what's best to be done in our schools and to our children, isn't that right?

Could you imagine if I criticized the way IBM was run and felt that I had a better idea on how to run that company? Would I be quoted? Would I have any authority to be consulted? Unfortunately it seems that everyone has an opinion about teachers and schools. Evidently teaching children is something that anybody with a viewpoint can write about in print or talk about on television. So rarely is that individual a working teacher. Most often it is a politician speaking for everybody.

Then to think that the College Board, which prides itself on being an entity devoted to quality in education, would make such a blunder as this.

I wonder, would they have used the quote if they knew it was little ol' me who said it? Would such a statement still warrant merit?

Oh, and by the way, this exact same quote from my book can be viewed on the Teaching Commission's own Web site . . . but it has *proper* attribution.

Funny, too, how I preach the gospel of honesty in writing to my own students. I have a lesson plan on plagiarism, using examples from former *New York Times* reporter Jayson Blair and noted historian Stephen Ambrose. Never in my wildest imagination did I think my own work would get stolen.

To the College Board's credit, once I brought the matter to their attention, they were apologetic and made the corrections. Perhaps plagiarism is the sincerest form of flattery. I guess I have finally "made it."

Such an injustice runs deep in the field of public education.

Teachers' thoughts and concerns are ignored, discounted, over-ruled. Teachers don't really matter to those in charge. Their principals and superintendents and politicians feed them the line about how important the classroom teacher is. But they don't mean it. For if teachers were truly at the top, those with the power would no longer have jobs, or certainly have significantly less power.

The time has come for teachers to grow up, to graduate. They need to be in charge of their own profession. Become National Board Certified, chair committees, lead state school boards, run for state superintendent. The president of the United States should create a new position of Education Czar that is independent of his cabinet, especially the Department of Education. The one requirement of the Education Czar? Several years of exemplary teaching experience.

What schools need is not more money. It's not even more teachers. And it's right within the four walls of so many of America's classrooms. The greatest resource a school has to offer is its finest teachers.

PART FOUR
The Way Schools Need to Be Funded

31

More Money Isn't the Answer

The more expensive the car the better the quality, right? A Lexus is better than a Honda, a Mercedes better than a Lexus, isn't that so?

An elegant French restaurant will use higher-quality ingredients than a greasy spoon café, correct?

The more money spent on education the better the students will learn? Not correct.

If schools were retail stores they would be Bloomingdale's in terms of expense but K-Mart in terms of results. You know that old saying of having champagne taste with a beer budget? The inverse is true with public schools, which have a champagne budget but with beer taste.

The one education area that the United States ranks high in when compared to other nations is its school funding, second only to Switzerland. Yet look at the fizzled bang we get for that buck.

Per-pupil spending has doubled during the last thirty years and in that time the percentage of students graduating from high school has remained unchanged.

In 2002–03, the average amount spent per child was $8,044. In 1961–62 that amount was $393; $2,382 when adjusted for inflation. Spending has nearly quadrupled in forty years yet the results remain stagnant. Washington, D.C., has the highest per-student spending in the country, yet it has some of the worst schools. Do you think children are being as well educated as they used to be—and at four times the cost?

Think about what public schools provide most parents:

- Full-day child care two-thirds of the year
- Child will learn (after all, something is bound to rub off)
- Cheap food
- Child plays with friends—a playdate every day!

Now look at what public schools provide those parents who demand more:

- The best teachers in America teaching their children
- The best-equipped classrooms
- The most up-to-date technology
- Principals who are at their beck and call
- Imaginative outside playgrounds
- Music- and arts-infused curriculum
- Healthy cafeteria menus
- And, ultimately, the best chance of their children attending prestigious universities

The idea that all students have access to the same education no matter the school has never been a reality. Parents in affluent communities like La Canada Flintridge and Orinda in California have a high bar of expectations and through tenaciousness and fund-raising efforts are able to meet their goals.

I'm not for punishing those schools whose parents have the wherewithal to raise millions in extra revenue. But is it not the job of government to ensure that basics like working facilities, sufficient books, and qualified teachers are maintained for all schools? Are libraries, sports programs, and counselors considered luxury items?

The problem isn't that schools don't receive enough money; it's how the funds are collected, doled out, and spent.

The advocates of increased funding for public schools, mainly districts and unions who become fast friends over this issue, keep asking for more and more money. If that additional funding actually bought better teachers then, yes, raise taxes. Instead, additional monies typically go toward creating new positions, new departments. Then when states face a budget crisis, districts claim that the cuts will hurt students in the classroom. That's bunk. It is going to mean that the principal who was given a new job title overseeing reading is now going to have to go back to being a principal of a school.

A recent California poll showed that most people believe that better use could be made of existing funds if local school boards had more control than the state.

Local control of schools is as anachronistic as a local Main Street full of mom-and-pop establishments. States pay for more than half of all education costs, and the federal government's share hovers around 7-8 percent.

Schools in New York, Texas, and California are mainly funded based on the Average Daily Attendance, or ADA. In other words, the more kids that show up at a school, the more money that school will receive. Other states like Florida still use attendance but only calculate it five times a year.

The word "audit" sends shivers down the spine of school personnel. That is why there are people who work at districts whose sole job is to keep track of the keeping track processes involving student attendance records.

Can you imagine the savings in terms of manpower and money if schools did not have to document the whereabouts of every single child for every single day of school?

The other problem with ADA is that it makes districts accept troublemakers just to get the bounty they bring into the school's coffers. It's the only reason why public schools use heroic measures to make sure kids are in school, that no matter the offense kids do not get kicked out or suspended, for that results in a loss of money. Who cares if a kid fresh out of juvenile hall may cause more damage than he is worth in attendance?

One parent's daughter was explicitly instructed by her homeroom teacher to come to school for that one period even if she was sick just so that the school could collect its ADA. Oh, and then she could go home?

Last year New York City Schools implemented a program called Opportunity NYC, which actually pays families up to fifty dollars a month if their children attend school 95 percent of the time, twenty-five dollars for attending parent-teacher conferences, fifty dollars for obtaining a library card, plus a four-hundred-dollar bonus for graduating. Who says education doesn't pay?

Schools should be funded based on how many teachers they need, not on how many students show up on a daily basis. That way a school wouldn't be forced to keep unruly children under its supervision.

Another funding source available for schools is grant money. My school received a $500,000 grant to take all ninth graders on an overnight camping trip on Catalina Island. Eight additional teachers could have been hired for that kind of money, but the grant didn't allow it. So instead the half a million got frittered away on some cockamamie idea that by paying for a weekend excursion with some psychobabble exercises thrown in somehow the grant would help students feel better about their school. Well, guess what? Any benefit from that experience was short-lived. Upon returning from the trip, students were supposed to attend weekly meetings with their "families," a teacher assigned to a small group of ninth graders, in order to strengthen their connection to school. Hardly any kids showed up for those meetings.

Usually more money for a school is a good thing but sometimes administrators feel pressured to spend the money just because it is there, not because there is a need for it. For example, due to a grant, the school could fund an extra advanced English class. Even though there weren't qualified students for such a class, the administration went ahead and pulled out students from regular ninth-grade classes and created a new one out of thin air, labeling it as advanced.

Another time my district received money to take students on field trips to a history museum. However, many teachers could not fit the trips into their lesson plans. Still, kids (and teachers) were strong-armed into going. The administrator in charge of the program sent the following e-mail out:

> These trips are sponsored by the local rotary club and not only is our superintendent a member but many of the members come from your school's neighborhood. And if these members' children do not go on these field trips it goes straight home!

These are the kinds of things that go on in our schools.

Then there are the out-and-out large donations from foundations. My hat's off to Mr. Bill Gates, who instead of going the route of his colleagues who donate profusely to universities took the road less traveled. Since 2000, his Bill and Melinda Gates Foundation has invested billions in public schools. He is by far the largest donor to K–12 education in the United States. However, when all his contributions and those of others are added up, it is estimated that private foundations' donations equate to one-third of 1 percent of all education spending. Therefore, asking wealthy benefactors to pay for schools isn't the answer.

Have you ever wondered, if money was no object, how much money should be spent on a quality public school program? That's what folks in California wanted to discover.

Since one out of every nine students in America goes to school in the Golden State, and one out of every ten teachers works there, it's important to study it. At a cost of $3 million and a length of 1,700 pages, a report came out in 2007 on the state of California's schools that estimated it would take an annual public school bill of $1.5 trillion in order to overcome all of the system's inadequacies. Don't forget, the whole country currently spends $0.5 trillion, so this amount solely for California is truly on steroids.

There is one area of untapped revenues that could go a long way toward adding quality to public schools, but it is considered so taboo that it requires its own chapter. Read on.

Bill Parents

Ask any involved parent what she expects from public schools and it is nothing short of a first-class, top-notch education without having to pay a private school price tag of $20,000 a year.

Well, guess what, folks? It ain't possible, it just ain't possible. All children in America are guaranteed a free education, not a free outstanding education.

With a population of three hundred million, and an annual education bill nearing half a trillion dollars, each man, woman, and child pays $1,666 a year for public schools. Not a bad bargain, actually, especially since everybody expects something miraculous from a government bureaucracy that is free and open to every single individual, one that has hardly changed over 150 years.

Frankly, it is remarkable that for such a backward, third-world system marvelous teachers do exist in America's classrooms, and that so many young people survive public schools unscathed, with some learning achieved.

Schools have been rightfully criticized for not having higher expectations of their students, and teachers have been rightfully criticized for not having enough rigor in their lessons. However, the outsiders—from politicians to parents to colleges to employers—have unrealistically high expectations.

If parents truly wish for an exemplary education experience for their child, then it is time to start charging for public education, something nominal like a two-hundred-dollar tuition per year. In a two-hundred-day school calendar, it works out to a single dollar per

230

day for a parent to educate her child. Even if half of the children's parents paid it, close to $5 billion would be generated. While equating to only 1 percent of the annual education bill, that money could be used by individual schools in any way they wish, from incentives for recruiting better teachers to reinstatement of art programs to office supplies.

There should be no sticker shock about this. Parents already pay for athletic uniforms, musical instruments, lab fees, school-embossed clothing, and field trips. How about different levels of tuition whereby five hundred dollars a year would cover all expenses so that parents wouldn't be nickel-and-dimed to death from schools week after week to give five dollars for the music program, order Domino's for science camp, or donate crayons and paper clips. Children would no longer have to go begging relatives and neighbors to buy coupon books or have their cars washed. The programs would receive the necessary funding through the tuition.

Frequently major office supply stores will print a list of supplies requested by individual schools so that parents can easily purchase them. These items typically aren't extra or unusual items to extend the education experience; instead, the requests are for staples such as reams of paper, colored pencils, and tape. At my children's schools, parents are asked to bring either a ream of copy paper or three dollars when visiting during Open House. You mean schools can't afford their own paper? They should be ashamed of themselves.

By having parents pay tuition schools would no longer have to go on their hands and knees for a ream of paper.

Parents who feel that cutting box tops of cereal boxes (which pays ten cents each), buying gift wrap and candy, or picking lottery numbers will help schools, think again. Who is profiting more from your purchases?

Ever get tired of the ROM (restaurant of the month) that will donate 10–15 percent of your purchases to the school? Well, let's see. If you spend twenty dollars on food that means the school gets . . . are you ready? . . . two dollars! Yippee! That will make an impact for sure. Why should people spend money at restaurants and buy inferior products from gift catalogs just so pennies from their purchases can go to their children's schools? Isn't giving money to schools outright to improve young people's education motivation enough? Why do we have to attach any giving to feeding our faces? What's up with that? I would rather (and many other parents would, too) forgo spending the twenty dollars on overpriced, undercooked pizza and instead hand over a five- or ten-dollar bill directly to the school. Schools would receive a lot more money that way. Wouldn't that be better for everyone (except the restaurant owners)?

Ask any parent who's participated in AYSO, the youth soccer organization. After parents pay the registration fee, it seems additional expenses pop up each week, such as a banner for the team, hardware for the banner, treats and drinks, and gifts for the coaches and team parent. Every week soccer parents are asked to bring in a few dollars more to cover an added expense. I would rather pay 50 percent more in the registration fee and have everything taken care of.

You know those food products that ask you to send in the box tops in order to help schools? Have you ever calculated how much cereal you have to buy in order for money to trickle down to your children's school? I checked my son's school online to discover that in one year a total of one dollar was donated to the school. Imagine that, a whole dollar! Why, with that kind of money the school could buy one-third of one ream of paper.

While Box Tops for Education was a nice idea, the problem with it is that its impact is miniscule. In ten years, $175 million has been raised. That averages out to $17.5 million in a year, or $1,250 per school district, not per school. Think of all the products people had to buy just for that and how much more could have been earned if people simply made a direct donation to the school. But that wouldn't have helped out the participating businesses.

It reminds me of how silly state lotteries are in terms of selling tickets in order to help out education. The amount states receive from lotteries for K–12 funding ranges from less than 1 percent to 5 percent, according to a study conducted by *The New York Times*.

The pittance schools get from lottery funds should be called guilt money for those who wish to be instant millionaires for wasting their cash week after week, selfishly gambling on a big payoff for themselves. And this is supposed to make people feel good because they are supporting the schools? How many people would stop buying lottery tickets if schools didn't receive a penny?

Another area parents foot the bill for is driver training. One of the budget cuts in many school districts in the last several years has been the elimination of driver ed classes in high school. Does this mean teenagers aren't getting driver's licenses? No, it means that parents are forking over two to three hundred dollars for their children to learn how to drive.

Besides paying tuition, students should buy their own books or CD-ROMs. Students are expected to bring their own pencils and paper, they are expected to buy their own lunch (whoops, over half of American children receive free or reduced lunches), so why shouldn't they buy their own books as well? If they don't want to lug around books, they can bring their own laptops to school like college students do. What? Laptops are expensive? Well, so are cell phones and iPods, yet young people seem to have no problem having Mom and Dad pay for those items.

When did everybody begin to assume that schoolchildren were entitled to free textbooks in the first place? Schools are frequently criticized for not having enough books or for having damaged books. Well, if you had parents take care of that expense, those problems would go away. If a student knew that his parents purchased the books, there would be less chance of the books getting lost or damaged since his parents would have to pay for replacements. The cost of books makes up a large chunk of a school district's annual budget.

Kids aren't stupid. They know the value of some things if they themselves, meaning their parents, paid for them rather than the school issuing them for free. Notice how upset teens get if their cell phones or iPods are confiscated by the school. It's like stripping them of their clothes; they feel naked without the technology. But lose a textbook? No big whoop. They didn't have to pay for it and now they don't have to lug it around. What a win-win situation. I wonder if kids would care that much about their cell phones being confiscated if schools gave one out free to every student just as they do books.

Attaching a price to "free" services will help students and parents understand the value of education. Psychologically it's interesting how people view something that is "free": They tend to place less value on it than if they have to pay for it. In my journalism classes we use the *Los Angeles Times* as a learning tool. Many newspapers offer similar education programs allowing teachers to receive free delivery of papers for their students.

The first time I did this I noticed how abused (if you can assign such a strong verb to an inanimate object) and unused the papers were; some left on the ground, some with sections still inserted clearly unopened. I told the class that the papers, while free to them, are not really free, that subscribers to the *Times* donate papers to schools. But since the kids didn't have to pay, the newspapers held no value to them. Now, instead of ordering copies for all students, I only have a handful.

Walk onto campuses right after lunch, especially at high schools, and notice the garbage strewn around. Would kids still do this if they (or more accurately their parents) had a vested interest in the property, if their parents actually wrote a check for that institution?

For years California community colleges charged no tuition. Then twenty years ago they started implementing a fifty-dollars-per-semester fee, which rose to a gigantic sixty dollars per semester in the 1990s. "How dare they" demonstrations broke out proclaiming the beginning of the end of community colleges. Well, today the colleges have more students than ever before, and the current fee is twenty dollars per unit. For an average class load of fifteen units, the cost of tuition for one semester of college is three hundred dollars. Nearly half of community college students get their tuition waived anyway due to their low-income status.

The more affluent public schools have high-powered parents who do serious fund-raising to the tune of millions of dollars. If some parents can afford $40,000 birthday parties, then paying a $200 tuition shouldn't be that much of an issue.

Unfortunately, expecting people to give out of the goodness of their hearts is a dream. That's why each parent has to be billed. Even the wealthiest people don't seem to make enough money to be liberally giving it away. In 2006, sixty wealthy Americans whose combined worth was $630 billion donated $51 billion of it, or about 8 percent. Does that sound like a good amount? Warren Buffett, quite an anomaly among philanthropists, was solely responsible for $44 of that $51 billion, meaning the fifty-nine others donated a grand total of $7 billion, or 1 percent of their value. Cheapskates, huh?

If schools continue to be funded based on average daily attendance, why not bill parents the cost of each day their children are truant? Just as more people these days get charged for using emergency services incorrectly, why not charge parents of children who don't use the schools they are supposed to attend?

One district in Santa Cruz, California, is doing just that: billing parents of children who miss a day of school due to nonillness reasons such as a vacation trip. The letter sent home entitled "If You Play, Please Pay" informs parents that one child absent for one day costs the Scotts Valley School District $36.13. In 2005–06, the district lost nearly one-quarter of a million dollars due to students missing school for reasons other than legitimate illnesses. While paying the bill is voluntary, many parents, perhaps out of guilt, gladly pay it, further proof that there are parents out there who would pay for school tuition.

Look, nobody enjoys paying for services that used to be free. However, a generation of people have grown up with cable television and don't even remember that TV used to cost nothing. Two hundred dollars a year is half of what the average person spends on watching television. Which is more important?

Cut Special Education and Title I

Here are two significant statistics:

- 12 percent of all students are categorized as special education
- 22 percent of all education funding goes to special education

It costs twice as much to educate a special education child as it does for a non–special ed child.

All parents thank God (or whomever) for having healthy kids. Unfortunately, not all children are. Those children with physical and mental disabilities are served in public schools under special education funding. What started out as a way to help these students get a better education has ended up hurting non–special ed kids.

For years special ed students were relegated to special schools. That changed in 1975 when President Ford signed the Education for All Handicapped Children Act, now known as the Individuals with Disabilities Education Act (IDEA). Suddenly over one million children previously kept at home or in institutions flooded the public schools, draining district budgets.

Originally, the federal government was to provide 40 percent of the extra costs. However, as recently as 2002, that participation amounted to only 18 percent, leaving local and state governments to make up the difference. This means less money available for regular ed students. In 2004, even though government sources provided over $4 billion for California's 700,000 special ed students, it was not enough. Another $1.6 billion was siphoned off the general ed

236

budget, according to the *San Francisco Chronicle*. Another way of looking at this is that California kids received over one-fourth less money than they should have because of special education.

IDEA also covers children from birth to twenty-two years of age.

Well, it's a bad IDEA. When it comes to special education, the needs of the few far outweigh the needs of the many. The pendulum has swung too far the other way. It is not unusual to find students on gurneys being wheeled to class by nursing personnel paid for by the school district. Is the purpose of public education to nurse students or to teach them? Why not have insurance companies and social services kick in for the needs of these students? Why is it wholly the school's responsibility? Because it's the law, one that is the fourth-most litigated federal statute in the nation, with $146 million spent by school districts to resolve disputes.

While it is not politically correct to say this, a cap needs to be put on special ed funding. The public needs to be informed of what is going on, how special education takes money that is already in the pipeline away from other areas that could positively impact many more children, and how certain parents selfishly exploit their children's disabilities in order for personal gains.

Parents used to campaign for their children to be labeled "gifted"; now, they desire the "special education" designation. Why? Because they get more services, such as additional time to complete standardized testing including AP and SAT tests. Plus, these parents quickly learn how to use the system. Want something for your child and not getting it? No problem. Just threaten to sue. Don't worry. Your demands will be met.

Not all parents of special ed students do this. However, a good number do hold their districts hostage and milk them for all they're worth. Meanwhile, as mentioned earlier, gifted kids continue to receive fewer services.

You see, there is plenty of money in education. It's just that some parents divert more than their fair share from the rest of the taxpaying parents. And they know that, so they hire attorneys who can manipulate the pockmarked laws to their benefit and to the

detriment of everybody else. And what politician in his right mind is
going to call them out on this? What is more politically incorrect
than taking a penny away from a kid in a wheelchair, right?

Some special ed services appear questionable, to put it mildly.
Riding horses may be fun and make special ed kids feel good, but
what the hell does that have to do with education? And if it is part of
an education-related curriculum, then why aren't regular kids getting the horseback riding as well? The choice a district ends up making, however, is one of damage control. Paying for horseback riding
is less expensive than holding a $40,000 hearing to question it. The
cheaper way out for districts is to settle out of court.

One California family hired an attorney who was able to strong-
arm the school district into paying for four years of tuition ($30,000
a year) at a private school in Maine as well as transportation costs
for the family to travel between both ends of the country. The incredible part of this story is that the school in Maine didn't even
have a special education program. *Un*believable. In the hearing over
this case the district was found to have overlooked filling out a form,
and so ended up paying for all the family's expenses, including their
$50,000 legal bill. Attorneys are diligently on the lookout for just
such omissions to make their clients victors over school districts.

Time magazine highlighted one family with an autistic child
who was enrolled in a special boarding school costing $135,000 a
year. The family asked the school district to pay the tuition since
federal law "requires school districts to provide an extended school
day and even residential services if a special-education student
needs them." When the district refused to pay for the twenty-four-
hour high-priced care, the parents sued and won. The loser wasn't
the district even though it put them back almost $200,000 in legal
fees, but the rest of the youngsters who disproportionately receive
less funding than special education children. As general counsel for
the National School Boards Association Francisco Negrón inter-
prets IDEA, the law "guarantees only a free 'appropriate' education.
It doesn't say . . . 'free *optimal* public education'" (emphasis added).

More special ed students are enrolling in private schools, then billing public schools. In the 2005–06 school year, New York City schools footed a $6.5 million bill for its more than two thousand unilateral placements (when parents place their children in facilities without the local school district's approval), half of those cases involving children who never attended the district's schools for even one day.

Last fall, the U.S. Supreme Court ruled on such a unilateral placement case involving Thomas E. Freston, cofounder of MTV, and the New York City school district. Freston believed the district should have paid for his son's private school tuition. Because the justices split their vote 4–4, the lower federal appeals court ruling in favor of Freston was affirmed. Incidentally, Mr. Freston supposedly received an $85 million severance package when he left his president and CEO positions at Viacom. Hmm, I don't know, but don't you think he could have afforded to pay the $22,000 tuition himself? Why suck a public school district dry?

Strict guidelines for proper screening of children need to be established to ensure that children categorized as "special ed" truly have special needs.

The President's Commission on Excellence in Special Education's 2002 report states that two million students get tagged as special ed "simply because they cannot read." Over 10 percent of New York District high school students were classified as special education in the 2005–06 school year.

Once a child is designated special ed, a paperwork juggernaut unfolds. There are hundreds of documents that need to be filled out, the main one called an IEP, Individual Education Plan, which involves a personal meeting with the student's teachers and parents present. In order to have this done substitutes are required to relieve the classroom teacher to attend the meeting.

Having teachers fill out logs and anecdotal forms and attend IEPs whittles away the time spent on teaching. And people wonder why special ed teachers are in such short supply.

The latest trend in special education is called "collaboration." Again, educators like coming up with terms that at first glance seem positive; collaborate, to work with others. However, the collaboration model involves placing a special ed teacher and a regular ed teacher together in the same classroom. The idea is that even though the teacher may only have three or four special ed students in a class of thirty-five, lessons need to be designed with the special ed students in mind.

Do you know how much this has got to cost to pay for two teachers in one room, serving only a handful of students? All the students in the class get lessons delivered in slow motion, taking a concept that should be completed in an hour and breaking it into smaller parts that stretch over days—not the rigor everyone is clamoring about that needs to take place in public education.

This would be like teaching a sixth-grade class but designing the lessons for kindergartners. Does anybody think about the vast majority of students sitting there who don't need large-print texts or slower-paced lessons in order to master the material?

Once more we have a situation where the good of the few outweighs the good of the many. How wrongheaded can you get?

When I wondered if this collaboration model was going to happen in the AP classes, the administrator shook her head adamantly: "Oh no, not in the AP classes." And you know why? Because those parents of those children would not put up with such nonsense.

Special education funding must be limited. Let the vast majority of children get more of their fair share of the education pie. Financially able parents as well as state medical agencies should help with the financial burden of this cost.

Besides cutting special education, another way of recouping money is canceling Title I.

After forty years of existence and nearly a quarter of a trillion dollars spent, the federal government's Title I program targeting economically disadvantaged children should be dissolved. Take the annual $13 billion and divide it equally among school districts based on population. No strings attached.

Despite being created to help out less-fortunate children, the Title I program has hardly had an effect on improving the education of the most impoverished children in America. Even former secretary of education Rod Paige said, "After spending $125 billion of Title I money over twenty-five years, we have virtually nothing to show for it."

All the computers, textbooks, and adult aides (which is where the money goes) have had little long-lasting impact.

Almost six out of every ten U.S. public schools receive Title I dollars. If a school is not officially declared Title I, meaning that at least 60 percent of a school's population is on the free or reduced lunch program (thirty million young people utilize this program funded by the Department of Agriculture), then any Title I funds that go to a school must be carefully monitored and used on items that will be exclusively for Title I students. So, let's say a teacher has ten Title I students in a classroom of thirty-five, leaving twenty-five non–Title I students, and wants another computer in the room. Title I will buy that computer, but only those ten students may use it. Do you honestly think the teacher is going to enforce such a restriction? Yeah, just like the copyright law that all teachers ignore when they photocopy everything from sample textbooks to newspaper articles. Or the software law that requires a site license for every single computer using a particular program.

You see, there is no way to enforce that only Title I students use Title I resources. For years people in charge of school budgets have played the shell game with categorical and grant monies, moving money from one account to the next. They fudge when it comes to which student population is being served with the expenditures.

Since Title I gives each state a portion in relation to that spending per pupil, poorer states with less funding end up with less Title I money. Yet again, poor students get less. Berkeley law professor Goodwin Liu refers to this as "education apartheid."

It's time to do away with nondiscretionary funding policies. Just give the money to the schools. Trust that the people in charge will do what's best for their particular student population.

PART FIVE

The Way Students and Their Parents
Need to Treat School

34

Kids Gone Wild

- A sixth-grade teacher at Simon Elementary School in Washington, D.C., was stabbed with a knife thrown by a twelve-year-old boy who had been spanked for attacking the teacher with a broken bottle.
- Teachers in the East St. Louis, Illinois, school system have become so terrified . . . that three out of four are carrying guns to class.
- A new wave of violence is sweeping U.S. classrooms. . . . Statistics suggest that more and more teachers are quitting their jobs out of sheer fear of their students.
- Students, realizing that punishment is unlikely, are soon out of control.

The above excerpts began an article in *Time* magazine from . . . 1969. See what I mean about how little has changed in public schools?

A big deal is made to inform parents that their children are in a safe and secure environment while at school. No one stops and thinks how important it is to have a safe and secure environment for teachers to work in as well.

For too long students have been getting away with murder (almost literally) with their antisocial behavior at school. If schools wish to provide quality education then those not showing any interest in school should be permanently expelled from the system.

In that *Time* magazine article, Philadelphia recorded over one hundred attacks against teachers for the entire 1968–69 school year. For the first half of the 2006–07 school year, over four hundred assaults on teachers were reported. Now there's a change. But here's the scary part: One out of every four assaults was perpetrated by a child in the *fourth grade or younger*. Even teaching the golden rule can't help some of these students.

The Pennsylvania Department of Education had to create a hot-line for teachers to report assaults since not all incidents are reported by principals. *Education Week* highlighted one of the more brutal attacks.

> A 15-year-old male student at Germantown High in north Philadelphia broke mathematics teacher Frank Burd's neck when he struck the teacher several times. Minutes before the assault, Mr. Burd, 60, had confiscated an iPod from a 17-year-old male student who . . . followed the teacher from his classroom into a hallway, threatening him. The 17-year-old either tripped or pushed Mr. Burd, who fell into the 15-year-old student. That student then hit the teacher two or three times, causing him to hit his head on a locker and fall.

Paul G. Vallas, the chief executive officer of the district, tried to downplay the number of incidents by saying that "some of these could have been a push or a brush up against a teacher." What? That's okay? It's no big deal if a student pushes a teacher? This guy needs training on what constitutes proper behavior toward a teacher. A push or a brush is inappropriate, got it?

As bad as that incident was, it is nothing compared to what was recently going on in Thailand. After the killing of two dozen teachers in an eighteen-month period, guns were purchased for teachers. But did they really want guns? Yes—two thousand educators requested them. But don't worry if teachers knew how to use the guns or not because the Thai government had its military provide training. Puts a whole new spin on that maxim "spare the rod," doesn't it?

Students and their parents should have to sign a code of conduct upon the children's enrollment that makes it clear that attending public school in the United States is a privilege not a right, and if a student does not follow proper behaviors (and the students themselves should be part of developing such a code), he will be permanently expelled, not just from a particular school but from the system. Just like when driver's licenses are taken away from repeatedly drunk drivers, if a young person repeatedly is in trouble, then he must be barred from school.

Quite clearly things are out of whack when teachers are penalized and students are not, when teachers are held accountable but parents are left off the hook.

We live today in an era where parents punch out hockey coaches and speak badly about their kids' teachers in front of their children.

Three out of four secondary teachers stated in a Public Agenda poll that dealing with misbehaved students makes them less effective teachers. One in three teachers either has thought about quitting due to unruly kids or knows of someone who actually did. As Public Agenda's president Ruth Wooden puts it in a *USA Today* interview, "A few troublemakers . . . tyrannize the rest of the class."

Teachers surveyed said that most of their problematic students throw in their face that they have rights and that their parents can sue.

Administrators need to do much more in supporting teachers. They like to create ways to make sure that teachers sending bad kids out is the absolute last thing that is done. If you're an administrator, do you want your office overrun with unruly kids? No. You want these hooligans to stay someplace; that is, in the classrooms.

It's troubling to see young teachers with incredible patience do the best they can with these kids who clearly do not want to be in school.

That is why hard-to-teach classes should be taught by veteran teachers, not so much because veteran teachers can do a better job, but a new teacher with so many innocent ideals should not be tainted by the worst kids at a school at the beginning of her career.

One new teacher discovered a student with a lighter and reported it, yet the kid didn't even get suspended. So after a while teachers get the drift—the administration doesn't support them; they just have to deal with these kids all alone. Again, these kids should go to work, do hard labor somewhere. Clearly, if a kid is in the back of a room gnawing on sunflower seeds, texting a friend, listening to his iPod, and causing mischief, he is no longer interested in school. So why force him to stay there? It's better for him if he's gone, it's better for the teacher if he's gone, and most important, it's better for the rest of those students in the room who wish to continue their education. It's maddening that schools cower and allow kids to dictate policy.

I had one student who was upset that I didn't give him a point—that's right, a single point—for reading his new ending to John Steinbeck's *The Pearl* to the class. Why didn't he get credit? Because he wrote about torture and alcoholism and wanted to get laughs from the class. He approached me after class to ask why he didn't get the point. I told him it was because what he wrote was inappropriate. Besides, a classroom is not a comedy club. He promptly turned around and said as loud as he could, "That's bullshit!" I immediately called him back into the room and he refused two times before I gave him the third and final warning, speaking to him as one does to a child: "I'll count to three and when I do you better be back in the room sitting down. One . . . two . . . three." He sat back down.

This was the same student whom I had reprimanded a week earlier for his poor behavior. When I asked him why he misbehaved, he said that I hadn't earned his respect yet. Imagine that. The teacher hadn't earned the respect of the student. My, my. I explained to him that he had our teacher-student relationship backward. It was his job to earn my respect, not the other way around.

I had an aggressive male student who would raise his hand to ask questions unrelated to what the class was discussing. If I didn't call on him he would blurt out, "I'm a student with a question and it's your job to call on me." If I did call on him, his wiseacre remark would cause a ripple of giggles.

After class I asked him to tell me why I had asked him to stay after class. He said, "That's the question I have for you. Why am I staying? I'm a student and you're a teacher and you're supposed to answer my questions." The only thing I could say at that point was "Have a nice weekend."

One student rushed out of my room shouting, "I can't believe this shit," loud enough for both floors of classrooms to hear, including her own thirty-five classmates sitting there. What caused her outburst? It was one of those tough situations for a teacher when you see a student in distress emotionally, who doesn't turn any work in and looks troubled. You basically have two options: One, ignore it and don't get involved, which, sad to say, is the safest route for a teacher. Or, seek help for the young person, which I did in this case. Because I spoke to a counselor about the girl, the counselor called my room to send for her. When the girl got the call to go to the counseling office, she must have sensed that I initiated the contact (damn me!) and so I was thanked with the obscenity-laced exit.

When I observe other teachers, I make a point not to interfere with the goings-on in the classroom. I try to be invisible. However, one time I had to intervene. A tenth grader was in the back of the room talking nonstop during class, using a cell phone as well as profanity, creating quite a disturbance. I told him to go outside. In a huff and a puff, he did. I asked for his phone. He refused. I then asked him for his ID. He claimed he didn't have one. When I asked him to walk with me to the office, he said, "Fuck this, fool." That's when I called for security. But wait, there's more.

When the security guard, a man in his fifties, and I walked the student to the office, he saw a friend on the softball field and yelled out to him. I told him to go quietly. He retorted hostilely, "Leave me alone, fool." The guard told him to stop speaking that way, and the fifteen-year-old yelled at this man old enough to be his father, "Kiss my ass. Fuck this goddamn shit," right outside the administration office, so several others heard him. Even when he was in the assistant principal's office, he brusquely threw down his ID card on the desk. It turned out that he was a frequent visitor to the AP's office. And what was his punishment? Only a five-day suspension. For speaking that way to authority figures? If inmates treated the guards the way students treat teachers, they would be placed in solitary confinement. This is a punk who doesn't deserve a free public education.

A somewhat funny episode of student misbehavior occurred in

2007 when a city bus carrying Mayor Antonio Villaraigosa and L.A. Unified Superintendent David L. Brewer III was tagged with graffiti right outside Santee Education Complex, a fairly new high school near downtown Los Angeles. The whole point of the officials riding the bus was to demonstrate to students how safe it was to take the bus now that it stopped right behind the school. Oh well. Fortunately the media was also on board; they took photos of the teen doing the tagging and eventually he was caught.

The disturbing part of the story was how the adults reacted to the vandalistic act. At first the mayor said the right thing, that the youth should have to perform one hundred hours of community service by cleaning buses, an apt punishment. A day later, however, he agreed with the school's principal that the youth's marking a public bus was "a cry for help." If that's the case, then around graffiti-scarred downtown L.A. there must be a river of tears. The principal, who was also along for the ride, said that what the student "needs the most is to be surrounded by people who are . . . nonjudgmental." No, what the kid needs is punishment. The mayor offered to personally mentor the youth, a hoodlum who already has counselors, social workers, and psychologists at his service free of charge. What more must be done *for* him before he starts doing things for himself?

Often parents are asked, in cases of unruly behavior, to accompany their children to school for a day. You can guess what results. The child with the parent there magically transforms into a model pupil. Once the parent exits so do the model behaviors.

You know how peace officers have cameras mounted near the front of their vehicles in order to have a record of how suspects act when pulled over? Perhaps cameras need to be mounted in classrooms as well. Teachers should videotape classes with badly behaved students and force parents to watch how their children act at school. Call it *Kids Gone Wild* or *The Super Nanny: School Edition*. I videotaped one veteran teacher's class and was amazed at how many kids acted out, even knowing I was videotaping them.

I observed one tenth-grade class where the students had a

complete disregard for their teacher. Even though the instructor made a concerted effort to connect with his students by circulating around the room to shake each and every one of their hands with a quick "how are you today," they took advantage of his goodwill. In one thirty-minute period I observed: two boys arm wrestling, two girls resting their heads on their fully closed backpacks (sitting directly in front of the teacher), four students continuously interrupting the teacher's lesson by complaining how hot the room was, three students having a private conversation laden with profanities about a party where one of them was going to get drunk. All these things were happening while the teacher was talking to the class. The fact that he did nothing to stop these interruptions meant that they must commonly occur and he has ultimately tuned them out or given up managing the class altogether (which is quite depressing).

When a classroom in Louisiana was left unsupervised a few students had sex as others watched. The most troubling aspect of this story? It was a fifth-grade class.

As mentioned in chapter 16, schools should be viewed as special places where certain behaviors are to be expected. Think of how much more enjoyable school would be if misbehaving kids faced real consequences: Shape up or stay home.

35

Meet the Worst Teachers: The Parents

While visiting a Barnes & Noble bookstore in Denver I noticed a huge sign posted above a Thomas the Tank Engine play set in the children's section of the store: "Parents, please keep your children in sight at all times." I thought to myself, "You've got to be kidding." Establishments have to actually post signs reminding parents to be parents? What's the next sign that has to go up? "Please pay for your purchases"? "Make sure to breathe in and out occasionally"?

The worst teachers are not found in classrooms but in homes. Disciplining one's children has become as out of fashion as typewriters, record stores, and unpierced body parts.

Surveys show an area that both parents and teachers agree on— that unruly children are a direct result of poor parenting and kids not being taught how to behave.

If parents did a better job parenting, schools wouldn't have so many students who exhibit poor behavior. Frequently when I've had students with issues I soon realize why the children act the way they do upon meeting the parents.

Meet today's modern parent: weak, out of control, litigious.

One mother deliberately placed one of her sons at a different school from her smarter son so that the struggling one wouldn't bother his brother. Yeah, but what about him bothering the other parents' children and the teachers?

I spoke to a mother about her daughter who was failing my English class. I reminded her over the phone that her daughter received an F on her report card issued weeks earlier. "Do you remember her grade?" Her reply, "No, I haven't had a chance to open her grades yet." After two weeks? What kind of parent is that? No wonder the student is failing if there is no accountability at home.

Too many parents cave in to the whines and demands of their children. One student I know was given a brand-new expensive car from his father on the condition that his grades improve. What do you think happened? The kid got the car and forgot about doing well in school. Despite poor grades, the teenager kept the car. What kind of lesson does that teach?

Once on a cross-country train ride I had a conversation with Randy, an Amtrak sleeper car attendant, about how children are not disciplined anymore. We were talking about parents traveling with young children who have to make many stops since it's hard for kids to tolerate a long drive. He said that his mother taught them how to tolerate long drives. "How?" I asked. "By simply not stopping."

One surefire way to get a student to turn against you is by suggesting that he has a bad attitude, a red-letter label for parents who likewise have one. They do not want teachers referring to their little loved ones as having a "bad attitude." It's one of those phrases like "please settle down" or "do not talk when someone else is speaking" that is nomenclature reserved exclusively for parents, never to be uttered by another adult, including a teacher.

One student who had a bad attitude embarrassed a young girl in my class, so I asked him to apologize to her in front of the class. This led to an all points bulletin–like megaconference in the administration office the following week. "How dare you tell our son that he has to learn how to act properly!" was how the meeting began. If only the conference could have been videotaped so the two of them could be forced to watch themselves and then, using a lie detector, admit that they, too, had bad attitudes. As if to show off her superior status to me, the mother proclaimed, "My husband works in the film industry and people don't treat other people like that." Oh, and that is a much more legitimate occupation than teaching, eh?

Sometimes it seems that parents just want to vent and are not interested in hearing the teacher's perspective. I had a student who refused to revise her writing. She decided that she wasn't going to change a single word in her paper. What bothered me, though, was the way she responded to my comments about her writing as if wondering who was I, Mr. English Majored, Master Degreed, National Board Certified Teacher and Published Author, analyzing a fifteen-year-old's essay? I told the young lady that she had a bad attitude and should rethink redoing the paper. Not ten minutes passed by after the class was over when I got a phone call from that girl's mother (ahh, aren't cell phones wonderful?). She took umbrage that I would say her daughter had a bad attitude. "Where do you come off saying that to my daughter?" Before I could breathe, she bulldozed her way through the conversation, not allowing me a word, hanging up with a "Happy Thanksgiving." By the way, the parent never appeared for the conference she herself had arranged and I never heard back from her again. Her daughter ended up failing the class due to over twenty truancies. Obviously, something else was going on in that household.

A Dallas mother, upset that her daughter's seventh-grade science teacher admonished the child for being in the hallway without a pass, walked right into the science class and beat up and kicked the teacher in front of everyone. P.S., the woman guilty of the attack was a teacher herself. You see, the self-hatred thing in action. Go figure.

Nowadays, many parents take a different view when it comes to deciding when it is reasonable for children to be absent. I had a parent who was very concerned about her child's low grade in my English class. Yet she scheduled his regular orthodontist appointments in the morning at the same time as my class. How could she not see the connection there?

Where I work April 24 is the day to remember the Armenian genocide and many Armenian parents allow their children to miss school. Supposedly these youngsters attend church or other remembrance activities. But just how many of the absentees actually do?

Schools already eliminate instructional time in order to hold schoolwide assemblies discussing the Armenian genocide and other atrocities. And on top of that kids get a day off? How inappropriate that so many young people use anniversary of genocide as their excuse to ditch school. As one would expect, the majority of students who don't go to school are just the ones who need even more days of instruction.

Why can't churches organize remembrances after 3:00 P.M., or hold them on weekends or in the evenings? Or, better yet, schools could have field trips to remembrance ceremonies. That way children can still be in their classes part of the day and the outing can be used in an educational way.

And how does the district respond? It looks the other way because by the time April rolls around attendance is no longer used to calculate payments to schools. However, when the Day of the Epiphany comes in January, and attendance is critical for receiving money from the state, the district decided to officially close schools down since it was losing one-quarter of a million dollars by having students choose to be absent. In other words, making sure kids are in school is not the main priority; the money is.

Members of my own family were not impacted directly by the Holocaust; however, my grandparents fled Russia in 1922 due to the Cossacks, who also killed a couple of my mother's siblings.

Even though I was aware of the tragedies that had befallen the Jewish people, my parents never instructed me to not go to school in order to observe a day of remembrance. If anything, in their eyes, the best way to remember what happened to the Jews was to make myself as successful as possible and that included attending school every day. That's the most fitting tribute young people can make to those who came before them and perished tragically.

Education codes do not allow teachers to penalize students for absences. In other words, a student who misses a whole week of school cannot be penalized for missing a whole week of school. How would that policy play out in the business world? Don't work for a week but still get paid for it. What educators do to get around this is give students participation points. So if a student doesn't show up, that is one day less of an opportunity to earn points. This is silly. Unless there is a legitimate reason why a student is absent, that student should be penalized for being absent.

With a longer school year, students could be given ten "free" days like any employee. These could be used for religious holidays, doctor appointments, vacation days. For the ten days, students could be given make-up work. Beyond that, there should be none; otherwise, students have no reason to attend school.

Schools are always clamoring for more involvement from parents. However, there are involved caring parents and then there are the in-your-face-I'll-sue parents.

How shameful that we have parents in this country who view school districts as cash cows and will come up with the most frivolous lawsuits to drain the legal resources of schools. Two Boston couples filed a federal lawsuit against the school district because a second-grade teacher read to her class *King and King,* a storybook about two princes who fall in love. The parents claimed that their civil rights were violated. But remember: In Massachusetts, same-sex marriage is legal.

If a student were to write a story about killing his teacher, should that student be suspended? Not if you're Rachel Boim, who as a sixth grader from Atlanta, Georgia, wrote such a thing in a journal. After she was initially expelled, her parents filed a lawsuit claiming that her right to free expression had been violated. The father, David Boim, told CNN, "What is appropriate writing? . . . Where does that erosion of civil liberties and our rights as American citizens . . . where does that begin and where does that end?" Well, it begins with having a daughter not writing about killing a teacher. Nice going, Dad.

Many parents have sued school districts over the right of their children to be valedictorians. One of the most famous cases involved Blair Hornstine, a New Jersey senior from 2003 who attended Morristown High School. She resisted being named a "co"-valedictorian, sharing the title with two other students whose GPAs were a little lower than hers. Due to her health, Hornstine had to study at home part of the day and was excused from taking physical education classes, which don't carry the same weight in calculating a grade point average. According to Superintendent Paul Kadri, "The level of competition . . . had been compromised."

Today's parents and their children have a difficult time accepting decisions they disagree with.

"You can't make a student feel bad . . . you can't tell a cheerleader she wasn't quite good enough," explains Adrienne "Andy" Kotner, president of the San Diego chapter of the group California Citizens Against Lawsuit Abuse. "We want kids and their parents to accept personal responsibility, and not sue their school when something doesn't go their way."

Did you hear the one about the parent who sued her son's assistant principal, the school, and, of course, the school district (hey, don't they realize how strapped for cash these places are?) for causing her son's suicide? Yes, you read that right. What happened was the administrator told students, many of whom were protesting illegal immigration legislation in the spring of 2006 in Los Angeles, that if any of them skipped school to join the protests they would not graduate. Poor guy, trying to do his job by letting kids know there are consequences to their actions. So what does the teen do? Kills himself. Now does this mean the district is going to be charged with murder? Then that would make the death a homicide, wouldn't it? With parents like these, who needs more parental involvement in the schools? And why didn't we see parents come out against their children being truant?

Such silliness takes precious money away from school districts. Even if districts win, they have to hire the lawyers to fight the claims. As Kotner says, "There are only so many pieces of the pie in education, and money spent defending frivolous lawsuits is money that isn't spent in the classroom."

The School Services of California did a study on this subject, backed by the Association for California Tort Reform, and discovered that it cost schools $80 million a year to defend these lawsuits, and that was a decade ago. As a preventive measure, administrators spend several hours a week documenting events in case of lawsuits.

Another tort reform advocacy group, the Common Good, commissioned Harris Interactive to conduct its own survey in 2003. "Sixty-three percent of teachers and sixty-five percent of principals said they believed an increased potential for legal challenges by students or parents had hurt their ability to do their job . . . resulting in less personal instruction and social interaction." A majority said that "fewer laws would improve their morale, the quality of education in their schools, and help them maintain order in the classroom."

You can't give a student a hug for fear of a sexual harassment charge.

Since the 1960s more and more parents have sued districts, in part due to the expansion of individual rights laws as well as federal agencies set up solely to assist people to sue.

Especially problematic are parents who are attorneys themselves. Their perennial client is their child and when something happens to their child that does not please them, the lawyer overtakes the commonsense side of the parent. And what are these parents teaching their children? If your Starbucks caffe latte is too hot then sue the company?

With any lawsuit, it is more expedient and less costly to settle a matter out of court rather than fight it. John Sullivan, president of the Civil Justice Association of California, says that "going to court means taking administrators and teachers out of their schools and classrooms where they ought to be. It means losing money and time. It's a waste."

In a reversal of roles, a Texas couple was actually sued by the school district for overburdening its staff with open-records requests, over two thousand of them, costing the district $600,000. The parents, who have a disabled son, filed over fifty complaints in a one-year period.

A growing trend in recent years has been the "helicopter parent," who continues advocating on behalf of his children beyond the school years. These parents complain to professors about their children's college grades, and some continue that defense attorney attitude in their children's workplaces, questioning company personnel about why their children didn't get a raise or promotion.

Parents need to understand that the same high standard of model behavior they expect from teachers should also be replicated in themselves. Ever notice how parents turn into maniacs in the morning when dropping their kids off at school? They park in no-stopping red zones or stop their vehicles in the middle of the street without any effort made to move their car toward the curb (and often there is a space to pull into). Even the simple basic polite gesture of putting their signal on to alert other drivers that they are about to stop and pull over to the side would be welcoming so that those directly behind them won't have to slam on their brakes in order to avoid a collision. Don't they realize their kids see this reckless behavior and could emulate it?

36

Would You Ever Question Your
Child's Pediatrician?

There are two reasons why parents feel they have every right to criticize a teacher and even tell her how to do her job:

1. "We pay your salary."
2. "We know better than you because you're just a teacher."

Manipulative parents know they can always go above the teacher's head, belittling what little prestige teachers have.

Have a problem with a teacher? No need to even bother talking to her. Call up the principal. Or, better yet, e-mail the superintendent. Threaten the superintendent that if this teacher doesn't have a talking-to, then you will remove your child and place him in a private school. Nothing gives supers more sleepless nights than the threat of declining enrollment, which translates to declining income.

Parents have actually done this, especially white native-English-speaking ones (quite a hot commodity in larger urban districts). These nasty parents know the leverage they hold over the heads of school boards and superintendents who cling to this shrinking population for its higher test scores and parent involvement.

How often do you walk up to a firefighter and say, "I'm not sure the way you put out the fire was the best way"? Firefighters get paid via public monies like teachers and many of them are not college graduates, yet chances are people would not approach firefighters that way. But with teachers, half of whom have master's degrees, parents seem to have no compunction whatsoever about suggesting ways to teach their children.

There's an inherent distrust of teachers because, after all, they're just teachers, right? You know the bumper sticker, THOSE WHO CAN, DO. THOSE WHO CAN'T, TEACH? Many fervently believe this is true.

Parents can be grouped into three categories: those who honestly care about their children's education and occasionally phone or e-mail teachers about how their children are doing, those who will demand a conference whenever their children dispute a grade, questioning the authority and knowledge of the teacher, and those in the silent majority who never contact teachers, who fully entrust their children (too much if you ask me) into the hands of the education system.

Once I had a parent walk right into my classroom while I was teaching. My immediate thought was, "How did the office allow her up here?" since the protocol is for parents to make appointments to see teachers. What really disturbed me was when I noticed she had a school pass, meaning the office gave her clearance to roam the campus. Despite the room being full of my students, including her own daughter, the woman said to me in all earnestness, "Can I talk to you right now about my child's grade or do I need to make an appointment?"

It's akin to a client bursting in a courtroom to visit his attorney who's right in the middle of trying a case.

One father I spoke to corrected me constantly whenever I didn't use the "Dr." title before saying his last name. But it was his demeanor that was demeaning, the way he spoke down to me as if I were some clerk in a department store. By the way, he was a veterinarian.

Each year I used to volunteer a complete Saturday from early morning to late evening to help out at the annual school carnival. The parents demand that all volunteers pay the same five-dollar admission price as someone who attends the event. Now they are already getting the labor of teachers on a weekend free of charge.

The most minimum gesture they could offer to show their appreciation is to waive the five dollars for volunteering. Nonetheless, I dutifully paid five dollars year after year until this one time.

What did it for me was when they cleared out the area before officially opening the doors. They asked all volunteers to leave the carnival area and go outside the perimeter where paying customers are waiting in line. I noticed that administrators and security personnel were paying their five dollars at the gate without having to wait in line and so I tried doing that as well. After all, why should I walk to the end of the line? Besides, I was supervising an area in the carnival. I didn't see the logic in having to go wait on the other side of the gate after spending several hours setting up.

However, when I attempted to pay at the gate this one parent barked at me, "You need to go to the back of the line," in front of everybody as if I were someone doing something really bad. "But I'm a teacher and have been here all day," I pleaded. "It doesn't matter," he said. And that statement reflects how many parents perceive the adults who work with their children all day long.

In the old days, parents would listen to what teachers and principals had to say about their children without questioning their expertise or authority. Today, the parents take the kids' side as the gospel truth.

As Evan Chase wrote in *Edutopia*, "Somewhere along the line [parents] have gotten the implicit or explicit message from administrators that, because they pay taxes for their child to attend public school, they are somehow entitled to unprecedented influence over what their child will learn . . . [and] think they know better than classroom teachers what's best for their kids."

I got an earful when one student's parents were upset that their daughter had to work on a project over the three-day Martin Luther King, Jr., holiday, which happened to be the same weekend as her birthday celebration in Las Vegas. They questioned my logic in assigning such a large project over a holiday period. It didn't seem to matter that their daughter procrastinated (the work was assigned two weeks earlier), only notifying her parents of the project two days before the holiday weekend.

The Frisco, Texas, school board let go a twenty-eight-year veteran art teacher in 2006 because during a field trip to a museum the fifth graders saw a nude sculpture. One parent complained about it and that was that.

One parent actually mailed me a lesson plan. How would my children's pediatrician react if I were to e-mail him directions on how he should treat my son?

The question is how many parents are ready for more professional teachers? Would parents be willing to look up to teachers, to respect their opinions on their children's learning abilities, if teachers earned more money and were truly given leadership roles? It is a major mind-set shift that needs to happen.

Perhaps it's the parents who need to go to school. And that is just what the Miami-Dade Public Schools (fourth-largest district in the nation) is doing with its program called the parent academy, or TPA, providing "hundreds of free workshops on study skills, test preparation, memory enhancement, reading, and creating a positive learning environment at home." Some of the classes offered include Family Museum Experience, Achieving the Dream: Owning Your Own Home, and Understanding and Overcoming Eating Disorders.

When surveyed, first-year teachers express that the one area they feel least equipped to perform in their job is communicating effectively with parents. I can't remember one minute out of all my credential coursework devoted to ways to communicate with parents. This should be a mandatory part of every teacher training program.

As both a parent and a teacher I can see firsthand what it's like to be both on the receiving end of a parent's concern and the person making the contact with the teacher.

Parents, too, should be taught proper etiquette in how to speak to teachers and other school officials. If nothing else, they could be given a brochure with guidelines on how best to interact with the school and participate, written in the most positive light. There is nothing more rewarding than parents who take getting involved seriously and do single-handedly improve a school. There is also nothing more dreadful than a busybody parent who feels that teachers are on twenty-four-hour call for the taxpaying parent.

Over the years, I've known mainly nice parents, parents who are willing to chaperone on a field trip, who are willing to bring coffee and pastries for an evening meeting, who wish to have meaningful discussions about how they can help their children succeed scholastically.

A teacher enjoys seeing parents who regularly check in on how their son or daughter is doing beyond the grading periods when reports are sent home. But there is a difference between regular contact and frequent, daily contact that interferes with the teacher's workday. I've had parents who have e-mailed me back and forth several times a day. I quickly learned to just answer these parents once a day; otherwise I'd be sitting at the computer in my classroom all day typing replies as my students chatted in their seats.

I had one parent pass along a bizarre message to me in an e-mail. Her daughter was failing my journalism class and I was highly recommending that she take a different class for the second semester. After thanking me for working with her daughter, the mother then went on for several sentences, trying to recruit me for her financial company, finishing with this: "I am also looking for people who would like to make an extra income working part-time or are looking for a career change."

That's the first time I've ever received an infomercial in an e-mail from a parent. By the way, was she suggesting that I change careers after working with her daughter? Hmm.

Parents need to take more responsibility for their misbehaving children for the sake of everyone else, and to respect those adults who watch over them, the same adults they should expect their kids to respect as well.

37

Johnny Can't Read Because Johnny's Parents Can't Speak English

Today's schools are not the schools you went to. The majority of students in the largest school districts in the nation are non–native English speakers or have parents who are non–native English speakers.

During the past thirty years, the number of minority students has nearly doubled, while whites make up a little more than half of all students in public schools. It's not too much of a stretch to envision a day not too long away where the majority of students attending public schools will be nonwhite. According to the U.S. Department of Education, one-third of students in western states are non–native English speakers. Between 1979 and 2003, the number of such students jumped 161 percent.

Families newly arrived in America these days, unlike immigrants from decades ago, are less likely to assimilate. Instead of the melting pot metaphor where all cultures blend into the American one, the salad bowl metaphor is more apropos today; all the parts still retain their individual texture. "Diversity" is the universal word used here. Don't learn the language. Don't associate with other cultures. Keep to yourself. Shop amongst yourselves. Don't bother translating business signs.

People are afraid to say anything about how some immigrants refuse to blend in for fear of being labeled racist or xenophobic.

For schools there is a dramatic negative impact, since families from other countries are less likely to participate in their children's education due to poor English skills. Parents have fears of the new place and lack self-confidence using English and so most of them don't even try to communicate with the schools.

Whenever I've had immigrant parents show up at Open Houses they have their children by their side serving as translators. More often than not, however, non-English-speaking parents keep to themselves.

They don't attend parent-teacher conferences.

They don't join the PTA.

They don't attend nighttime school events.

They don't volunteer in the classrooms.

And, most critical of all, they don't provide a home environment where English is spoken. Nearly half of all California's students speak a language other than English at home, over half in the L.A. area.

With so many students not speaking or hearing English at home, where it can be constantly reinforced, these children are unfamiliar with famous American idioms and sayings, not to mention common vocabulary and customs.

The less often parents speak, read, and write using English, the less practice their children have. Non-native-English-speaking students are deprived of extra practice outside of school. This has a deleterious effect on these students' reading and writing skills. I've had plenty of intelligent, hard-working young people in an honors English class who, due to their nascent knowledge of the English language, could not match the same complexity of reading and writing assignments as their English-only counterparts.

This high number of immigrants coming into the public school system partly explains the fluctuation in test scores and why it's insanity to try to compare scores of one school with another. It's not like testing is administered on a stable population of English speakers at every school in America.

The lack of parental involvement passes down to their children, who are less likely to join clubs, participate in after-school sports, or attend school events. Parents coming from other countries did not grow up with American school traditions. These parents are more than likely to shield their children due to language and cultural barriers.

And if the parents aren't connected to the school, you can wager successfully that their children aren't, either. And that's a bad situation, not conducive to a healthy learning environment. When students don't have a sense of belonging to their schools, certain problems surface: Littering happens, vandalism rises, fights erupt.

Despite the large percentages of immigrant students, PTAs are mostly comprised of white native-English-speaking parents whose children may only represent a fraction of the school's population.

Where I work there is a predominant Armenian immigrant population, along with some Latino and Korean students. Yet, to look at the parent booster organization, you'd think only white, nonimmigrant students attended the school. Few immigrant parents are involved even though the school began changing ethnic composition over twenty years ago. So, it's not just a "don't know English" situation. Part of the problem is cultural.

Another reason why parents who don't speak English or don't speak it very well hurt the education system is because they can't be advocates for their children's education. Too often these parents feel insecure about their command of the English language so whenever a problem arises they tend to ignore it and not do anything.

One morning when I was being dropped off at work via a car dealership's shuttle, the man driving the van, who was a native speaker of Spanish, tried to tell me in his broken English a story about his daughter and this incompetent teacher. (It's funny how once strangers know that one's a teacher, they unleash a flood of school stories, usually pertaining to their children.) As the Spanish-language radio station played in the background, he tried as best he could to tell me how one of his seventh-grade daughter's teachers would mistakenly mark her as absent and not give her credit for homework. I informed him of how important it is that he speak to the principal of the school about the matter. As I spoke, I tried using the simplest vocabulary I could come up with, yet still I don't think he understood what I was saying (and, perhaps, I didn't quite get the details of his story, either).

One time I was in a meeting with administrators and department chairs. The principal was engaged in a conversation with another teacher in their shared native language. No one else knew what they were saying. Besides being a rude thing to do, this isolates people from one another.

I also wish that school districts would inform parents from other countries about possibly providing American nicknames for their children in order to avoid ridicule from other kids. Case in point: I had a student named Dong. I must admit that I purposely mispronounced his name closer to "dung," thinking that would be less embarrassing to him, especially in a room full of teenaged boys.

It's interesting how everyone in a school district is forced to learn how to be sensitive to other cultures and in some cases to learn others' languages, yet those who come to this country are not asked to return the favor. Why not teach them English, along with American customs? The Dallas, Texas, school board forced its principals to learn Spanish if they wanted to keep their jobs. Society goes too much out of its way to accommodate strangers (such as printing ballots in a variety of languages) with little asked in return.

School districts do make the effort of involving these parents, but depending on the culture some parents are resistant and even suspicious of such endeavors.

It's like cultural isolationism, with each group keeping to itself with little interaction, and even less motivation to change this pattern.

Efforts should be made to include non-native-English-speaking parents into the school fold. Why not hold a school fair with various booths signing parents up for English classes, for volunteer work? Introduce parents to the traditions of the school, the carnivals, the football games, etc. Assign these parents a "buddy" parent who can guide them through the learning process of American schooling.

If more parents got involved, their children would, too. How many kids would play soccer or T-ball or participate in scouting if not for their tireless parents who push them to do these activities? That same parent push needs to happen throughout schooling.

Suppose 90 percent of all parents decided not to get their children vaccinated against measles, chicken pox, or hepatitis. What would happen to our society? Disease would run amok. The following statement in print would look like this: "90 percent of all parents do not take an interest in their children's health." The other 10 percent would be aghast at this if it were true; thankfully it is not.

Now, take the same sentence and substitute the word "education" for "health" to read "90 percent of all parents do not take an interest in their children's education." I wish I could say this is also false, but, alas, it is not.

Most parents do not attend PTA meetings, most parents do not volunteer at their children's schools, most parents do not help with their children's homework. Even the two nights of the entire year when parents are invited to the school, Back to School Night and Open House, have many absentee parents who can't even show up for a couple of hours. Parents of the best students are the ones who usually attend. While it's nice for parents to hear compliments about their children, teachers would rather have a chance to converse with parents of struggling students.

This is why parents—all parents, not just immigrants—should have to sign contracts with their children's schools. One of the stipulations should be that no report cards get released without parents coming to the schools and personally picking them up.

Force parents to come to the schools during the student-free Friday that teachers would have. Otherwise, look what happens.

At Birmingham High School in Van Nuys, California, after widespread media attention on the school's dropout rate (only one-third graduated), the principal held a special nighttime meeting for parents to discuss this problem. As reported in the *Los Angeles Times,* "Teachers and school staff members outnumbered parents at the meeting by at least 2 to 1." What a surprise. Did Principal Marsha Coates do a good enough job informing parents about the meeting? Well, let's see. All she did was mail flyers home, send e-mails out, and leave automated phone messages. Such weak parent attendance is quite common.

Representative Wayne Smith from Austin, Texas, has taken the idea of mandatory parent involvement one step further by proposing legislation that fines parents five hundred dollars if they miss teacher conferences. That's the same punitive mentality that is heaped upon students by the public school system. Motivate through punishment. Well, it doesn't work.

As a working parent myself, I know how hard it is to voluntarily do something for your child's school. That's why such involvement must be made mandatory. Just as students have contracts whenever they are on academic probation, parents should sign a contract with a school, saying that they will help out in some way during the school year. Parents can be offered a menu of activities so that they can choose the ones that best fit their schedule: work the school carnival, bring refreshments to a PTA meeting, read to students, assist the teacher, or chaperone on a field trip.

Unfortunately, being well intentioned is sometimes not enough to volunteer at a school. Remember the story about the boy who scrawled graffiti on a bus with the L.A. mayor on it and Villaraigosa offered to mentor him? Santee Education Complex principal Vince Carbino said that the mayor would have to go through the same procedure as anyone else who wanted to volunteer in L.A. Unified by getting fingerprinted. Carbino told the *Los Angeles Times* that "we can't just let anybody come in through the door, I don't care what title they wear." Can you believe that?

In Charlotte, North Carolina, parents need to be interviewed and get a criminal background check before being approved for volunteer work. And sometimes the security check has to be paid for by the volunteer parent herself.

In some cases, parent involvement has gone extreme. *The New York Times* spotlighted the PTA at Collins Elementary School in Livingston, New Jersey, which has fifty-five committees "charged with everything from running kindergarten orientation to landscaping the school garden," the largest of which is the Pizza Lunch Committee, made up of forty-two parents. What could possibly be a downside to all this parent involvement? After all, isn't this what parents getting involved with their kids' schools is all about? Well, yes and no. It's good to have parents show up for meetings and volunteer their time to help out, most definitely. But some parents take it further by being bossy, especially if they come from careers holding "positions of authority and are very much used to giving orders" said Assemblyman Richard L. Brodsky of Westchester County. It is not uncommon to have parents bring their laptops, not box tops, to meetings "where refreshments are catered rather than homemade."

A 2002 study published by the Southwest Educational Development Laboratory called *A New Wave of Evidence: The Impact of School, Family, and Community Connections on Student Achievement* found that "when families of all backgrounds are engaged in their children's learning, their children tend to do better in school, stay in school longer, and pursue higher education."

The best way to combat bad parents is to force them to volunteer at their children's schools. Put them right in the middle of things because frequently their views of teachers and schools are based on myths and not reality. Before we begin demanding that students perform community service, let's expect parents to perform parenting service by being aware of their children's work in school.

38

Vouchers, Charters, and All That Jazz

For parents unhappy with their public schools, five alternatives are available: private schools, vouchers, homeschooling, online courses, and charter schools.

PRIVATE SCHOOLS

Except for religious reasons and spiffy uniforms, there is no sound argument for educating children in private schools.

Which environment mirrors the real world, public or private schools? Do parents choose where their children will work and who they will work with?

Because of their selectiveness, private schools shelter children from the environment they'll face in life, whereas kids in public school are better prepared to enter society, having been exposed to a wide array of people.

Since most private schools pay less in teacher salaries, they hire people who aren't as qualified. Private school teachers do not have the same training or credentials as public school teachers. The best teachers out there know this and that is why they work in public schools where they can command higher salaries.

What private school advocates like to point out is that, percentage-wise, more public school teachers send their children to private schools than the general public, 21 versus 12 percent, based on a Fordham Institute report.

All this proves is that teachers naturally spend more time carefully choosing the right school for their children. If teachers truly felt that private schools were the right choice, then the statistic would be off the chart.

However, to deduce from this that it's due to lousy public schools is simplistic. The teachers I know who send their children to private schools do so because class sizes are smaller, a religious framework is desired, or the environment is more controlled. I have never heard a public school teacher say it is because the teachers are better. They're not.

Public school parents should take comfort in knowing that nearly 80 percent of public school teachers still send their children to public schools. Has anybody ever looked into the percentages of local, state, and federal politicians who send their own children to private schools? My guess is that a higher percentage of politicians than teachers use private schools. And, if so, people should feel more outraged that politicians, those who are truly in charge of setting education policies and mandating curricula, are avoiding those very same institutions that they shape.

Additionally, no private school has ever won the U.S. Academic Decathlon since its inception in 1980. Every year a public school has been crowned champion.

And for those of you who abhor testing, well, to gain entrance into the best private middle and high schools requires doing well on the Independent School Entrance Exam, the Secondary School Admission Test, or the High School Placement Test. This means ten-year-olds go through the same angst as do seventeen-year-olds taking their SATs, not to mention the tutoring sessions parents spend money on.

The only reason I see for choosing private over public is that kids who don't follow the program get the boot. Remember the "beauty and the beast" duality of America's public schools: Every child is accepted and educated regardless of how they behave.

It's not that public school teachers do a worse job of disciplining than their private school counterparts, but that teachers often don't get the administrative and parental support they need.

If public schools were able to expel the bad apples—and having each parent sign a code of conduct as mentioned in chapter 34 would be a big step toward that—there would be a rush of parents removing their kids from private institutions and placing them in public ones, in turn saving themselves thousands of dollars.

Viable option? No.

VOUCHERS

Vouchers have turned into the Betamax of school reforms. What started out as a promising honest alternative way of educating kids—give parents the choice of sending their children to a private school rather than a public one if given money or a voucher—hasn't taken off as its advocates had hoped. Cleveland, Ohio, Milwaukee, Wisconsin, and Washington, D.C., are the most prominent cities that offer parents up to $7,500 in vouchers if their children attend private institutions.

In 2004 at a cost of $14 million, the D.C. School Choice Incentive Act was implemented by Congress, making Washington, D.C., the only city with a voucher program supervised by the U.S. Department of Education. Although vouchers were developed for parents whose children attend failing schools, a 2005 study discovered that of the one thousand students who received the $7,500 vouchers, only 6 percent fell into that category.

The voucher movement has been hit by several setbacks in recent years.

- One of Florida's three voucher programs, the A+ Opportunity Scholarship Program (seven hundred students, $4,350 vouchers), was ruled unconstitutional by the U.S. Supreme Court in January of 2006.
- A Colorado Opportunity Contract Pilot Program was found unconstitutional in 2002 before it went into effect.
- A study analyzing Cleveland's voucher program (begun in 1995) found that students not only scored the same as their non-voucher peers, but scored worse in math.

But perhaps the biggest setback to vouchers has been the tremendous rise in popularity with charter schools. Charters embody the concept of choice that voucher proponents keep clamoring for.

Viable option? No.

HOMESCHOOLING

It is very hard to get a true number of children who are homeschooled in America; however, most believe it to be close to two million. If accurate, that's roughly 4 percent of the country's student population. An estimated $750 million is spent by parents buying materials for their homeschooled children.

Why do parents choose this route? According to a study by the National Center for Education Statistics, 31 percent "said they were concerned about drugs, safety, or negative peer pressure in schools." Another 30 percent wanted to provide a particular moral or religious experience that public schools don't offer.

Demographically, most homeschooled children are white and middle class, which leads one to believe that race may play a large unspoken role in parents opting out of public schools.

Since states don't require parents to submit data, little is known in terms of how well homeschooled children do academically, though many participate in national spelling bees.

The main disadvantage to schooling children at home is actually one of the advantages for some parents: that kids avoid interacting with other kids. Sometimes homeschooled kids have a rocky transition if they later attend public schools.

The bottom line is that homeschooling isn't a threat or viable option to public schools, and for most people who have to work it isn't even possible.

Viable option? No.

ONLINE COURSES

Think about this: More students take online courses than use vouchers. And the numbers grow exponentially each year.

Over one million public school students took a class online in 2006, with half of the states offering distance learning. In fact, in order to graduate from a certain high school in Michigan, students need to take at least one class on a computer.

The main reason why high school students take online courses has to do with the classes not being available at their regular school. In other words, teachers take heart; it's not because they don't like what or how you are teaching.

Teachers don't like the online alternative for fear it will put them out of business. What's funny is that back in the 1960s teachers were frightened by the prospect of students being taught by a teacher on a TV. Think of all the jobs lost! One teacher's lecture can be viewed by thousands of students. Such a concept never materialized and teachers fretted over nothing.

If students want to take a course online because their school doesn't offer it, then they should be encouraged to do so. Just how many students would be self-motivated enough to take it at home by themselves? Only the best students, right? I say let them. There will still be plenty of jobs for teachers.

Online courses have a limited role and will never replace the classroom experience.

Viable option? No.

CHARTER SCHOOLS

Clearly the largest growth market in public school alternatives is the charter school movement. Since the first charter school appeared in 1991, more than 3,600 schools have opened for business in 40 states and the District of Columbia, serving over one million students. More than 600 charter schools are in California, with 220,000 students enrolled, making one out of every 15 public schools in the state a charter school.

Charter schools can remain part of a public school system, or can be run by private companies.

USC studied effective characteristics of charters, including "project-based learning, parent involvement, and the infusion of arts in the curriculum." In other words, charters go against the tide of most public schools.

The Woodland Hills Academy in California offers lessons in law from a retired judge, in health care from a hospital, and in the food business from a restaurant, representing a few of over thirty electives students can choose from.

Since 1994, Boston schools have had their version of charter schools, called "pilot" schools, which perform better than traditional schools. These pilots have a longer school year and longer school days, ideas expressed earlier in this book.

One common characteristic among charter schools is an emphasis on character. The KIPP (Knowledge Is Power Program) schools whose fifty campuses dot the northeast have two slogans: "Work Hard" and "Be Nice." According to *The New York Times*, "They want their students to be well behaved and hard-working and respectful because it's a good way to live but also because the evidence is clear that people who act that way get higher marks in school and better jobs after school." Aha, the golden rule works.

As a sign of parents' preferences of charters over vouchers, Ohio has 5,700 students who receive vouchers versus 249 charter schools that serve 62,000 students.

Los Angeles Unified School District (LAUSD) opened its one hundredth charter school in 2006, and is the district with the most charters in the country. Of course the school board, as a way to celebrate such numbers, wanted to place a moratorium on any more schools turning charter.

That same year, LAUSD withheld $85 million from charter schools even though legally the district needs to share its resources with them. Caprice Young, head of California's Charter Schools Association, told the Los Angeles *Daily News* that the district's "record has been absolutely abysmal. They treat charter students like second-class citizens." Due to a scarcity of space for charters, they have makeshift classrooms at places such as church while they wait on new construction. Each Monday teachers set up their room, then by Friday dismantle the whole thing.

School districts, in a weird way, want charters to fail in order to make the noncharter schools look better. However, publicly they need to support charters because of their popularity with parents. So what has happened is that charters are given some freedoms but not complete autonomy.

And teachers unions are enemies of charter schools. (That's reason enough to support charters.) They don't like it that teachers working at charters are not union members. Recently, some are doing an about-face. At first, unions were hoping for charters to just go away or remain a tiny cluster of schools. Now that charters have exploded in numbers, unions are after those same teachers whom they vilified for leaving the district schools, campaigning for them to unionize. Why? To regain the loss in union dues.

Of all the alternatives, charter schools hold the most promise, but while many of them have attractive elements—some incorporating ideas in this book such as longer school days and a longer year, incentive-based pay for teachers, and more principal autonomy—they don't go far enough in transforming the education experience for children, who are cocooned in bureaucratic red tape.

Viable option? Possibly.

But will it fly?

No.

That's what most people will say after reading this book. Too many unanswered questions, too much fuzzy math, too simplistic, it can't be done.

But I don't see anyone else coming up with a top-to-bottom plan. All I know is that just focusing on a few parts of the system (accountability and testing are the reforms du jour) leaves the system securely in place.

Of course, it's easier just to leave the system alone. Oh, things will come along like NCLB that will tinker with it, push it, prod it, but the structure will remain steadfast.

This thinking reminds me of a message sign in front of an elementary school: "Reading Comprehension Is Our Focus." Well, I should hope so. But do we need signs that state the obvious? How about hanging "Abiding by the Law Is Our Focus" in front of police headquarters? Would that make everyone feel more secure?

By the way, that sign never changed the whole year. Whether it was because the school took its mission seriously or they didn't have someone to climb a ladder, after the first few weeks people ignored the sign. What a microcosm of the public school system.

Most of the ideas in this book cost no money. The only price is to the egos of certain individuals and groups who must admit past mistakes and be willing to share decision-making with teachers.

Are teachers ready to take on a more authoritative role?

Are administrators ready to take on a more supportive role?

Are politicians ready to relinquish power to teachers?

It is a powerful awareness that so many kids are under the control of such a behemoth structure like public schools. These kids are capable of doing so much more. They are capable of becoming much more. They are capable of reaching more goals, goals more relevant to their interests.

Why aren't we doing anything about this? Zombie-like, public schools march on.

Remember the Million Man March? If one-third of all public school teachers were to organize themselves in similar fashion (during the summertime, of course; I'm not talking strike here), and congregate in Washington, D.C., if nothing else, national attention would be paid to changing schools. The president wouldn't be able to ignore such a powerful message.

I strongly believe in public schools; otherwise, I wouldn't want to make them better. This country is stronger because it provides education to all children.

I'd rather have a broken public school system than have millions of kids stay home to be schooled. I'd rather deal with bureaucratic headaches than have vouchers given out to millions of parents who are even less equipped than educators when it comes to learning strategies.

The nobility of teaching a room full of children from various backgrounds is heartwarming and life affirming. It takes one back to a simpler time in one's life when all of us believed that we were all equal and that everyone had a chance to succeed. However, it is increasingly more difficult to ensure everyone's success.

One day my son Benjamin and I were playing cashier and customer, respectively, with his toy cash register. On the toy is a scan gun that my son would use around the house, scanning everything he could reach with it. Each time an item is scanned a robotic voice says the price: "fifty cents," "twenty dollars." As he carefully scanned everything in his room, we both noticed that every single toy, including the cash register, was made in China.

The world is changing. But America's public schools are not.

If nothing else, may this book spark a national discussion on how we need to prepare America's children for the future.

A transformed public education system would make our country stronger. Often it is said that a country is as strong as its army. I say a country is as strong as its young people.

Every day forty-seven million children attend public schools and they do so for thirteen straight years. What type of experience do we want to provide America's youth?

Imagine the possibilities of what they could achieve. Imagine the America they could build. Imagine the Americans they could become. Imagine that this can happen today. It *can* happen today. It *should* happen today. Let us all make it happen today.

Acknowledgments

This book would not have been possible without the support of important individuals. Thank-yous to: my agent, Ron Goldfarb, who continues to believe in spreading the word of my message; Thomas Dunne, who gave the project the "go"; Mark LaFlaur, Lorrie McCann, Christian Vachon, Erin Brown, and Julie Gutin, for strengthening the manuscript; Colleen Schwartz, for ensuring an audience; and my friends and family, especially Sherry, Ben, and Max, for encouraging me to explore my inner writer.

Index

AASA. *See* American Association of School Administrators

absenteeism. *See also* attendance, school
parental allowance of, 254–55
penalty system for, 255–56

ADA. *See* Average Daily Attendance

Adlai E. Stevenson High School (Illinois), 73

administrators/principals, 10*n*
admonishment of teachers by, 155, 156–57
communication issues related to, 145, 148–49, 154–55, 279
disconnection by, 52–53
evaluation of teachers by, 155–56, 189–93
power/responsibilities of, 48–49, 190
subservience promoted by, 159–63
teachers' meetings and, 152–53
teachers' relations with, 50–55, 143–44, 145, 148–57, 159–63, 247–48, 279
teaching performed by, 53–54
training of, 54
trust of teachers by, 50–52, 55, 148, 150–52, 154–55, 158
wages of, 49–50, 55, 178

admonishment
of students, 106–9
of teachers, 155, 156–57

Advanced Placement (AP) classes, 124
dumbing down of, 127–33
GPA influenced by, 130
qualification of students in, 64–65
special education and, 237, 240
stipends for teachers of, 178
teacher competence and, 125–26, 187
tests related to, 129–31, 206, 219, 237
trends in, 125–27, 132

AEA. *See* American Education Association

aesthetic, school
dress code and, 9–10
environmental, 6–7
negativity toward students and, 8–9
prisonlike, 3–6

AFT. *See* American Federation of Teachers

After School Matters program, 28

after-school programs, 29
Navigators, 28
After School Matters, 28

women, 10*n*
  discrimination, teacher, and,
    159–63
  union leadership and, 162–63
Wooden, Ruth, 247
Woodland Hills Academy
  (California), 277
Woodrow Wilson National
  Fellowship Foundation, 169

Woods, Tiger, 129
World Health Organization,
  18

yard duty, 157
year-round school, 21–25, 278
Young, Caprice, 278

Zobel, Tom, 33